The State and the
Industrialization Crisis
in Turkey

The State and the Industrialization Crisis in Turkey

Henri J. Barkey

Westview Press
BOULDER • SAN FRANCISCO • OXFORD

Westview Special Studies on the Middle East

Published in 1990 in the United States of America by Westview Press, Inc., 5500 Central Avenue, Boulder, Colorado 80301, and in the United Kingdom by Westview Press, 36 Lonsdale Road, Summertown, Oxford OX2 7EW

ISBN 0-8133-8025-1

Printed and bound in the United States of America

 The paper used in this publication meets the requirements of the American National Standard for Permanence of Paper for Printed Library Materials Z39.48-1984.

10   9   8   7   6   5   4   3   2   1

To Alvin Z. Rubinstein

Contents

Tables

Acknowledgments

This book would not have been completed had it not been for the help, encouragement and advice of a great number of friends and colleagues. I would like to express my appreciation to Youssef Cohen, Ahmet Ö. Evin, Frederick Frey, Rajan Menon, Bruce Moon, Şevket Pamuk and Karen Barkey for the comments, insights and advice; and to Eda Amado for taking the time to do the cover. I would also like to express my gratitude to Milica Zarkovic Bookman and Richard J. Bookman, whose friendship over the years has been truly indispensable.

In addition, my debt to Jak and Tuna Barkey, who have endured this process longer than anyone, is incalculable. As it is to Alvin Z. Rubinstein who pushed me relentlessly.

Finally, I would like to thank Cathy Barkey, without whose extraordinary patience, support and time commitment this book would never have seen the light of day.

Henri J. Barkey

Glossary of Acronyms

DP. Democratic Party, *Demokratik Parti.*

DISK. Confederation of Revolutionary Workers' Unions, *Devrimci Işçi Sendikalari Konfederasyonu.*

DPT. State Planning Organization, *Devlet Planlama Teşkilati.*

ECLA. Economic Commission for Latin America.

ISO. Istanbul Chamber of Industry, *Istanbul Sanayi Odasi.*

ITO. Istanbul Chamber of Commerce, *Istanbul Ticaret Odasi.*

JP. Justice Party, *Adalet Partisi.*

NAP. National Action Party, *Milli Hareket Partisi.*

NDP. National Democracy Party, *Milli Demokrasi Partisi.*

NSC. National Security Council.

NSP. National Salvation Party, *Milli Selamet Partisi.*

ODTÜ. Middle East Technical University, *Orta Doğu Teknik Üniversitesi.*

OECD. Organization of Economic Cooperation and Development.

PP. Populist Party, *Halkçi Parti.*

RPP. Republican People's Party, *Cumhuriyet Halk Partisi.*

SOB. Union of Chambers of Industry, *Sanayi Odalari Birliği.*

SPO. State Planning Organization.

TISK. the Turkish Confederation of Employers' Unions, *Türkiye Işverenler Sendikalari Konfederasyonu.*

TOB. Turkish Union of Chambers, *Türkiye Odalar Birliği* or *Türkiye Ticaret Odalari, Sanayi Odalari ve Ticaret Borsalari Birliği.*

TÜSIAD. Turkish Industrialists and Businessmen's Association *Türk Sanayicileri ve Iş Adamlari Derneği.*

1

The Political Economy of Import Substituting Industrialization

Introduction

The emergence of the Bureaucratic Authoritarian State in Latin America in the 1960s and 1970s has been linked to the failure of import substituting industrialization (ISI). Guillermo O'Donnell[1] and others have argued that the hopes engendered by import substitution were dashed as this method of industrialization ran out of steam causing severe economic and political crises. Balance of payments deficits, inflation combined with the political activation of popular classes strained the political system beyond its capacity. As a result, Argentina, Brazil and Chile, which have had remarkably similar industrialization policies, succumbed to brutal military dictatorships. The new rulers jettisoned the inward-looking economic policies in favor of more orthodox and outward-looking ones. The Bureaucratic Authoritarian State spelled the end of the import substituting regimes.

The case of Turkey has been interpreted in the same light. The politico-economic crisis at the end of the 1970s — reminiscent of its Latin American counterparts — first gave rise to the transformation of the economic relationships on January 24, 1980 and then culminated in the September 12, 1980 military intervention which established a Bureaucratic Authoritarian State. Again industrialization policies were blamed for the failures. Did import substitution deserve such blame?

This book re-evaluates the politics of this much maligned industrialization strategy and examines Turkey's attempts to implement it in the 1960s and 1970s. It argues that ISI itself is *not* responsible for the failure of Turkey's industrialization efforts. It points instead to the state and its inability to successfully implement the development policy.

Faced with the emergence of powerful and competing vested interests among those segments of the private sector directly affected by import substitution, the state was deprived of its autonomy. Consequently, it lost its ability to lead, correct for the shortcomings of ISI and ensure that long-term goals are not sacrificed in the pursuit of immediate ones. The Turkish case therefore demonstrates how political-economic cleavages in the private sector contribute to the politicization and paralysis of industrialization policies, reducing the state to the role of a spectator unable to take the necessary decisions. In Turkey, as elsewhere, it is the army's intervention that restored the state its autonomy, enabling it to rise above societal divisions, redirect and execute its economic priorities.

This book contributes to the theoretical literature on the role of the state in industrialization processes, specifying the need for an autonomous state in the implementation of ISI. It questions the role of ISI as a key factor in the rise of the Bureaucratic Authoritarian State, and provides a more complete explanation by introducing state autonomy as a variable to contend with. The new specified model argues that the success of ISI is dependent on the existence of an autonomous state capable of undertaking initiatives to correct ISI's inherent problems. It also elucidates the particulars of the Turkish case by bringing to light new sources of information regarding private sector cleavages and linking these to the loss of state autonomy.

This chapter starts the analysis by placing ISI in the broader context of industrialization. It then discusses the problems inherent to ISI and concentrates on the causes for its exhaustion as elaborated in the literature.

Industrialization

The success of industrialization is influenced by two factors: timing and the political-economic context in which the effort is undertaken. The timing of each successive wave of industrializers played a critical role in determining the nature of the process. As Alexander Gerschenkron and Albert Hirschman show, there were qualitative differences between the first set of industrializing countries and their immediate successors. Differences between the third wave and their predecessors were even more pronounced than those separating the first two. The timing of the undertaking, in turn, influenced the political and economic environment: societies had to contend with different forms of external competition and domestic political and class structures.

England was the first country to industrialize. Its experience was therefore unique. Since then, at each successive stage of historical development, any other country attempting to industrialize has had to contend with the existence and impact of its predecessors, either because of the precedents set forth or because of the competition originating from them. Therefore, each society's experience has contained an element of uniqueness due not only to the timing of industrialization, but also to the necessarily different political, economic and socio-cultural conditions prevalent in each. In Europe, late-comers to the industrialization process employed different methods and marshalled the power of new institutions to make up for lost time.

In a series of six propositions, Gerschenkron has argued that the more backward a country's economy, the more likely its industrialization was to (1) start discontinuously as a sudden great spurt, (2) rely on larger plants, (3) emphasize investment rather than consumer goods, (4) divert resources away from consumption, (5) rely on "special institutions" to aid in raising capital for new industries, and finally, (6) rely less on the agricultural sector to provide it with surplus labor.[2]

From a political-economic perspective, the most interesting of the above propositions is undoubtedly that concerning the role of "special institutions." Gerschenkron was concerned with developments in countries such as Germany, France, Italy and Russia, where the nature of "special institutions" differed considerably. In France, during the Second Empire, and in Germany, banks played a major role in mobilizing capital for the industrial sector. In Russia at the end of the 19th century, the state had two interests. Its primary motive was to enhance its military strength for which it needed to industrialize. However since, as Gerschenkron points out, "the scarcity of capital in Russia was such that no banking system could conceivably succeed in attracting sufficient funds to finance a large scale industrialization,"[3] the state, through the Ministry of Finance, was crucial in creating the conditions for the rise and sustenance of industrialization.

The examples of Russia, the French state under Napoleon III and Bismarck's Germany demonstrate the role political institutions can and must play in the attempt to modernize. Napoleon III eliminated the protectionist barriers erected around French industry and Bismarck's "iron and rye" coalition gave a boost to the steel industry. With the exception of England, where the industrialization process occurred more or less autonomously from state bodies, political decision-making has played a major role in starting and/or enhancing the process. Even there, it can be argued that state support for colonialism and other mercantilistic policies was crucial to maintaining British industry's supremacy. In contrast to these examples, where state elites were anxious to promote industrialization, the Ottoman state hampered the growth of commerce and industry during most of the Empire's existence (See chapter 3 for details).

If state support was important and sometimes vital for newcomers such as Russia and Germany, the need for active state intervention in support of industrialization was even more apparent in the developing societies of Latin America, South Asia and the Middle East. The late-late comers — as Hirschman calls Latin American societies — suffered from a multitude of additional disadvantages than their industrialized predecessors. This was true of all three types of late-late comers. For those societies remaining under colonial rule into the 20th century, it is the "mother" country's political power that kept them in their respective position as suppliers of raw materials. For those which had become independent of colonial mastery earlier, such as Latin American societies, political and economic power remained in the hands of small oligarchic elites wedded to their respective export sectors and the prevailing international division of labor. Finally, for societies which had never been colonized but had fallen into a state of disrepair, such as Turkey, the pull of the international division of labor had a similar effect to those of the former colonies. And time itself made matters worse for all three cases as the European, American and Japanese industrialization took off, thus increasingly widening the gap between late and late-late comers.

If lateness had some advantages in the 19th century, being late-late in the 20th had none. When the gap between the first and the late-comers was relatively small, Germany and others benefited from the fact that England had invested large sums of money in industries where production techniques were rapidly changing, thus saddling it with obsolete technologies.[4] Satisfied with their status in the international division of labor, elites in late-late comers did not seek to industrialize and take advantage of developments in Europe. Instead, they allowed their markets to be completely penetrated and even controlled by the industrialized West. By the time the world plunged into the Great Depression of 1930, which forced all to take a second look at their dependent status, the industrialization game had been lost. As James Kurth points out, by the time producer goods industries developed in Latin America, the natural and traditional markets for steel and iron had vanished. That is, while railroad construction had spurred these industries in Europe, the Latin American steel manufacturers found that the European steel industry had already built the Latin American railroads. Similarly, the secondary market for European industry, the arms race, was essentially irrelevant for Latin America.[5]

The developing countries' response to the Great Depression was quite dramatic. A great many of them — especially in Latin America —

decided to vigorously implement a new set of industrialization policies designed to reduce their dependence on the more advanced nations. Based on the premise that some previously imported consumer goods could be manufactured locally, this strategy, which came to be known as Import Substituting Industrialization or ISI, was protectionist in nature and relied heavily on government interference and initiative. Starting in the 1930s and sometimes later, import substitution became the favorite method of industrialization for countries as diverse as Argentina, Turkey, India and the Philippines, each in its own way, seeking to catch up with the developed world.

Import substitution proved to be a different course than the one taken by Gerschenkron's late-comers. Hirschman argues that only the last of Gerschenkron's six propositions — the one concerning the impact of agriculture — can be considered to apply unconditionally to Latin American countries. "Special institutions designed to supply capital and entrepreneurial guidance (point 5), became important in most of Latin America after the ISI process had already been underway as a result of private, decentralized initiative for a considerable time. As to the remaining four points, almost the opposite could be said to hold for our late-late comers."[6]

Where there was a developed but not particularly strong private sector, the state's role as the "special institution" in ISI was limited to selective, although extensive, interference in market operations. Elsewhere, if the private sector was not strong or diverse enough to sustain an industrialization drive, the state played a more direct role in creating the conditions and infrastructure for industrialization. Turkey was such a case. Whereas Argentina and Brazil had fairly well-developed private sectors,[7] Turkey's was nonexistent. Hence, following the 1930 collapse of the world economy, the Turkish state marshalled vast resources to advance the course of industrialization. Two decades later, when the Turkish private sector eventually began its own import substitution efforts, it was in part due to this early phase of state-sponsored industrialization.

The late-late comers, whose import substitution drive started in the aftermath of the Great Depression or the Second World War, while differing from their predecessors, by and large followed similar patterns: each focused on substituting of consumer goods imports with products of domestic labor-intensive industries. However, despite their valiant efforts, most of these countries continued to suffer from serious balance of payments difficulties. Where import substitution policies were accompanied by populist regimes, this mode of industrialization became entrenched, and survived until serious economic and political crises undermined the regimes' very existence and led to military takeovers. Despite the late emergence of its private sector, this also applied to Turkey. Only Far Eastern countries such as South Korea and Taiwan significantly varied their implementation of import substitution so as to quickly adjust their respective manufacturing sectors for exports. While their success — evidenced by the economic powerhouses they have become — is indisputable, they are atypical of the late-late comers in terms of institutions, history, linkages to the international economy and timing.[8]

To the extent that Latin American societies and Turkey have been unable to redress the imbalances in their economies, they have had to contend with severe political-economic crises. The culmination of these crises was often marked by military interventions attempting to accomplish what civilian politicians could not. This problem was not one envisaged by Gerschenkron. The question that needs to be answered is why could these countries not manage to deal with the problems resulting from import substitution? The answer is a multi-layered one: it starts with the nature of ISI and culminates with the impact of state-business relations.

Import Substituting Industrialization (ISI)

Induced by the Great Depression, the long and protracted decline in the economic fortunes of the industrialized nations precipitated the adoption of import substituting industrialization among the developing countries. These, which had hitherto specialized in exports of primary products to their more advanced counterparts, suffered a great deal from the depression. Faced with disappearing export markets and the resulting severe foreign exchange shortages, these countries had no choice but to drastically curtail the importation of goods necessary for domestic consumption. When the effects of the world depression appeared to be long-lasting, some countries reluctantly, others more eagerly, turned to import substitution as a solution. By domestically manufacturing previously imported simple consumer goods, countries could achieve two desirable aims: they could save the foreign exchange which was previously expended to purchase such goods, and simultaneously they could provide an impetus to the development of an industrial base.

As envisaged by its practitioners, ISI was to consist of two stages: the early, easy phase, and the second, more difficult one. The easy stage was to be characterized by the substitution of simple consumer goods for which internal markets existed and labor-intensive production methods could be employed. Textiles was the industry of choice. The second stage was to involve the development of intermediate and capital (or investment) goods industries, such as steel and machinery. Although more difficult since it required the establishment of capital-intensive industries, the second stage was a necessary step to becoming truly industrialized in the long run.

All in all, ISI was a simple idea which promised to (1) contribute to the solution of the chronic balance of payment problems since it relied on the production of previously imported goods, (2) increase import capacity by saving foreign exchange, enabling the country to import goods which were previously unavailable due to foreign exchange limitations, (3) develop domestic industries, (4) lead to the economy's vertical integration and hence to the rise of intermediate and investment goods industries through backward and forward linkages, (5) create and develop an industrial entrepreneurial class, (6) increase available technology and know-how, (7) expand employment (as more and more labor is absorbed by the labor-intensive consumer goods enterprises), (8) diminish dependence on the export sector, where primary commodities are continuously subjected to the vagaries of an unpredictable international market, and, finally, (9) develop the internal market and raise domestic standards of living, which, in turn, would help develop a momentum of its own by reinforcing the backward and forward linkages and giving rise to new ventures. Not surprisingly, therefore, in Latin America, South Asia and in parts of the Middle East, ISI's implementation was accompanied by great expectations.

According to Hirschman, there are four general impulses for the initiation of ISI in late-late countries: "wars, balance of payment difficulties, growth of the domestic market (as a result of export growth) and official development policy."[9] Typically, wars and balance of payments difficulties contribute to shortages of manufactured goods, increasing the attraction and profitability of their domestic production. Whereas these constitute external stimuli, "as incomes and markets expand in such a country and some thresholds at which domestic production becomes profitable are crossed, industries come into being without the need of external shocks or government intervention."[10] Where the private sector is too weak or unwilling, official development policy can encourage import substitution. Where the private sector is simply nonexistent, the state can conceivably initiate the process itself.[11] In general, "it was only after World War II that ISI became a deliberate policy tool for economic development. Most of the larger countries in Latin America implicitly or explicitly accepted the ECLA [Economic Commission for Latin America] analysis of the hopelessness of gearing their economies toward the traditional world division of labor."[12]

In Turkey, ISI became the official instrument for economic development following the 1960 military intervention. In post-World War II Latin America and post-1960 Turkey, the role of the state was one of encouragement, of providing inducements and help for import substitution, with investments representing the direct involvement. The inducements mostly took the form of fiscal measures and instruments related to the import regime, such as quotas, tariffs, exchange rate regulation and the like. In other words, the state was content with limited interventions into the marketplace.

On paper at least, the implementation of ISI seemed as simple as the strategy itself. ISI's protectionist nature did not alter the fundamental relations in society. In fact, Gourevitch points out, "one important characteristic of protectionism. . . is that protectionism keeps the state's involvement in the economy at a distance: although the purity of the market has given way to government interference, that interference still works directly through the marketplace."[13] The intellectual rationale for import substitution was provided by the infant industry argument: the notion that new and nascent industries, specifically those that compete with imports, ought to be protected from foreign competition — until they are strong enough to face foreign competition. To protect such industries or enterprises, governments institute tariffs or quotas on imports for which domestic substitutes exist. While tariffs generally increase the cost of an imported commodity immediately at the point of entry, quotas, by comparison, set import quantities. Therefore by making imports scarce, quotas reduce competition and indirectly affect the domestic price of imports. If domestic production is sufficiently large to meet the needs of the country, a government can elect to completely arrest the importation of all competing products, thereby assuring local manufacturers a free reign.

Quotas and tariffs are not the only instruments available to governments. By reducing the cost of imports, overvalued exchange rates also benefit importers. When used in conjunction with quotas and tariffs on consumer goods, overvalued exchange rates can be targeted to reduce the cost of intermediate and capital goods imports. In addition, governments can make use of a multitude of other direct inducements, such as negative real interest rates, investment credits, favorable treatment at the central bank, and discretionary loans.

As the manufacturing sector grows in response to these inducements, it displaces the agricultural and commercial sectors in importance. Its relative share of employment also climbs, attracting more and more workers into the urban and industrial regions. In turn, the resulting changes in these relative shares brings these different sectors into conflict with one another, heightening the significance of the political factors and issues.

The Politics of Import Substitution

If the economics of import substitution seemed relatively simple, its political rationale and perceived ramifications made it irresistible. First and foremost, ISI was interpreted and implemented as a strategy to build up the domestic market. Speaking to a group of manufacturers in 1946, Juan Peron argued, "no market can replace the internal market. Regardless of how big, how beautiful they may be,...[other markets] are always aleatory, never safe. . . If something is left over, we will sell it somewhere, but the Argentine people come first."[14]

Import substitution carried with it a strong nationalist message; goods which previously seemed to be the exclusive preserve of advanced countries would now be within developing countries' reach. As such, it was also appealing to their militaries, a fact not lost on political leaders. Getulio Vargas, for one, declared in 1944 that the first lesson of World War II was that "the only countries that can really be considered military powers are those that are sufficiently industrialized and able to produce within their own frontiers the war materials they need."[15] The implication was unmistakable: for Brazil to be considered a power it had to develop its own industrial structure.

Politically, the expansion of manufacturing industries stood to benefit a great number of people, chief among them an unlikely couple: industrialists and workers. Increased manufacturing activity meant new jobs, which fueled internal demand, giving rise to more production and employment. The focus on the internal market required the broadening of society's aggregate consumption levels to support the new domestic industries. Since the working class and urban consumers, in general, represented the bulk of the new consuming public, the expansion of societal consumption necessitated an increase in working class incomes.

The nationalist, inward-looking, economically expansionary attributes of ISI were well suited to populist leaders and coalitions. Leaders such as Peron could construct coalitions against the old oligarchic interests, coalitions that included the middle classes and the newly emerging urban working class. In Brazil, Vargas who, during his earlier Estado Nôvo dictatorship did not share the populist ideas, would later embrace this industrialization strategy with the backing of significant segments of the national bourgeoisie. As Gourevitch points out, protectionism — the essential component of ISI — "avoids a zero-sum political game with respect to class divisions of society. In economic terms it pits domestically oriented producers against internationally oriented ones, and this is by no means a cleavage that brings capitalists and workers to confront each other. Rather, it joins the two groups together in conflict against another cross-class coalition."[16]

The high point of populism in Latin America became associated with the expansionary or the consumer goods phase of import substitution. In fact, as Kurth maintains, "populist politics were probably well-suited to the consumer phase of industrialization in Latin America as liberal politics had been to a similar phase in Europe. Indeed, for a time, populist politics meant higher wages and higher welfare benefits and thus higher domestic consumption of consumer goods than would have been in a strictly liberal state."[17] A political contract between the state, the middle classes and the emerging urban working class became crucial to ISI's success and allowed for the satisfactory division of the spoils of industrialization. By embracing ISI-based policies, populist leaders could use the effects of protectionism, as Gourevitch suggested above, to construct multi-class coalitions.

Populism was not, at least in Latin America, a democratic force. It was comprised of corporatist controls, significant working class co-optation and state-controlled mobilization. Compared with the oligarchic regimes it supplanted, populism was, nonetheless, more inclusionary, especially with respect to such groups as urban dwellers. Despite its ideological vacuousness, populism left an enduring legacy in the form of a mobilized urban working class, which, at times, has successfully threatened the state. These populist arrangements between industrialists, workers, the state and its leaders did not withstand the pressures of economic downturns. In Argentina, for example, by 1955, as Peron's economic policies increasingly resembled the orthodox plans he had so openly despised, his worker support evaporated. In the years to follow, the legacy of populism — represented by Peron's return to power in 1973-74 and the electoral successes of others in the populist mold — became an almost nostalgic search by a significant segment of Latin American populations for the "good old days" of bountiful energy and expectations. Yet, in many ways populism had also planted the seeds of these societies' own decline since, as Malloy argues, "the period saw an increase in the state but a decrease in autonomy, power, and efficiency of governmental apparatuses."[18]

The Exhaustion of ISI

Despite some modest successes in Latin America and elsewhere, ISI's great expectations remained unrealized. In the 1960s and 1970s, many countries which had experimented with ISI faced serious economic shortcomings. Among these were continued balance of payments deficits, severe foreign exchange shortages, low growth rates, inflation, unemployment, overcapitalization, and an inefficient industrial structure. In other words, most of the ills which ISI was supposed to remedy re-emerged with a vengeance. The crises faced by such countries as Brazil in 1964, Argentina in 1966 and 1976, Chile and Uruguay in 1973, Turkey in 1980, and even India in 1975, were triggered not only by the economic problems listed above, but also by the heightened political expectations engendered by ISI.

ISI seemed to have exhausted itself. The euphoria that had greeted the early stages of quick growth was replaced by the sudden realization of limits and policies gone awry. This realization's political ramifications were manifested in new divisions in society, acrimonious and bitter debates about future courses of action, the polarization of views and, ultimately, a paralysis of the state decision-making structures. The resulting stalemate was almost always broken by military interventions which brought to power officers intent on restructuring societal economic relations, and, in some cases, as O'Donnell has suggested in his model, society itself.[19]

There are four reasons — the first three being inherent to ISI — which help explain this strategy's tendency to run out of steam and lead to crises: (1) excessive protection, (2) exchange rate controls, (3) the imitative nature of import substitution, and (4) the relatively small size of markets.

(1) The first and probably most significant criticism concerns the levels and duration of protectionist policies. While it is necessary to defend newly established enterprises, long-term protectionist policies give rise to inefficient industries. In turn, these tend to contribute to the general distortion of the price mechanism affecting other industries and their output. Instead of concentrating on industries and factors of production where the developing country enjoys a comparative advantage, protectionism tends to lead to an economy-wide misallocation of resources. Depending on the type of instruments employed to achieve the desired level of protection, the distortions vary. Tariffs directly lead to increased prices for the consumer and exchange controls generally give rise to misallocation of resources. Because their size are determined by industry's productive capacity, quotas directly encourage the formation of domestic oligopolies.[20]

In the absence of foreign competition, market distortions continue to occur, even where the number of domestic firms is relatively large.

Consider the case of the Chilean automobile industry where, in 1964, 19 different companies combined to produce a total of only 7,558 units[21] (an average production of 398 units per enterprise).   Under such circumstances it is difficult to imagine this industry to be either price or cost competitive, let alone have any export potential.   Protective barriers that eliminate incentives for efficiency ultimately also defeat one of the main purposes behind ISI: to develop industries capable of competing with the outside world and thus contribute to a country's export earnings.

(2) Exchange rate controls constitute another important cause for ISI's exhaustion.   By maintaining artificially high exchange rates, developing countries reduce the cost of imported inputs for domestic manufacturers. While reducing the cost of imports, an overvalued exchange rate increases the price for that country's exports.   Historically, the main victim of this policy has been the agricultural sector.   A decline in agricultural exports with no commensurate increase in the exports of other products diminishes a society's ability to earn foreign exchange. The high cost of the domestic currency further discourages the new enterprises' export possibilities.

Because the cost of investment goods imports is driven down by an overvalued exchange rate, domestic industrialists are encouraged to invest in capital-intensive manufacturing techniques, thereby contributing to the overcapitalization of their industry.   The resulting increases in incremental capital output ratios negatively affect the rate of labor absorption.   Therefore, in these societies, increases in employment have not kept pace with increases in manufacturing output,   missing an opportunity to benefit from the abundance of labor.   During the 1950-68 period, whereas industrial output in Latin America grew at an average annual rate of 6.0 percent, the growth in industrial employment amounted to 2.8 percent.   In some countries this discrepancy was more pronounced: Brazilian industrial employment grew by 2.2 percent, while its manufacturing output expanded by 7.3 percent.[22]

In later stages of substitution, especially with the introduction of consumer durables, overcapitalization gives rise to a segmented industrial working class, where those working in capital-intensive sectors earn considerably more than their counterparts in other parts of manufacturing.

In the longer term, upholding overvalued exchange rates defeats another purpose of ISI: the transition to the second and more difficult stage of the industrialization drive.   Instead of progressing toward the vertical integration of industry, firms prefer horizontal expansion.   In other words, instead of investing in the production of sub-components or intermediate goods necessary for the final product, firms will opt to jump to a new and unrelated finished product line, switching, for example, from refrigerators to radios. With imported capital and intermediate goods prices kept artificially low, domestic producers have little incentive to invest in such industries. The resulting distorted industrial structure is not only more dependent on imports than before, but also lacks adaptability to changing conditions. According to O'Donnell, the Bureaucratic Authoritarian regimes which dotted the Latin American landscape in the 1960s and 1970s had among their immediate goals the desire to redress this very imbalance, which he has termed the absence of 'deepening.'[23]

(3) A third major cause for exhaustion lies in the imitative nature of import substitution. As a replication of conventional capitalist methods of industrialization, ISI, as Hirschman points out, is a "tightly staged process," and, as such, it is "a matter of imitation and importation of tried and tested methods" and is, therefore, "far less" learning intensive.[24] This imitation process does not restrict itself to production, but as a result of what Ragnar Nurkse calls the "international demonstration effect,"[25] it takes a step further as LDCs — especially their elites — emulate the consumption patterns exhibited by the industrialized societies. This explains the tendency of import substitution efforts to gravitate towards the production of consumer durables. As LDCs imitate the more developed societies' consumption patterns, the incentives to domestically manufacture such products increase, especially since their imports are either banned or severely restricted by the import regime. These industries tend to be capital intensive and discourage savings. The development of the automobile industry in Latin America and other semi-industrialized countries constitutes a glaring example of this "imitative" characteristic. For instance, American automobile corporations entered Western European countries when their per capita GNP had reached $1000 (1965 dollars). Similarly, large-scale direct foreign investments in Spain's automobile industry occurred at a comparable income level.[26] In Brazil, by contrast, foreign investment in this industry doubled between 1964 and 1970, when 1966 per capita Brazilian GNP was only $340.[27] Turkish automobile production got underway in 1970 at a time when the per capita GNP was merely $273. With insufficient export possibilities and domestic demand to sustain them, these industries were condemned to a state of permanent inefficiency.

(4) Finally, another contributing factor to ISI's exhaustion is the relatively small size of domestic markets. This is nowhere more apparent than in consumer durables when "...the relative market growth

becomes mainly vertical, that is, it is based on the purchasing power of the high income sectors.   This is due to two main factors: (1) the high capital density per unit of output precludes the large scale absorption of labor; (2) the high unit value of the goods produced permits the entry into the consumer markets of small sectors of the population."[28]

While none of these problems was insurmountable, the inherently political nature of ISI made them difficult to tackle together.   It is precisely to this aspect of the decline of import substitution that this chapter turns to now.

The Political Implications of the Crisis of Import Substitution

As argued earlier, the most visible casualties of the exhaustion of import substitution were the populist leaders such as Peron, Vargas, and the coalitions which had helped them capture their citizens' political imaginations. However, the damage done to those countries' incipient democratic systems was far more important. Despite the significant contribution of ISI's exhaustion to the emergence of BA regimes in Argentina, Brazil, Chile and Uruguay, it is fair to say that the strains of industrialization and rapid change had been in evidence for much longer. Behind Peron's fall from power in 1955 and Vargas' suicide in 1954 was a sense of deep disenchantment and frustration with economies suffering from unbalanced growth and unrealized (and maybe unrealistic) expectations.[29]

In general, ISI's exhaustion has been credited with worsening economic and concomitant political crises that ultimately led to the praetorianization of society and the unraveling of many countries' political systems.   Whereas crises were resolved previously by revamping internal alliances through relatively small changes in distribution priorities and emphases, O'Donnell has argued that ISI-induced crises have only been resolved through dramatic breaks with the past. Accordingly, the BA states — as opposed to other military regimes — are representative of this dramatic break. The military interventions of 1966 and 1976 in Argentina, 1964 in Brazil, 1973 in Chile and Uruguay and 1980 in Turkey brought about the fundamental restructuring of domestic and international alliances: the state, foreign capital and the internationally oriented elements of domestic capital assumed a predominant role, and the "national bourgeoisie," while still important, was relegated to a lesser position. In effect, the BA states represented the final undoing of the cross-class coalitions that Gourevitch maintained were the natural result of protectionist policies.

In O'Donnell's model, the military intervenes to achieve three objectives: (1) by instituting new economic policies, it seeks to vertically integrate (or 'deepen') the industrial structure. These measures involve increased investments in capital goods industries and the implementation of more orthodox economic prescriptions, such as devaluations, tightening of money and credit, return to "free market principles" and export stimulation.

(2) These BA states also work to achieve domestic stability, which had been endangered by the stagnating economy unable to cope with demands from below. O'Donnell argues that the military leaders and their technocratic civilian allies believed that if international capital is to participate in the transformation of these societies and invest in 'deepening,' then a conducive domestic atmosphere must be attained. This means that those segments of society that had been politically activated by the exuberant phase of ISI must be depoliticized and curbed. In addition to political stability, the military must also try to ensure economic stability: "if one of the aims was to begin a flow of industrial exports it was necessary to guarantee stability in some of the institutional mechanisms — typically, promotion systems and exchange rates — that had varied erratically in the previous period."[30]

(3) In addition to deepening, the depoliticization of economic decision making, O'Donnell argues that the BA state aims at the economic exclusion of the popular classes and incorporates in the higher echelons of the government former members of the armed forces and public and private bureaucracies.[31] In other words, the state gets staffed by technocrats who can depoliticize and ultimately de-praetorianize of society.

How valid is O'Donnell's BA state? The issue that has invited the greatest amount of scrutiny has been the "deepening" hypothesis. Robert Kaufman and Jose Serra, among many others, have pointed out that in most of the cases where the BA regime model would be applicable, i.e. Brazil in 1964, Argentina 1966 and 1976, Chile 1973 and Uruguay 1973, deepening did *not* occur after the coup. The only exception is the period following the 1966 takeover in Argentina. All these cases, according to Kaufman, shared some common characteristics: "sharp restriction of public contestation, each government changing the prevailing rules of the game in ways that were quite clearly *authoritarian*;" "the use of the state apparatus to depoliticize organized labor;" and "a technocratic policy style."[32] Similarly, Serra found that in Brazil deepening did not materialize after 1964, and that, in actual fact, deepening in this country had started in the 1950s.[33] Hirschman, also addressing himself to the same issue, remarked that:

the economic problems of which the policy and coup makers

were most conscious were, first, inflation and second, balance of payments disequilibrium especially when foreign exchange reserves were threatening to run out. Those who were responsible for turning Latin American politics in the authoritarian direction, partly under the impact of those twin crises, had some notion about the political and economic problems that were in turn responsible for the immediate emergency.[34]

Irrespective of the questions surrounding the validity of the 'deepening' hypothesis, the concept of the Bureaucratic Authoritarian state cannot be easily dismissed. Even if the "commitment of BA governments to the development of a vertically integrated industrial sector was at most partial — often set aside in favor of other, more conventional objectives, such as facilitating the importation of supplies necessary for the expansion of existing public and private enterprises,"[35] they represent radical departures from the past and a peculiar response to the political and economic problems gripping their respective countries. Intent on restructuring society so as to avoid a repetition of the chaotic conditions that preceded their entry, the military seeks to rearrange the domestic distribution of political forces. In so doing, it also revamps the alignments between state and domestic classes so as to include capital only at the expense of the popular classes.

Rethinking the Inevitability of Exhaustion

There is little doubt that the implementation of ISI ran into serious difficulty in many of the countries in Latin America and elsewhere. What is less clear cut, however, is the extent to which ISI's shortcomings are due to its inherent tendency toward exhaustion. Albert Hirschman has raised this question and taken the concept of exhaustion to task. He acknowledged the natural resistance of industrial elites to vertically integrate their industries. Instead they prefer to continue importing their intermediate product needs, and thus resisting deepening. Nonetheless, he also argued that if limits were placed on horizontal expansion, firms would find vertical expansion profitable and also the most natural way to increase size.[36] In addition, he blamed the inability of the various sectors to export on the fact that the allocation of resources at the national level had been based on "customs protection. . . internal inflation, overvaluation of the currency, and exchange controls."[37]

In later works, Hirschman argued that policies as well, and therefore policy makers, were to blame for bringing about ISI's exhaustion. He suggested that deficient policies, especially extravagant public works spending projects, such as the construction of Brasilia, contributed significantly to the failure of import substitution. Hirschman argued that, while ISI declined in its effectiveness, policy makers and industrialists alike failed to detect new possibilities and patterns that were emerging, including the expansion of manufacturing exports, the broadening of the tax base, and the financing of development through the use of industrial sector profits.[38] These opportunities were missed in large part not because, as O'Donnell claims of a lack of deepening, but from the absence of a transition to more orthodox economic policies. Michael Wallerstein, though not exactly echoing Hirschman's thoughts, also claims that, at least in the case of Brazil, state policies were responsible for the demise of the democratic regime in 1964. However, it was not Goulart's, but, his predecessor, Kubitschek's conduct which is to blame[39] for creating conditions under which economic policy-making options were polarized and where there was "no policy that would be both economically feasible and politically acceptable."[40] Similarly, Youssef Cohen points a finger at the political system in Brazil for contributing to the polarization of issues and the regime's eventual demise.[41]

The implication of the above discussion is clear: errors were committed at the political level when opportunities were missed to effect change. A transition to greater economic orthodoxy — which may have eliminated the need for a BA coup — requires action and leadership on the part of either industrialists, who, in the long-run, stand to benefit the most from the change, and/or state authorities. With the exception of Colombia, where export subsidies, mini devaluations and reductions in the levels of protection were successfully implemented without recourse to the draconian measures of the BA state,[42] most Latin American countries resisted the change, as did Turkey. Hirschman attributes to the nature of exporting the unwillingness on the part of industrialists to demand from state authorities policies aimed at expanding their exports. Exports, unlike selling to the domestic market, involve considerable amounts of investment in research, packaging and design. Exporters, therefore, require both stability and some measure of control over the key policy instruments of the governments. Hence, "only a cohesive, vocal and highly influential national bourgeoisie is likely to carry industrialization beyond relatively safe import substitution to the risky export-oriented stage." And, since "in no country of that continent do industrialists feel securely in control of vital economic policies affecting them. . .[and] policy makers positively cultivate unpredictability and distance from interest groups,"[43] transitions from import substitution to more export oriented strategies never materialized.

Paradoxically, export-oriented strategies could have ensured industrialists the predictability, since "if governments are serious about exporting manufactures, their freedom to intervene is restricted by the exigencies of keeping manufactures internationally competitive and by trade conventions and sanctions that limit permissible methods of trade promotion."[44] From the perspective of industrial growth, countries which opted for export promotion have, in general, achieved more satisfactory results and, as Anne Krueger points out, with such policies "stop-go patterns do not seem to emerge due to foreign exchange bottlenecks; efficient low-cost firms can expand rapidly well beyond the limits of the domestic market."[45]

If industrialists were unwilling to push for change, state officials were equally complacent about their existing policies. This *status quo* oriented approach explains why countries involved in import substitution were "characterized more by an absence of a coherent and long-range plan for industrialization than by import substitution as an affirmative strategy of *industrialization*."[46] Respective political authorities did not pay necessary attention to their policies' ramifications, as import substitution for the sake of import substitution became the apparent *modus operandi* in most places. As Edward Mason argued in the case of India, "it is only a slight exaggeration to say that in India, official opinion holds that no domestic cost is too high a price to pay for import saving."[47]

In the face of deteriorating conditions everywhere, how can we account for the absence of initiative on the part of industrialists, and for the complacency of state officials overseeing these economies? If ISI's exhaustion was not a foreordained outcome, then why were measures not implemented to remedy problems? If such initiatives were designed, why were they not successful? The next chapter attempts to answer these questions by looking at the relationship between the state, the private sector and import substitution.

Notes

[1]Guillermo O'Donnell, "Corporatism and the Question of the State," in James M. Malloy (ed.), *Authoritarianism and Corporatism in Latin America* (Pittsburgh: Pittsburgh University Press, 1977); Guillermo O'Donnell, "Reflections on the Pattern of Change in the Bureaucratic-Authoritarian State," *Latin American Research Review*, Vol 13, No. 1 (1978) pp. 3-38; Guillermo O'Donnell, *Modernization and Bureaucratic Authoritarianism* (Berkeley: University of California Press, 1979); Guillermo O'Donnell, "Tensions in the Bureaucratic-Authoritarian State and the Question of

Democracy," in David Collier (ed.), *The New Authoritarianism in Latin America* (New Jersey: Princeton University Press, 1979), pp. 285-318.

[2]Alexander Gerschenkron, *Economic Backwardness in Historical Perspective* (Cambridge, Mass.: Belknap Press, 1962), pp. 452-454.

[3]Gerschenkron, *Economic Backwardness in Historical Perspective*, p. 19.

[4]Peter Gourevitch, *Politics in Hard Times: Comparative Responses to International Economic Crises* (Ithaca: Cornell University Press, 1987), pp. 90-91.

[5]James Kurth, "Industrial Change and Political Change: A European Perspective," in David Collier, *The New Authoritarianism in Latin America*, p. 358.

[6]Albert Hirschman, "The Political Economy of Import Substituting Industrialization," in Albert Hirschman, *A Bias for Hope* (New Haven: Yale University Press, 1971), p. 95.

[7]John Sheahan, *Patterns of Development in Latin America* (Princeton: Princeton University Press, 1987).

[8]In both of these cases, the state — an authoritarian one — played a significant role in directing enterprises and marshalling resources.

[9]Hirschman, "The Political Economy of Import Substituting Industrialization," p. 90.

[10]Hirschman, "The Political Economy of Import Substituting Industrialization," p. 89.

[11]While the Turkish state, unlike its Latin American counterparts, felt obliged to establish industries on its own, its efforts in the 1930s were of limited duration and scope. The private sector responded only after the Korean War boom's collapse.

[12]Werner Baer, "Import Substitution and Industrialization in Latin America: Experiences and Interpretations," *Latin American Research Review* (Spring 1972), p. 97.

[13]Gourevitch, *Politics in Hard Times: Comparative Responses to International Economic Crises*, p. 47.

[14]Quoted in Carlos H. Waisman, *Reversal of Development in Argentina* (Princeton: Princeton University Press, 1987), p. 134.

[15]Thomas Skidmore, *Politics in Brazil, 1930-1964: An Experiment in Democracy* (New York: Oxford University Press, 1986), p. 45.

[16]Gourevitch, *Politics in Hard Times: Comparative Responses to International Economic Crises*, p. 47.

[17]Kurth, "Industrial Change and Political Change: A European Perspective," p. 358.

[18]James M. Malloy, "Authoritarianism and Corporatism in Latin

America: The Modal Pattern," in James M. Malloy (ed.), *Authoritarianism and Corporatism in Latin America,* p. 15.

[19] "It [BA State] had to be an *expansive* state, not only to impose great transformations..., but also to guarantee for the future the consolidation of the new 'order'. . . " O'Donnell, "Corporatism and the Question of the State," p. 59.

[20]Often a government will determine the quantity of an input to be imported on the basis of existing total productive capacity in the country. Oligopolies arise when the government divides import permits among firms on the basis of individual capacity, independent of efficiency considerations.

[21]Leland L. Johnson, "Problems of Import Substitution: The Chilean Automotive Industry," *Economic Development and Cultural Change* (January 1967), p. 205.

[22]Baer, "Import Substitution and Industrialization in Latin America: Experiences and Interpretations," p. 102.

[23]O'Donnell, "Reflections on the Pattern of Change in the Bureaucratic-Authoritarian State," p. 6.

[24]Hirschman, "The Political Economy of Import Substituting Industrialization," p.92.

[25]Ragnar Nurkse, "Some International Aspects of the Problem of Economic Development," in A.N. Argawala and S.P. Singh (eds.), *The Economics of Underdevelopment* (New York: Oxford University Press, 1971), pp. 264-271.

[26]James Kurth, "The Political Consequences of the Product Cycle: Industrial History and Political Outcomes," *International Organization,* Vol. 33, No.1 (Winter 1979), pp. 28-29.

[27]Kurth, "The Political Consequences of the Product Cycle: Industrial History and Political Outcomes," p. 31.

[28]Economic Commission for Latin America, "The Growth and Decline of Import Substitution in Brazil," *ECLA* (March 1964), p. 8.

[29]In 1955, abandoned by the urban working class which represented the foundation stone of his populist coalition, the military removed Peron from office with ease. This was a remarkable turn of events since they had been the ones who had snatched him away from his military jailers in 1943. Similarly, in August 1954, alone and besieged on all sides, Vargas was bitterly disappointed by the lack of support he enjoyed, despite his phenomenal 100 per cent rise in the minimum wage. He chose to take his own life rather than face the ignominy of being deposed for a second time in his career by the military, which had swept him into

office in the first place.

[30]O'Donnell, "Reflections on the Pattern of Change in the Bureaucratic-Authoritarian State," p. 12.

[31]O'Donnell, "Reflections on the Pattern of Change in the Bureaucratic-Authoritarian State," p. 6.

[32]Robert Kaufman, "Industrial Change and Authoritarian Rule in Latin America: A Concrete Review of the Bureaucratic-Authoritarian Model," in Collier (ed.), *The New Authoritarianism in Latin America*, pp. 187-189.

[33]Jose Serra, "Three Mistaken Theses Regarding the Connection between Industrialization and Authoritarian Regimes," in Collier (ed.), *The New Authoritarianism in Latin America*, pp. 99-164.

[34]Albert Hirschman, "The Turn to Authoritarianism and the Search for Economic Determinants," in Collier (ed.), *The New Authoritarianism in Latin America*, p. 76.

[35]Kaufman, "Industrial Change and Authoritarian Rule in Latin America: A Concrete Review of the Bureaucratic-Authoritarian Model," pp. 233-234.

[36]Hirschman, "The Political Economy of Import Substituting Industrialization," pp. 106-114.

[37]Hirschman, "The Political Economy of Import Substituting Industrialization," p. 117.

[38]Hirschman, "The Turn to Authoritarianism and the Search for Economic Determinants," pp. 73-74.

[39]Michael Wallerstein, "On the Collapse of Democracy in Brazil," *Latin American Research Review*, Vol. 15, No. 1 (1980), p. 33.

[40]Wallerstein, "On the Collapse of Democracy in Brazil," p. 7.

[41]Cohen shows that the 1964 Brazilian coup resulted from political polarization and not an economic crisis. Youssef Cohen, "Democracy from Above: The Political Origins of Military Dictatorship in Brazil," *World Politics*, Vol 40, No. 1 (October 1987), pp.30-54 and Youssef Cohen, *The Manipulation of Consent: The State and Working Class Consciousness in Brazil* (Pittsburgh: University of Pittsburgh Press, 1989).

[42]Hirschman, "The Turn to Authoritarianism and the Search for Economic Determinants," pp. 78-79.

[43]Hirschman, "The Political Economy of Import Substituting Industrialization," pp. 119-120.

[44]Donald Keesing, "Outward-Looking Policies and Economic Development," *The Economic Journal* (June 1967), pp. 303-304.

[45]Anne Krueger, "Inflation and Trade Regime Objectives," in W.

R.Cline and S. Weintraub, (eds.) *Economic Stabilization in Developing Countries.* (Washington, D.C., Brookings, 1981), p. 88.

[46]Stefan H. Robock, "Industrialization Through Import Substitution or Export Industries: A False Dichotomy," in J.W. Markham and G.F. Papanek (eds.), *Industrial Organization and Economic Development* (Boston: Houghton Mifflin, 1970), p. 361.

[47]Robock, "Industrialization Through Import Substitution or Export Industries: A False Dichotomy," p. 361.

2

The State and the Crisis
of Import Substitution

The decline and exhaustion of import substitution is the result of a complex and dynamic political process which both feeds upon and accentuates ISI's inherent weaknesses. The protectionist aspects of ISI lead to economy-wide distortions, distortions that also create extraordinary gains for those involved in import substitution. These benefits, which result from state intervention in a market-oriented economy, are what Anne Krueger calls "economic rents."[1] While the elimination of these rents is critical to the successful implementation of an ISI-based strategy, the beneficiaries of rents are not only reluctant to abandon their spoils, but are also willing to organize and fight to retain and maximize them.

As a result, the state finds itself trapped among the different private sector groups vying for these economic rents, a fact which undermines its autonomy. Thus, it is unable to adjust its economic policies and resolve or even arrest the distortions associated with import substitution. The state's contribution to ISI's decline is a consequence of its inaction, which exacerbates the adverse conditions and indirectly prepares the ground for the armed forces to intervene. I argue, therefore, that import substituting industrialization fails for political — not economic — reasons; that its success rides more on the strength of state autonomy and less on its inherent economic weaknesses.

ISI, Economic Rents, and the Private Sector

Import substitution is predicated upon government interference in the market to guide firms, individuals and sectors to produce goods which contribute to the saving of foreign exchange. By intervening in the market and manipulating the supply and demand of commodities, the

23

state creates artificial conditions which result in some individuals and/or groups benefiting more than they would usually, often at the expense of other individuals or society as whole. For instance, a quota banning the importation of widgets translates into extra gains for domestic widget makers who no longer have to contend with better made or cheaper foreign competition.[2] These extra economic gains derived from government intervention in the workings of the market system are "economic rents."

The impact of rents on an economy is fourfold:

(1) From a free trade perspective, interventions in the market result in sub-optimal operating conditions and, in turn, represent a misallocation of resources. Hence, rents are societal welfare losses. Estimates of government-induced rents can represent substantive portions of a country's income. For instance, in 1968, rents derived from Turkey's system of import licenses was estimated at 15 percent of GNP.[3] Distortions will also be reflected in the favored sector's inflated share of the national output. For instance, in Argentina, "national accounts show manufacturing to be 31.3 per cent of gross domestic expenditure in 1958, but if production had been valued at world prices this ratio would have been only 22.5 percent."[4] Societies, however, will tolerate such losses and distortions generated by state interference if the ultimate goal, such as the development of an industrial infrastructure or achieving economic independence, is perceived as being legitimate.

(2) Rents distort the behavior of firms and individuals. Irrespective of state aims, all protectionist devices that reduce competition and distort market operations with the intended or unintended effect of generating rents, induce individuals operating in such markets to naturally gravitate towards activities that maximize their share of these gains. In other words, even though at the micro level the firm may be maximizing its profits, from the macro level perspective, what is being maximized is a share of state-generated rents. What is paradoxical about rents is that they must be sought by all firms operating in a competitive or even semi-competitive environment. This is because if one firm does not, another will and hence, capitalize at the expense of the former. Rent seeking, therefore, is perfectly rational, but its final outcome is one of rent — and *not* profit — maximizing. Thus, government "interventions lead people to compete for rents although the competitors often do not perceive themselves as such."[5] If quotas determine market size, then competition focuses on capturing the largest share of such quota. Where other forms of protection prevail, firms and individuals will attempt to maximize the level of protection in their own sector while attempting to deny it to others. Such competition among the private sector's constituent groups

necessarily leads to added inefficiencies of production and distribution since a great deal of effort is expended by rent seeking activities. The resulting distortion in behavior means that ventures which require long-term commitments of resources and time will also be sacrificed for the more immediate and, in many ways, surer gains from short-term rents.

(3) The pursuit of economic rents and the resulting distortion of "economic behavior" has far-reaching implications for the private sector itself and for its relations with other forces in society. Since rents can only be appropriated from society or a rent producer (e.g., an exporter), rent seeking alters the nature of competition and, hence, of conflict in society. Depending on the specific character of government policies, a sectoral (e.g., agriculture vs. industry) or intra-sectoral (e.g., textiles vs. electronics) dimension is added to conflict in general. As a result, new societal cleavages and their conflicts share the stage with traditional divisions, such as those based on classes. This, in effect, extends Gourevitch's argument, which proposed that protectionism considerably reduces class tensions within a society by externalizing conflict.[6] Populism in Latin America demonstrated that protectionist policies could form the basis of cross-class coalitions because, when it came to the foreign trade regime, sectoral solidarity cut across class lines. Thus, in seeking to maintain trade barriers which will benefit them and their employers, workers in protected enterprises fail to support less fortunate members of their own class in other industries who stand to profit from an export expansion. Hence, the affinity of views between industrialists and their workers on such issues should not surprise us. In fact, the glue of Juan Peron's coalition in Argentina was precisely an understanding of this linkage. What prevailed in the Argentine Peronist state, as in the Turkish state of the 1960s, was a mentality which can best be described as a "philosophy of protection" advocated by interested segments of the private sector, labor unions, and the state.

Nonetheless, just as Peron's coalition finally succumbed to internecine disharmony and friction, most other such political alliances also followed suit. It was not only the cross-class component of the alliances that failed, but also the intra-sectoral affinity predicated upon protectionist and other such policies that collapsed. The lack of an enduring coalition brings up the fourth and final proposition regarding the impact of rents.

(4) Rents interject an element of politics into what hitherto were economic decisions in their purest form. While this theme will be elaborated in greater detail later in this chapter, suffice it to say here that since it is the state that creates rents, competition between two widget makers for a share of a quota allocation will necessarily involve the state. Hence, rent seeking assumes a political dimension. Charles Lindblom

characterized market-oriented systems as those in which, "a large category of major decisions is turned over to businessmen, both small and larger. They are taken off the agenda of government. Businessmen thus become a kind of public official and exercise what, on broad view of their role, are public functions."[7] The allocation of economic rents, therefore, should invite increased participation of businessmen, further politicizing what already is a political process.

The Political Dimension of Rent-Seeking

At the root of the politicization of economic decision making lies economic rents. Capable of distributing these in a controlled fashion, the state falls victim to pressures from various private interest groups, each of whom is fighting for a "bigger share of the rent pie." Losers in the competition for rents almost always know that they have one last recourse: political action. In other words, they demand compensation from the state. Transfer payments, such as agricultural support payments, are thinly disguised attempts to buy off those groups most often harmed by protectionist schemes. In effect, when the loser is compensated for the cost of a particular group's rent seeking activities, the loss has been transferred to the society as a whole. Under such circumstances, rents can be said to have been socialized.[8]

Although the socialization of the costs of rent seeking behavior dilutes the burden, rents themselves are not infinite. The state's ability to continuously distribute rents is limited. When rents are bountiful, the fashioning of multiclass coalitions à la Peron or Vargas is considerably easier than maintaining them when rents are scarce and the demand for them extensive. The scarcer the rents, the greater the intensity of the inter- and intra-sectoral conflicts. In fact, crises can be described as instances when the cost of rent seeking can no longer be socialized, either because of determined resistance from segments of society or sparseness of available rents.

What is the origin of these rents? For import substituting industries the obvious source of rents is foreign exchange, since what they most desperately seek is access to "inexpensive" supplies of foreign currency. For a firm, foreign exchange represents the means by which a variety of inputs, intermediate and capital, are satisfied. For an economy, foreign exchange embodies the means through which all other needs of society, from defense to medical, can be fulfilled with purchases from abroad. Yet, it is precisely the limits created by the shortage of foreign currency which, in the first place, led countries to look at import substitution as an alternative. Other sources of rents include cheap credit; the regulation of bank interest rates so as to have depositors subsidize the borrowing by business enterprises and other government programs directly subsidizing manufacturing activities.

As competition for rents intensifies in times of foreign exchange scarcity, firms' energies will increasingly be directed at influencing government actions and intentions. This political struggle and its impact will explain why, in the final analysis, import substitution regimes falter.

Two preliminary conclusions can be drawn. First, the presence of rents helps explain the industrialists' and others' reluctance to undertake potentially risky ventures, such as exporting to foreign markets. Those who benefit from rents are unlikely to voluntary ask for their removal. Second, rents give the state the potential to shape and direct the industrialization drive. Hirschman, as we saw in the previous chapter, concluded that industrialists in Latin America felt that they did not possess enough means to control or influence state policies for any length of time. The state's discretionary power regarding the creation and distribution of rents confirms his conclusions.

While the first conclusion is clearly correct, the second is *premature*. Although rents are primarily derived from state intervention in the marketplace, the creation and allocation of rents involve a separate dynamic which, contrary to expectations, diminishes the state's power to bargain. This is because of two characteristics inherent to rents. First and foremost, unlike public goods which are indivisible, rents can be targeted at specific segments of society. If the state can create one set of rents for one industry, it can also extend them to another or eliminate them altogether. This control, however, poses a problem for the state: how to provide a clear rationale for its decisions. In turn, this leads us to the second characteristic of rents: although import substitution and, more generally, the infant industry argument have a certain degree of theoretical justification, they lack the internal ideological consistency of free market principles and ideas.

Import substitution policies are a great deal more susceptible to interpretation and argument, and, consequently, vulnerable to challenges and politicization. The competition for rents assumes an intensely political dimension, and "...even if they *can* limit competition for the rents, governments which consider they must impose restrictions are caught in the horns of a dilemma: if they do restrict entry, they are clearly 'showing favoritism' to one group in society..."[9] Similarly, if the state intercedes directly to help one sector at the expense of another, it can, arguably, find alternative means of compensating the loser. In Turkey, the most obvious example of such practices consisted of agricultural support prices disbursed primarily to offset the agricultural sector's exchange rate losses.

This dilemma is complicated by private sector cleavages. In newly industrializing countries, divisions are accentuated by the transitional nature of these societies; the agricultural and often the commercial sectors are in the process of being supplanted in importance by a more dynamic industrial sector.[10] The latter, regardless of its own lack of unity, possesses significant resources and clout because of its potential promise and the pro-industrialization ethos of the modern era. Paradoxically, despite its dynamism, the industrial sector in most such societies accounts for a minor share of both GNP and labor employed. It is pitted against the usually more numerous landed elites and commercial groups. In a competitive political system, this can be a great disadvantage since voting power belongs not to industrialists, but to their sectoral competitors. Additionally, the transitional nature of these societies implies that state officials often continue to maintain strong ties to traditional elites, agrarian and/or commercial. It is because of such factors that industrialists often perceive themselves to be in a precarious position. There is not, therefore, any single dominant sector capable of imposing its preferences on state and society. Caught amidst competing interests, the state has to satisfy very diverse and often contradictory demands, contributing further to existing economic dislocations.

Paradoxically, the glaring inefficiencies and distortions, tolerated in the name of import substitution, have helped defeat the idea that new industries could gain an international comparative advantage in their own right. John Sheahan finds that some distortions were not accidental. With Argentina in mind, he argues that, "they [distortions] reflect punitive domestic strategy aimed against landowners, a deep rooted aversion to international trade that worked against promotion of industrial exports as well as primary, and the natural pressures of industrialists seeking both protection in their own interests and low-cost access to imported equipment."[11] In the end, however, these distortions, intentional or unintentional, posed significant dangers to the well being of societies engaged in ISI.

State Autonomy and the Exhaustion of ISI

Historically, state authorities as well as participating interest/economic groups have not been oblivious to these potential dangers. As countries plunged from one balance of payment crisis to another,[12] the state, besieged by its various constituencies, had difficult choices to make. These entailed the reduction of tariffs and quotas, the denial of preferential access to foreign exchange and other such mechanisms of protection, and the introduction of an element of rationality and competitiveness to business decisions.[13]

In Latin America, Turkey and elsewhere, the state did not act with determination and vision when it came to promoting exports or limiting protection. Instead, as country after country tumbled into the type of prolonged crisis that brought about military interventions, it became clear that state authorities were incapable of addressing ISI's imperfections and inherent biases. When solutions were devised, they consisted mostly of small and delayed devaluations, multiple exchange rates and complicated export rebate schemes — all of which proved to be of temporary and minimal effectiveness.

What stood between the state authorities and these obvious remedies? Why did these state not take a more active role? What has historically impeded states from relieving an import substituting economy's bottlenecks and distortions? Why has import substitution been transformed into a strategy that simply fuels the expansion of the domestic market, often at the expense of increased indebtedness?

The key to these questions rests in the absence of state autonomy. An autonomous state is free of dominant class interference and is powerful enough to impose its own solutions on an independently minded civil society and/or segmented private sector. Empowered by its control over the creation and distribution of economic rents, the state is uniquely placed to devise and implement the sort of corrective and long-term policies necessary to avoid the degeneration of economic conditions. Otherwise, when such measures are instituted, they tend to get abandoned or scuttled before they can become effective.

By contrast, the Bureaucratic Authoritarian (BA) states, which emerged from the crisis of ISI in Latin America in the 1960s and 1970s, brought with them what their parliamentary counterparts had lacked: a degree of freedom of action. The authoritarian states could impose solutions — whether "deepening" à la O'Donnell or more traditional and orthodox ones — on the populace at large and, more importantly, on the divided private sector. The more serious the crisis preceding the coup, the more severe was the ensuing authoritarian regime, for it needed all the power at its disposal to impose its own vision of the future.

This authoritarian response was as much about the serious economic decline as it was about the inability of government bodies to arrest it. The societies, devoid of a consensus on what future courses of action should be followed, were adrift. With relatively short histories of parliamentary and democratic institutions, Latin American societies were quick to succumb to paralysis and immobility. In 1980, in Turkey a stalemated parliament and paralyzed state institutions contributed to the complete collapse of social order. Similarly, in 1964, a divided Brazilian state apparatus prompted the military to intervene to "preserve" the state and itself.[14] In 1966, in Argentina the serious divisions within society were acutely felt at the political level as one segment of the private sector was actively encouraging the military to intervene in order to implement economic measures which had not being considered by elected administrations.[15] It is the BA state which has succeeded in restructuring the economic relationships, often by totally abandoning ISI.

Any solution envisaged by governments or state institutions, even authoritarian ones, would necessarily include measures that are not welcomed by segments of the populace. Stabilization programs in particular have, more often than not, aroused the ire of some segments of the population and private sector. Thomas Skidmore's study of post-World War II stabilization attempts in Latin America shows that, in comparison with authoritarian regimes, governments in competitive political systems tend to have an especially difficult time confronting and meeting the many demands thrown at them. He argues that "even authoritarian governments must have a high degree of internal consensus to carry through a successful stabilization."[16] For the Southern Cone, post World War II economic history is "littered with failed stabilization plans. . . A plausible hypothesis is that, *ceteris paribus*, the longer the history of failed stabilization plans, the smaller the chances of success (and/or the greater the costs of success) of any new plan."[17]

The Turkish case is a prime illustration of how, faced with internal divisions, all viable economic measures are obstructed and the state is rendered impotent. In 1970, Turkey introduced a stabilization program to limit the damage done by excessive reliance on substitution.[18] Despite the private sector's opposition to its implementation, this program was generally successful in that it achieved the results the state sought; an increase in exports of manufactured goods, a rise in foreign exchange reserves, and, in some industries, an increased level of competitiveness and rationalization. However, these successful economic measures could not be sustained as the various elements of the private sector, alienated by the stabilization program, defected from the ruling conservative Justice Party, depriving it of its parliamentary majority. Faced with domestic opposition this — and future governments — crafted solutions that consisted of a patchwork of concessions to various groups, and thus were ill-conceived and executed.

The failure of these regimes rested on the state's relative weakness vis à vis the private sector in implementing necessary — but admittedly unpopular — measures. The domestic political repercussions in 1970 proved to be a prohibitive price to pay for an elected regime. Therefore, in the case of Turkey, import substitution failed because its governments were unable to take timely and decisive action to remedy the ISI-induced dislocations.

In more general terms, for a state to be proactive in face of potential crises, it needs a great deal of latitude in decision making. Precisely because the competition for rents tends to instill a short-term goal projection onto the participants, the state must take the longer view. In other words, it needs to be autonomous. It is this autonomy which enables it to avert problems, and to convince the dominant classes and/or society in general that it is acting in their long-term interests.

What do we mean by an autonomous state? The debate on state autonomy has preoccupied a great many scholars' attention in the past. Both Marxist and non-Marxist approaches to the state have postulated the state's ability to act independently.[19] For Eric Nordlinger, the state is said to be autonomous "to the extent that it translates its preferences into authoritative actions,"[20] independent of societal preferences. He conceptualizes three types of autonomy. Type 1 refers to cases where state-society preferences are different and the state is not dissuaded from altering its course. Type 2 refers to situations where state and societal preferences, while being divergent at first, are made to coincide as state officials successfully manage to shift the societal preferences to conform with their own. Finally, Type 3 refers to those situations where both sets coincide and, thus, the state can freely pursue its choices.[21]

In contrast to Nordlinger's emphasis on societal preferences, Nora Hamilton approaches state autonomy from the perspective of dominant classes. Accordingly, there are three distinct manifestations of state autonomy; 1) when the state pursues specific "state ends," 2) when it acts independently of dominant class interference, and 3) when the state acts "for ends *opposed* to the actual or perceived interests of the dominant class."[22] While both view the state as an independent actor with its own interests, Hamilton's state is more constricted in that it is not considered autonomous if its interests do not diverge from those of the dominant classes.

From both perspectives, the state, as an actor, has a stake in its own and in the regime's survival. Self-preservation, therefore, is a primary responsibility. An autonomous state, in the words of Hamilton, can "transcend structural boundaries, eliminating old structures and creating new ones..." These new structures or conditions arise only because, as Theda Skocpol suggests, the state, despite its broad commonality of interests with the dominant groups, such as "keeping the subordinate classes in place," in the final analysis perceives a duty to maintaining political order and peace. This fundamental interest may lead the state, "especially in periods of crisis — to enforce concessions to subordinate-class demands. These concessions may be at the expense of the interests of the dominant class, but not contrary to the state's own interests in controlling the population and collecting taxes and military recruits."[23]

While Skocpol was concerned with revolutionary situations, the above characterization is transferable to crises of a different kind: those that are triggered by the impending exhaustion of import substitution. These crises threaten both the regime's and the dominant classes' stability and well being. As O'Donnell also suggested, the crises have two interlinked dynamics. On the one hand, the state faces the prospect of an economy entering a period of protracted stagnation and even decline, which threatens the process of industrialization and capital accumulation. On the other hand, a long-term economic crisis engenders political disorder on the part of an organized and mobilized populace, which often leads to praetorian politics undermining the regime.

Accordingly, if state autonomy is heightened, as Hamilton suggests, by the degree of weakness in the dominant classes' position, the possibility of an alliance of the state with the subordinate class(es) and the degree of internal cohesion within the state apparatus itself,[24] then periods of prolonged crisis should serve to enhance the weakness of the dominant class. It would also follow that the more segmented and bitterly divided the dominant class, the weaker it is and, consequently, the stronger is the state; and, finally, the deeper and the more threatening the crisis, the more autonomy the state ought to have. Similarly, Dietrich Rueschemeyer and Peter Evans consider the divisions within the dominant class to be the most obvious structural condition favoring greater state autonomy.[25]

I would argue, however, that the opposite was true in the case of Turkey. As the crisis deepened, the state found itself weaker rather than stronger. The exercise of state power was also found to be wanting in Argentina, where private socioeconomic groups have "enormous political veto power," which help defeat stabilization attempts. Paradoxically, as in Turkey, such Argentine groups "do not possess sufficient power to impose a 'project' of their own."[26]

An autonomous state has two options: 1) it can unilaterally impose its preferences or, 2) it may seek to reach a compromise solution with Nordlinger's societal forces or with Hamilton's dominant classes. Depending on the level and intensity of the opposition to state policies, both choices represent difficult courses of action and each is fraught with its share of perils for the state. Both sets of choices may lead to the further alienation of dominant groups or weaken the state in society's eyes. With either option, it is not just state preferences but also state behavior which will determine outcome; in other words, how the state plays the game is as important as what it requires of society.

Even where the state has traditionally been weak, as in the United States, some scholars have shown that its importance in setting the agenda, taking the initiative and convincing relevant groups to go along with it has been underestimated.[27] Judith Goldstein maintains that, along with other factors, state ideology is instrumental in enforcing its own policy choices on unruly elements of the private sector. In the case of the United States, the state's unifying ideological stance on the preservation of an international free trade system was crucial in defeating protectionist forces and sentiments.[28] This, of course, is in marked contrast to market-oriented countries, such as the Latin American ones and Turkey, where state involvement in support of protectionism and import substitution dilutes the ideological commitment to free trade and market principles. In turn, this considerably weakens the state's ability to confront competing private sector interests pleading for rents.

ISI, Economic Rents, and the State: Conclusions

What constrains state action is the combination of the segmented civil society and competitive party politics, where the parties vie for control of the state apparatus. Because import substitution gives rise to economic rents, any strategy to alleviate ISI's ill-effects needs to reduce or redistribute these rents. If the state cannot convince the different groups to relinquish a share of their rents, then it needs to forcibly mandate the change. To convince or to mandate change, the state in a parliamentary system needs the help of political parties. Parties, especially those that purport to represent the views of the dominant classes, are crucial to this endeavor. Through their interest aggregation and coalition building capabilities, they have to "sell" the private sector on "new foreign trade regimes."

Concurrently, the presence of competitive party politics acts in the opposite way by creating conditions under which disaffected segments of the dominant class can defect from a ruling coalition. This behavior is quite rational from the perspective of the "rent seeker." Since the dominant class does not constitute a unified block, and because each sub-group is actively involved in competition for a bigger share of "economic rents," political parties come under a great deal of pressure to grant their demands for these extra economic gains. Once in power, governmental parties can use the state bureaucracy to advance these goals, by obtaining necessary permits, licenses, exemptions and funds for investments, etc.

Failure to do this may be perceived by the different segments as cause for abandoning the party or parties in power.

The stage is thus set for furious party rivalries and party-private sector clashes that ultimately serve to paralyze the political system and deny the state its autonomy. And this is exactly what occurred in Turkey in the 1970s as parties scrambled to attract the alienated segments of the industrial, commercial and agricultural elites, thus denying the ruling pro-business party its majority in parliament and society. The intense fragmentation of the Turkish state which rendered it incapable of decisive action was not unique. In Argentina, O'Donnell argued that the "state apparatus [was] extensively colonised by civil society. . . As a consequence, this colonised state was extraordinarily fragmented, reproducing in its institutions the complex and rapidly changing relationship of dominant and subordinate classes — classes which could use the institutions to fuel the spiralling movements of civil society."[29]

Therefore, the military interventions, which followed ISI-induced crises, have to be viewed in light of the fragmentation of the state apparatus and the need to impose a dominating vision on the unruly segments of the private sector. Thus, as Irving Louis Horowitz and Ellen Kay Trimberger have argued, the military in late-late countries has acted as the "pivot, guaranteeing state autonomy and creating the same conditions of state power that obtain in older industrial powers."[30]

In effect, the conclusion this book draws from the Turkish experience is that, the 1980 military coup served as the means through which the state could untie the Gordian knot to rearrange domestic economic coalitions and get the stalemated system moving again.

This book takes a close look at import substitution in Turkey — from its historical background and roots, to its implementation, demise and eventual abandonment. Was a military intervention the only remedy for economic ills that ensued from ISI, economic rents and a severely divided private sector? By focusing on the interactions within the private sector and between the state and the various business groups, the book shows how debilitating the segmentation of these groups was to economic decision making . In the process, the book offers an alternative explanation to the demise of import substitution and the importane of the intensely political nature of the industrialization process.

Notes

[1] Anne Krueger, "The Political Economy of Rent Seeking Society," *The American Economic Review*, Vol. 64 (1974), p. 291.

[2] Another example can be represented by the following: let us suppose

that an industrialist receives an import license for $100,000 to purchase TV screens. If his projected need is for $50,000, he will sell the remaining $50,000 at a 10% premium to a competitor, whose allocation from the state proved insufficient for his needs. The 10% gain represents a rent; a gain derived not from any value added, but rather from the manipulation of scarcity.

[3]Krueger, "The Political Economy of Rent Seeking Society," p. 294.

[4]John Sheahan, *Patterns of Development in Latin America* (Princeton: Princeton University Press, 1987), p.86.

[5]Krueger, "The Political Economy of Rent Seeking Society," p. 302.

[6]This is not to say that class conflict disappears altogether within a protected sector. The emergence of cross-class coalitions, a point also made by Gourevitch, was examined in Chapter 1 of this book.

[7]Charles Lindblom, *Politics and Markets* (New York: Basic Books, 1977), p. 172.

[8]The exception to this rule would occur if and only if there were transfer payments from abroad for the explicit purpose of off-setting these welfare losses. Only in rare exceptions does foreign aid come with such an explicit objective.

[9]Krueger, "The Political Economy of Rent Seeking Society," p. 302.

[10]In industrializing societies, where the transition from landed and commercial interests to the industrial sector has not been completely accomplished, the state is confronted by these different sets of interests. Markos Mamlakis, for instance, suggests that sectoral clashes result when the "government intervenes in a deliberate attempt to promote a particular sector beyond the limits set by a transfer of resources and funds from other sectors," Nikos Mamlakis, "Theory of Sectoral Clashes," *Latin American Research Review*, Vol. 4 (1969), p. 11. Mamlakis' model distinguishes between a dominant sector, which was aided by the government; a suppressed sector, whose growth was discouraged; and a neutral sector, which was devoid of a "well defined role." However, as the discussion on economic rents indicated, the sectors are by no means unified, and the cleavages that exist within them are as important, if not more so, than those that stand between them.

[11]Sheahan, *Patterns of Development in Latin America*, p. 93.

[12]For a discussion of these crises see the section entitled, "Rethinking the Inevitability of Exhaustion" in Chapter 1.

[13]As Anne Krueger argued, export promotion policies were also required. Some countries, such as Colombia, adopted more balanced industrialization policies which combined elements of classical import

substituting type measures with some of the remedies suggested above. Alternatively, periodic and, if necessary, severe stabilization measures, to re-establish a modicum of equilibrium between the outside world and the domestic economy, could have reduced the need for the desperate acts which accompanied the BA regimes. In the absence of such state-sponsored, actions the economy, as argued in Chapter 1, becomes progressively more inefficient, which leads to the exhaustion of ISI as sources of foreign exchange disappear. Hirschman too thought, early on, that the state had a role to perform in avoiding such an outcome. One such suggestion of his had the state nationalize the foreign trade sector. "A less radical and more promising solution would be for the state to simply to take an active role in promoting exports by private enterprise." Albert Hirschman, "The Political Economy of Import Substituting Industrialization," in Albert Hirschman, *A Bias for Hope* (New Haven: Yale University Press, 1971), p. 121.

[14]For an analysis of the Brazilian case, see Youssef Cohen, *The Manipulation of Consent: The State and Working Class Consciousness in Brazil* (Pittsburgh: Pittsburgh University Press, 1989).

[15]Marcelo Cavarozzi, "Political Cycles in Argentina since 1955," in Guillermo O'Donnell, Phillipe Schmitter and Lawrence Whitehead (eds.), *Transitions from Authoritarian Rule: Latin America* (Baltimore: Johns Hopkins University Press, 1986), p. 28. In this respect, Brazil also had its share of politicians and others who tried to instigate the military to intervene and rid the country of Vargas — and later of Vargas' followers, the most obvious of whom is Goulart. The most prominent anti-Vargas and anti-Goulart politician was Carlos Lacerda (See Thomas Skidmore, *Politics in Brazil, 1930-1964: An Experiment in Democracy* (New York: Oxford University Press, 1977). Yet, unlike the Argentine "liberals," whose main preoccupation was with economic policy or the lack thereof, Brazilian liberals were as concerned with politics as they were with much as economics, which enabled them when in power to emulate and adopt the policies of their arch-enemies. Carlos Lacerda was one such prominent example when as Governor of the state of Sao Paolo, he implemented policies he had so vigorously combatted all his life.

[16]Thomas Skidmore, "The Politics of Economic Stabilization in Post-War Latin America," in James Malloy, *Authoritarianism and Corporatism in Latin America* (Pittsburgh: Pittsburgh University Press, 1977), p. 181.

[17]Carlos Diaz-Alejandro, "Southern Cone Stabilization Plans" in W. R. Cline and S. Weintraub (eds.), *Economic Stabilization in Developing Countries* (Washington, D.C., Brookings, 1981), p.120.

[18]This package will be discussed in greater detail in a later chapter.

[19]The question of state autonomy has its roots in the debates on the nature of the state, the most important of which pitted Ralph Miliband against Nicos Poulantzas. See Ralph Miliband, *The State in Capitalist Society* (New York: Basic Books, 1969); Ralph Miliband, "Poulantzas and the Capitalist State," *New Left Review*, No. 82 (November-December 1973), pp. 83-92; Nicos Poulantzas, *Political Power and Social Classes* (London: New Left Books, 1973).

[20]Eric A. Nordlinger, *On the Autonomy of the Democratic State* (Cambridge, Mass: Harvard University Press, 1981), p. 19.

[21]Nordlinger, *On the Autonomy of the Democratic State* , pp. 28-29.

[22]Nora Hamilton, *The Limits of State Autonomy* (Princeton: Princeton University Press, 1982), p. 12.

[23]Theda Skocpol, *State and Social Revolutions* (New York: Cambridge University Press, 1979), p. 30.

[24]Conversely, limits on state autonomy are increased, accordingly, by the contradictions inherent in an alliance with subordinate classes, degree of opposition from the dominant class(es), and inter-relationship that may exist between the state and elements within the dominant class(es), Hamilton, *The Limits of State Autonomy*, pp. 281-284.

[25]Dietrich Rueschemeyer and Peter Evans, "The State and Economic Transformation: Toward an Analysis of the Conditions Underlying Effective Intervention," Peter Evans, Dietrich Rueschemeyer and Theda Skocpol (eds.), *Bringing the State Back in* (New York: Cambridge University Press, 1985) p. 63.

[26]Robert Ayres, "The 'Social Pact' as Anti-Inflationary Policy: The Argentine Experience since 1973," *World Politics* (1976), pp. 494-495.

[27]G. J. Ikenberry, D. Lake and M. Mastanduno (eds.), *The State and American Foreign Economic Policy* (New York: Cornell University Press, 1989). The one exception in this volume is Jeff Frieden who stresses the importance of sectoral clashes as a source in the formulation of U.S. foreign economic policy.

[28]Judith Goldstein, "The Political Economy of Trade: The Institutions of Protection," *American Political Science Review*, Vol. 80 (March 1986), pp. 161-184; " Judith Goldstein, "Ideas, Institutions, and American Trade Policy," in G. J. Ikenberry, D. Lake and M. Mastanduno (eds.), *The State and American Foreign Economic Policy* , pp. 179-217. The American state, however, has not been immune to the effects of domestic sectoral clashes. As Jeff Frieden shows, a great deal of the confusion in the post World War I years with regard to United States foreign economic policy was primarily due to the bitter struggle between the "internationalist" and

"isolationist" elements in US business. Each group had succeeded in forging links to segments of the US state, thereby giving rise to conflicting and contradictory policies, and since neither side was "strong enough to vanquish the other" "the central state apparatus found itself torn between conflicting interests," Jeff Frieden, "Sectoral Conflict and U.S. Foreign Economic Policy," in G. J. Ikenberry, D. Lake and M. Mastanduno (eds.),*The State and American Foreign Economic Policy* , pp. 67-68.

[29]Guillermo O'Donnell, "State and Alliances in Argentina, 1956-1976," *Journal of Development Studies*, Vol. 15 (October 1978), p. 25.

[30]In late-late comers, "an autonomous state apparatus is nearly always authoritarian." Irving Louis Horowitz and Ellen Kay Trimberger, "State Power and Military Nationalism in Latin America," *Comparative Politics* (January 1976), p. 233, 226.

This conclusion is even corroborated in the one exemption to this rule: post-1957 Colombia. There, following a devastating civil war, known as La Violencia, the two main political movements, the Liberals and Conservatives, came to a gentleman's understanding, where power was shared through alternating electoral victories, leading to what observers have called "an oligarchic democracy." A. Wilde, "Conversations among Gentlemen: Oligarchical Democracy in Colombia," in Juan Linz and Alfred Stepan (eds.), *The Breakdown of Democratic Regimes: Latin America* (Baltimore, Johns Hopkins University Press, 1978).

3

The Historical Antecedents of Import Substitution in Turkey

This chapter analyzes the historical antecedents of the 1960-1980 period in Turkey and identifies the key themes to understanding its contemporary political economy. The industrialization efforts of the 1960s and 1970s and their consequences, which are the focus of this book, have their origins in both the underdevelopment of the Ottoman Empire and the initial industrialization efforts of the Republican government during the Etatist period in the 1930s.

The pre-1960 era of planned import substitution is preceded by three distinct eras; (1) the Ottoman Period, (2) the early days of the Republic and the Etatist Period of the 1930s, and (3) the Democrat Party Era, 1950-1960. The contribution of each era has been equally distinctive. The Ottoman Empire, especially in its ascendancy, may have symbolized the apex of the Ottoman-Turkish civilization, but its practices and actions sowed the seeds of future underdevelopment. Because of its Ottoman past and its former leading role on the world stage, Turkey had the privilege of never having been colonized. Nonetheless, this privilege came with neither high rates of capital accumulation, nor an infrastructure, nor class development. In fact, the contrary was true: the Ottoman Empire, with its strong state apparatus, discouraged development à la Western Europe.

Being different in this respect from its European and Latin American counterparts, Turkey's experience did not conform to either Gerschenkron or Hirschman's late and late-late model of industrializers, but rather contained attributes of both. Industrialization did not start with a sudden great spurt. Rather, it started with the state undertaking the initial steps at developing a basic industrial infrastructure. Given the particular historical reasons and situational context, the Turkish state had little alternative but to act in the manner of Gerschenkron's "special institutions." During the Etatist era of the 1930s, the state assumed the primary responsibility for capital accumulation.

The Turkish state's efforts at commencing the industrialization process came after the shock of the Great Depression, the very same event that galvanized Latin American countries to initiate their import substitution processes. An important difference was that while a great number of Latin American countries could rely on an incipient industrial class with its origins in the export sector, the Turkish state had no such domestic group to fall back upon. Its incipient industrial class did not emerge until the mid-1950s, or the Democrat Party Era. In other words, unlike Argentina which had an infrastructure sufficient to accommodate ISI, Turkey could not effectively transform its industrial structure by simply altering its international trade practices. It is, therefore, appropriate to trace the roots of this deficiency in domestic resources back to the nature of the Ottoman Empire and its economic policies.

The Ottoman Legacy

The Ottoman Empire, the historical predecessor of Turkey, left behind a complex legacy of agricultural, commercial and industrial development. Once a formidable empire, the Ottoman state was first and foremost conquest-oriented and not unlike the feudal states of Europe, it derived its revenues from increased territorial acquisition for booty and the exploitation of land resources. The similarities with Europe, however, end at this very point. In fact, Max Weber distinguished between the two systems and categorized the Ottoman as prebendal (strong central government control) and Western Europe as feudal, "systematically decentralized domination."[1] While the European states were an agglomeration of different and contending sources of political power, the Ottoman state was a unified whole where the Sultan exercised complete and uncontested authority. Furthermore, with its divided jurisdictions, feudalism in Europe did not interfere with private property in the general sense, whereas almost all of the land belonged to the state in the Ottoman Empire. In 1528, for instance, 87 percent of all of the empire's land was state owned (*miri*).[2]

The Ottoman landholding system has to be seen as an integral part of the administrative apparatus set up to fulfill not only economic and political but also military needs of the empire. The prebendal domain (*timar*) was the basic administrative unit in the provinces. Not hereditary, it was granted to officials who, in return for revenues obtained from the holding, were held responsible for supplying cavalry to the army and also for ensuring the welfare of the peasants under their jurisdiction. The hierarchically organized provincial system with the *timar*, as the smallest unit, was imposed on all newly-acquired territories. Set up as such, the state not only guaranteed revenues for itself, but also maintained a large army which was in no way a burden on the treasury.[3]

Starting in the mid-16th century, the land tenure system began to break down. As a result of the "price revolution" in Europe which, in turn, had been caused by the discovery and conquest of the Americas, the Empire itself came under serious economic difficulties. Also, trade routes which had previously passed through the Empire's domains were diverted, thus denying the imperial treasury valuable funds. Lacking funds, the treasury continuously debased the currency which affected the fixed income groups most, that is, the elite military class. Concurrently, the increasing tendency to use firearms in warfare put the cavalry class into disuse and forced the state to hire mercenary companies of vagrant peasant origins. These kinds of companies created dislocation in the rural social structure, as well as as a sizeable financial burden on a treasury which was already decimated by financial troubles.[4] The problems of the Ottoman state and army were exacerbated by the need to fight larger and larger campaigns away from the center, and hence undertake costlier operations as the Empire reached its zenith and territorial limits.[5] The financial breakdown contributed to rural unrest fuelled partly by companies of brigands and unemployed soldiers. By the end of the 17th century, the slow disintegration of the land tenure and its replacement by various forms of tax farming contributed to the rise of powerful *ayans*, local notables. The notables would later contest the center's authority and power. The system further degenerated as the bureaucratic elite of the center became corrupt and participated in schemes to appoint favorites to local posts.

The empire's industrial make-up did not fare any better. The industrial system, if it can be called as such, was tightly organized under a guild system which enabled the imperial authorities to control and set prices and production figures as well as quality levels. The guild system was also burdened by the traditional Islamic ideal that competition and incentives for profit were essentially disruptive of the system.[6] The Turkish artisans were priced out of the markets both with respect to the final goods produced and to the procurement of raw materials.[7] The state's main incentive in controlling prices was to meet the requirements of the population, specifically that of Istanbul where discontent could have "far-reaching political implications."[8] These controls rendered the guild system inefficient. Thus, when reversals on the front or declines in trade revenues created conditions of need for the Empire, the guild system was incapable of rising up to meet the challenge.

While aided by the rapid changes in Europe, the underdevelopment of the Ottoman Empire was in essence the result of the particular political order which actively discouraged the development of capitalist social formations. The nature of political control was such that there was practically no activity independent of the imperial center's control. Unlike feudal Europe where autonomous cities would emerge and flourish independently, and sometimes even in opposition to the political structures, no such development could take place in the Ottoman Empire. Other factors that mitigated against the accumulation of capital included the transformation of Istanbul, the imperial center, in the mid-16th century to a consumption-oriented, unproductive metropolis. State ownership of land, and the consequent absence of a landed aristocracy, also undermined capital accumulation. In addition, the threat of confiscation or expropriation by the state of the wealth amassed by office holders was a very real fear which had to be contended with, especially during times of crisis when the treasury was devoid of funds.[9] Finally, the "stigma attached" to all commercial occupations precluded Muslims from participating in ventures conducive to capital accumulation. Instead, if fortunes were made, as Bernard Lewis argues, it was through political means, that is, the sale of public offices and the like. Hence no investments in a real economic sense were made.[10] Even with the advent of tax farming and the commercialization of agriculture, neither bureaucrats who invested in these schemes nor most local notables resided in their regions. They lived instead in the imperial center, and thus became absentee landholders with expensive European tastes.[11]

As the level of corruption increased, the state mechanism faltered. The financial predicament of the Empire contributed to the degeneration of authority. Losses in the battlefield, especially on the Western front, further accelerated the drain on the treasury as more and more territories were conceded to adversaries. As Lewis points out, by the 17th century the Ottoman Empire was incapable of competing with the modernizing states of Europe because "fundamentally, [it] had remained or reverted to a medieval state, with a medieval mentality and a medieval economy — but with the added burden of a bureaucracy and a standing army which no medieval state had ever had to bear."[12]

In the 19th century, the precarious domestic and external conditions forced the adoption of a series of reforms aimed at rebuilding the administrative-political structures, but not its economic base. In the capitulary agreements signed with European powers, little attention was paid to the economic ramifications of the economic stipulations. In the 1838 Anglo-Turkish commercial treaty, the customs duties were fixed at 5 percent on imports, while exports were taxed at 12 percent.[13] Osman Okyar further argues that real and meaningful economic reform did not take place until the end of the 19th and early parts of the 20th centuries, when the state decided to offer some protection to domestic industries emerging from the ruins of the guild system.[14] One significant change of attitude came about with the enunciation of the *Gülhane* Edict in 1839, and that was the recognition of private property. This was a revolution in conceptual terms, although external powers, such as Britain and France, had a great deal to do with these and military reforms that were primarily conceived as a means of strengthening the "Sick Man of Europe" against advancing Russian armies.

Even the Young Turk Revolution of 1908, which supplanted the despotic regime of the Sultan with a reform-minded bureaucratic elite, did not significantly alter the socio-economic make-up of the empire. The outgrowth of the reform attempts imposed from above was an expanded bureaucracy in a society that was already highly bureaucratized. The new Turkish Republic, which emerged from World War I in 1923, inherited this bureaucratic-patrimonial state.

The Early Years of the Republic and the Etatist Period

The new regime under the leadership of Kemal Atatürk was a one-party state. The People's Party, later renamed the Republican People's Party, RPP, ruled for almost thirty years. It was composed of an alliance between what Frederick Frey calls a secular, modernizing and statist national elite in control of the military and the bureaucracy on the one hand, and a traditional, conservative and provincial elite, comprised of mostly local notables on the other. "However, its apparatus was often weak outside the main urban centers. It needed support at the grass-roots level and found it through the local notables. These were persons of great sway in their local areas, wielding influence based on landowning, tribal position, familial prestige, and so on."[15]

During the first years of the Republic, the Kemalist regime was primarily concerned with instituting political and social reforms, such as the establishment of secular institutions, the abolition of the caliphate, the changing of the dress code and the adoption of Latin script. Issues of political economy in general played a minor role.

The lack of importance attached to economic issues can be attributed to two factors: first, the new regime's primary concern was its own survival and the adoption of new rules and customs befitting a modern state in the 20th century. Second, the 1923 Lausanne Treaty required the Turkish government to make concessions regarding customs duties and debt payments, in exchange for the Allies' willingness to dismantle the capitulations imposed during the previous century. In essence, the new Republic relinquished its right to establish tariffs and customs duties until 1929. These concessions effectively undermined the government's ability to adopt trade policies in line with its needs and, as Zvi Hershlag points out, "the outcome was the vast curtailment of the government's income from customs, lagging industrial development owing to the restriction of protective measures and an unfavourable trade balance that persisted until the expiration of the agreement."[16]

An overwhelmingly agricultural country, Turkey had to rely on imports to satisfy its needs for manufactured goods. In 1927, when the gross domestic industrial production was around 550 million TL, imports of manufactured goods alone totalled 187 million TL. In other words, one out of four liras spent on manufactured goods was spent on imports.[17] As Table 3.1 shows, Turkish balance of payments were in deficit during the whole period.

Table 3.1: Balance of Trade, 1923-1929 (million, TL)

Year	Imports	Exports	Trade Balance
1923	144.8	84.7	-60.1
1924	193.6	158.9	-34.7
1925	241.6	192.4	-49.2
1926	234.7	186.4	-48.3
1927	211.4	173.5	-53.0
1928	223.5	173.5	-50.0
1929	256.3	155.2	-101.1

Source: Çağlar Keyder, *The Definition of a Peripheral Economy: Turkey 1923-1929* (New York: Cambridge University Press, 1981), p. 76.

Given the restrictions of the 1924 Lausanne Treaty, the government could do very little to influence the flow of trade, and the deficits had to be made up by borrowing abroad. The new regime had committed itself to a laissez faire system. Keyder calls the Turkish state of the twenties "exemplary in its non-interventionist stance."[18] The state even abolished the 12.5 percent traditional tax on land output, the tithe. State attempts at encouraging industry by enacting a special law were for the most part ineffective. The capital required for industrialization did not exist and, in the absence of a well integrated national economy, it could not possibly be raised by the private sector. In this vein, the most significant development of this early period was the founding of the Turkish Iş Bank by the private sector The bank, which had two branches in 1924, quickly expanded to 15 and then 51 in 1928 and 1934 respectively.[19]

The Great Depression of 1929 radically altered the state's approach and understanding of political economy. The impact of the crash was felt both on exports and imports. With the decline in the price of basic agricultural commodities, Turkey's main source of foreign exchange, the government had no choice but to drastically curtail imports. The import bill, which had reached a high point in 1929 with 256 million TL, declined to 147 million TL, 126 million TL and 85 million TL in 1930, 1931 and 1932 respectively.[20] The reduction in imports meant that the domestic industry, as modest as it was, was further hampered in its efforts to expand. As real incomes declined, tax revenues were also adversely affected. "Taxes were heavily increased in the early thirties. In spite of this, tax revenue fell quite sharply from 222 million TL in 1930 to 186 million TL in 1931, 169 million TL in 1932 and 170 million TL in 1933, indicating a fall in the national income."[21] Having accomplished some of the political reforms they had sought, Atatürk and his political party turned their attention to the economy to face the unpleasant realities of the depression. They proposed a novel way to approach the economic crisis.

This was the promulgation of Etatism, and almost overnight the Turkish state, which had previously relinquished its role in the political-economy, reclaimed it with a vengeance. The authoritarian one party state was particularly well suited for their purposes. Atatürk and his associates, "though imbued with new ideas, were by status and habit men of the old ruling *elite*, with centuries of military and Imperial experience. Even after the destruction of the Empire and the banishment of the dynasty, they still had the assurance and authority to demand and receive — obedience not needing neither to court popularity or enforce submission."[22] Under Etatism, the state would serve two functions. In addition to its traditional regulatory duties, it would assume the task of producing goods for the national economy. Thus, the Etatist state undertook to enhance the country's basic infrastructure, while also engaging itself in almost all facets of manufacturing. Even though it was theoretically not intended to supplant the small private sector, the Etatist state stretched its capabilities into sectors of considerable private sector activity. The case of the textile industry, with its sizeable private sector plants, demonstrates that no aspect of the private sector was immune from competition with state industry.

Through Etatism, the state sought to alleviate the one major shortcoming of the private sector: its ability to generate large amounts of capital. Unlike the private sector, the government could — and did — issue Treasury bonds, use the Central Bank machinery, increase taxation, and issue new money against the "government guaranteed bonds" for state enterprises.[23] Etatism was a reaction to the *laissez-faire* or liberal capitalist approaches, and not — as many had heralded — an alternative to capitalism and socialism. Etatism has come to represent the foundation of Turkey's mixed economy, even though its actual application went far beyond the conventional notions of mixed economy. Although the Turkish leaders had been impressed by the planned measures instituted by the Soviet Union, the Republican People's Party itself was not clear on the definition of Etatism, as different segments of the party interpreted the concept differently. Nonetheless, Etatist policies helped, at least temporarily, to fuse the ruling party and the state.

A short and limited experiment with multi-party democracy in 1930 followed the introduction of the Etatist policies. The Free Party, which was led by a close friend and associate of Atatürk, vigorously defended liberal economic thinking. As a result, opposed to the Republicans' more interventionist approaches, the Free Party's emergence intensified the struggle and debate over economic policies. This party's success in municipal elections and constant criticism of the ruling Republicans put a great deal of political pressure on the latter.[24] The Free Party was not allowed to survive long and was banned five months after its inception. Nevertheless, the politicization of economic policies and the havoc created by the depression forced the Republicans to re-evaluate their policies. The conclusion reached stressed that the way out of the economic depression was through autarchy and rapid industrial development.

By contrast, if Latin American economies did not consider autarchic solutions to their similar problems, they nonetheless envisaged solutions which also called for rapid industrial development. The Latin American example closest to Turkey is Vargas' Estado Nôvo in Brazil. The Estado Nôvo combined some of the autarchic aspects of the

Turkish Etatist state with the pursuit of industrial development through the active participation of the private sector. Thomas Skidmore argues that protection of the emerging industrial sector in Brazil "did not result from popular demand or from pressure brought to bear by the entrepreneurial sector, rather, it was the response of a political elite. The only group that solidly backed the industrialization was the higher military, who badly wanted a steel industry."[25] The Estado Nôvo went one step further than Etatism While institutionalizing the state's role in the development of an industrial structure, it nonetheless also created in its corporatist framework a place for the private sector.

Etatism was far from a cohesive theory or ideology. Two different interpretations of the notion were continuously debated within the ruling People's Party circles. One group, organized around the monthly review *Kadro*, consisted of those who could be called "hardliners." Arguing that private enterprise had failed in Turkey during the 1920s, they championed the right of the state to acquire the principal means of production. The *Kadroists* believed that since the Turkish Revolution was not a class-based movement, the final outcome ought to be different from such class-based systems as socialism and capitalism. This emerging new system would have little or no class conflict.[26]

Etatism was the means to achieve such a harmonious arrangement. They argued that the state should involve itself in the comprehensive planning of all aspects of society, including the health, education, social and economic realms.[27] Despite is intellectual nature, the *Kadro* movement enjoyed support from within the Republican People's Party. Significantly, Ismet Inönü, the Prime Minister, had even contributed an article to the review.

Inönü's support for a more extensive, comprehensive and interventionist view of Etatism was resisted by Celal Bayar, the Minister of the Treasury, who became President of the Republic during the 1950-1960 era. Bayar, the first general manger of the Iş Bank, interpreted Etatism to be a transitory phase designed to supplement and strengthen the Turkish industrial structure in which the state's endeavors would, in the final analysis, be supplanted by private enterprise.[28] Atatürk, himself the ultimate arbiter, was ambiguous in his definition and interpretation of Etatism. In 1935 he argued;

> Turkish Etatism is not a system which borrows ideas that have constantly been harped on by socialist theoreticians of the 19th century; it is a system peculiar to Turkey, which has evolved from the principle of private activity of the individual, but places on the State responsibility for the

national economy, with consideration of the needs of a great nation and large country, and of many things that have not been done so far. The Turkish Republican State wanted to do quickly things which had not been done throughout the centuries in the Turkish motherland by individual or private activity; and, as we realised, it succeeded in doing this in a short time. This road which we have followed is, as we have seen, a system different from liberalism.[29]

However, in practical matters, the indications are that he sided with the more moderate group of Celal Bayar. Atatürk not only appointed Bayar to the Ministry of the Treasury in 1932, and later to the Prime Ministership to replace Inönü, but at a crucial point cast his support in favor of the Iş Bank and private sector groups.

The application of Etatism was ad hoc, concentrating solely on the creation of an industrial base, to the total exclusion of agriculture. In a country where 80 percent of the population was involved in agriculture, this narrow Etatist focus was, from both political and economic perspectives, an error. "The large mass of the peasants...remained detached from the development trends of the new regime. Illiteracy and general cultural backwardness — the main obstacles to development — persisted in the atmosphere of isolation and destitution of the villages."[30] Twenty years later the Republicans would pay the political price for their neglect of agriculture. A productive and vibrant agricultural sector could have yielded the surplus needed to nourish the industrial sector the state so desperately sought to foster.

As part of the Etatist edifice, the state created a number of State Economic Enterprises (SEEs) which principle to be governed as private profit maximizing firms. The two most important SEEs were the Sümerbank, which was established in 1933 as a holding company to oversee industrial production; and Etibank, which was established in 1934 to supervise mining activities. These two companies quickly expanded and, by the end of the thirties, became vast conglomerates with numerous subsidiaries in various sub-fields.

Although Sümerbank's inception in reality preceded the Plan's implementation date, the creation of Sümerbank and Etibank were part of the First Five Year Industrial Plan, which went into effect in 1934. The five year plan was the first such attempt by a developing country outside the Soviet Union. It was limited to industrial production and, given the narrow means of data collection of the time, it could not account for all factors of production. To save foreign exchange, the plan called for the rapid creation and development of a consumer goods industry in general, and a textile industry in particular. It also called for investments in intermediate goods sectors, such as chemicals. The first plan was followed by a Second Industrial Plan which went into effect in 1938. The second plan sought to develop the capital and intermediate goods sectors. However, the 1939 outbreak of World War II in Europe undermined its aims. Overall, the plans were unsuccessful and they failed to improve the standard of living of the population and especially that of the peasantry.

In 1938 the government introduced a law (No. 3460) to standardize the operations of SEEs. Accordingly, state enterprises were allowed to enter into partnerships with private enterprises, to have autonomous managers who were to run the enterprises as regular business firms.[31] The law also provided for the possibility of the sale of SEEs to the private sector. The SEEs, however, were essentially imposed on the private sector. The "mixed economy" created with their development was a curious one, as the two sectors — private and public — coexisted within the national boundaries, but had little to do with each other directly. Even when SEEs were established in areas where private plants were in operation, such as textiles and cement, there was no competition between the sectors. In general, the SEEs enjoyed many more advantages than private sector firms, such as access to the limited foreign currency reserves, Central Bank loans and credits, and new and modern equipment. At the same time, the SEEs were saddled with higher overhead costs and an inefficient bureaucracy.

The autonomy of the SEEs was eroded with the advent of the Second World War when the government instituted price controls and, over time, when the various ministers started to interfere in the running of individual enterprises. In view of these facts, the Etatist system came under severe criticism. Robert Kerwin, for instance, argued that Etatism in general, and the SEEs in particular, seriously undermined the development of the private sector which was fearful of the state and its aims.[32] By taking away scarce capital, the SEEs had an indirect influence on the operation of private firms. They also benefited a number of private concerns without necessarily helping the whole of the private sector. The textile industry is a good example. Here, the government enterprises' sale prices were taken as the market price at which the private firms, with their lower production costs, sold their own products, thus deriving unusually high profit margins.[33] The private sector also benefited from the protection granted by the state through the foreign trade regime and especially import restrictions. This was especially true of sectors where the private and public sectors coexisted.[34]

Etatism was primarily an attempt by the ruling bureaucratic elite-embodied in the Republican People's Party to impose change from above. It was also an instrument to fuse the party with the state, as was first exemplified by its incorporation into the party's six principles (or arrows as they were called) in 1931. Later, when the Constitution was amended in 1937, all six principles — including Etatism — became part of this document.

A significant portion of the RPP and its cadres did not have much faith in either the peasantry or business elites. The disregard for agriculture was part of the dominant thinking, despite Atatürk's belief that the War of Independence had been fought and won by the peasantry. The rural masses were viewed as inconsequential to the modernization efforts, and their loyalty to the regime was viewed as suspect. With the death of Atatürk in 1938, these tendencies were reinforced. If the peasantry was viewed as anti-modernization and backward, business elites did not exude much confidence in the eyes of the bureaucratic elite. This was primarily due to the disproportionate presence of non-Muslim minorities in commerce. The *Varlik Vergisi* (Capital Levy) imposed in 1942 on business groups, which discriminated heavily against religious minorities and had disastrous consequences for them, not only alienated the general commercial elites but revealed the arbitrariness of the authoritarian rule imposed by the Republican People's Party.[35] Keyder points out that,

> in ideology and practice the etatist regime was very close to fascism — a similarity that was observed by many contemporaries. However, it never succeeded in building a popular base: the Republicans remained elitists who did not trust the masses. It is not possible to imagine any RPP leader addressing a popular rally in the style characteristic of Mussolini or Peron. The factor determining this impossibility was the absence of a potentially mobilizable urban petty bourgeoisie.[36]

The RPP's policies during the war years did not endear them to the populace. Despite the fact that the Capital Levy benefited Muslim entrepreneurs, it nevertheless demonstrated the power and autonomy of the state as embodied in the Party. The state directed compulsory purchases of a portion of the peasantry's crop at fixed prices and thus intensified the alienation of towns and rural areas. Following the death of Atatürk in 1938, during the leadership of Inönü, the RPP seemed to lose its reformist spirit and the state became more rigid and harsher: "After the death of Atatürk there was some deterioration. In the hands of lesser men than himself, his authoritarian and paternalist mode of government degenerated into something nearer to dictatorship as the word is commonly understood."[37]

Despite its rigidity, the RPP would not remain immune to changes outside and inside Turkey. The Party had hedged during World War II by remaining "neutral." The Allies' success in this conflict, and the possibility of obtaining United States aid, helped spur moves to end what was now anachronistic single-party rule. On the domestic front, the RPP, by virtue of its position as the sole party, contained diverse and contradictory elements within itself. No longer dominated by a towering figure such as Atatürk, the party's hierarchy was unable to manage its internal divisions as these came to the fore with the Land Reform Bill submitted to Parliament in 1945. The law was passed after an acrimonious debate and after the proposal had been rendered ineffective and its application limited to state owned lands.

Land reform would, nonetheless, remain a hot political issue in the coming decades. The Land Reform Bill of 1945, on the other hand, served to crystallize the different factions within the ruling party. Finally, in 1946, with the onset of US aid plans for Europe, the President Ismet Inönü relented and allowed a new party, the Democrat Party (DP), to form under the leadership of Celal Bayar and Adnan Menderes.

The Democrat Party espoused ideas which made it very popular in both rural and urban areas. The new party declared itself against Etatism, promising to establish a free market system and to dismantle the SEEs by selling them to the private sector. The party was for freedom of speech and parliamentary democracy, and against the authoritarianism which had accompanied the etatist policies. The bourgeoisie, even if predominantly merchant in origin, was coming of age. The inflation of the war years had enabled it to accumulate a sizeable amount of capital which allowed it be more "assertive."[38] This group threw its weight behind the new party. The 1946 general elections, the first since the inception of the new "multi party system," were conveniently called for so as not to allow the new party time to get itself organized nationally.

The RPP emerged victorious, but not without the Democrats scoring some impressive victories. The unexpected popularity of the Democrats and other pressures moved the Inönü governments to relax some of the etatist policies. In its 1947 General Convention, the RPP's leadership decided to heretofore limit the establishment of SEEs to fields where the private sector could not succeed on its own. This was an idea the Democrats had advocated from the start. In 1947 an attempt to introduce a new five year plan was unsuccessful. It faced internal as well as external criticism.[39] Etatism had run its course and even the RPP had attempted, in the 1948 Economic Congress held in Istanbul, to redefine the concept and liberalize it. The new formulation was renamed, not unexpectedly, "New Etatism." All these steps and changes were designed to reduce the differences between the Republicans and their opposition, the newly constituted Democrat Party. The final blow to Etatism came with the Republicans' decisive defeat at the polls in 1950.

If Etatism collapsed in 1950, its remains continued to exert a great deal of influence on the society and its economy. The most important result of Etatism was the strengthening of the political center. This center had faced a number of challenges at the beginning of the Republic from centrifugal forces in the periphery. There were numerous revolts against the authority of the state, including Kurdish secessionist ones. Together with the social reforms of Atatürk, Etatism, by providing a basic economic infrastructure, consolidated the power of the state and increased its relative autonomy and influence. If in the waning days of the Ottoman Empire the state was strong in name only, Etatism helped recreate the strong state apparatus that was the hallmark of that Empire. Paradoxically, the strong state would prove to be illusory, one that was autonomous only when it suppressed and dominated all aspects of civil society. As the 1960s and 1970s will show, the Turkish state was incapable of dealing with the diversity of society when the rules of the game were modified.

The Democrat Party and the 1950s

The Democrat Party came to power with an impressive array of supporters: the intelligentsia which had had enough of the autocratic rule of the RPP; the new business elites which, in the aftermath of World War II were eager to dismantle the restrictive policies of Etatism; and, more importantly, the peasantry and the urban workers. The party had committed to establishing a free enterprise system where the onus of industrialization would fall upon the shoulders of the private sector. Furthermore, they also promised to bring the agricultural sector back from the position of neglect the RPP had relegated it to.

The Democrats, however, lacked a cohesive approach or strategy and simply expected the economy to develop by "leaps and bounds" once the private sector had been freed from the confines of Etatism. Although the private sector did demonstrate an unprecedented flurry of activity, in the final analysis, the results expected by the new party in power did not materialize, and by the end of the fifties the economy plunged into a serious crisis.

The initial period of Democratic rule was characterized by high growth rates. Helped by the favorable international conditions created by the Korean War, Turkish GNP growth exceeded 10 percent per annum for the first three years of the new government. As promised, Democrats emphasized the development of agriculture. An ambitious mechanization program was started. Tractor use increased from 9,170 units in 1949 to 24,000 in 1951, 35,000 in 1953 and by the end of the decade the number reached 42,136.[40] Taxes on agriculture were eliminated, and an extensive road building program was undertaken with the help of US aid. By integrating the villages with the major population centers, this road program enabled the peasantry to market their produce with greater ease. The government also increased "the supply of credit and instituted a policy of high minimum prices by state purchasing agencies, so as to boost the resources available to the farmer."[41] Thus commercialization of agriculture achieved a peak, especially in Western Turkey which constituted the most solid base of support for the Democrat Party and contained some of the most productive lands. Yet, despite the increases in cultivated land areas and mechanization, agriculture remained dependent on weather conditions, as the latter contributed to a disastrous harvest in 1954. In turn, this event had serious implications for the fortunes of the party.

On the industrial front, the relaxation of import restrictions and government encouragement fueled production. Industrialization attempts were also bolstered by the Industrial Development Bank, (Türkiye Sinai Kalkinma Bankasi), IDB, which extended long- and medium-term credit to the manufacturing sector, and made foreign exchange more accessible. Originally created in 1950 by the Republicans with an infusion of capital from the World Bank, "IDB accounted for a high proportion of the total industrial investments which occurred in the decade."[42] The prosperity enjoyed by the industrial sector was also helped by rising agricultural incomes which increased the general level of consumption. The rise in consumption levels also pushed the manufacturing sector into establishing consumer goods industries. The IDB encouraged this trend since it viewed it as a means of reducing imports. In other words, this was the beginning of import substituting industrialization. However, these efforts at substitution were not the result of the government's clearly thought-out and executed policy decisions, but rather a reaction to changes in the internal economic conditions as well as the foreign exchange difficulties experienced after 1953. As such, early attempts of ISI were very much in line with Hirschman's characterization of the haphazard nature of import substitution's beginnings (see Chapter 1).

The Democrats' attempts to expand the output of agriculture and their investments on infrastructure led to fiscal deficits which had to be financed by borrowing from domestic and external sources. Especially after 1953 the contraction in international markets following the collapse of the Korean War boom, the setbacks in agriculture and the general sluggishness witnessed in manufacturing created a dilemma for the Democrats. Despite their promises to undo the institutional structures of Etatism, they increasingly relied on SEEs to make up for the lack in private sector investments. As political considerations played an increasingly important role in investment decisions, whether these related to types of investments or their locations, they resulted in increased inefficiencies. The Democrats used the public sector investments and SEEs' outlays as a means of halting any erosion in their domestic support base. Their agricultural policies also contributed to the general decline. As Dwight Simpson argues "...in order to encourage the agricultural sector the government abandoned the tax on agricultural income in the 1954 budget. However valuable such a step may have been politically when 77 percent of a population and 40 percent of a gross national product is exempted from taxation it becomes very hard to finance a large investment program without a corresponding deficit."[43] These deficits were offset by foreign aid, the use of gold and foreign exchange reserves and Central Bank outlays. Despite the government's attempts to attract foreign private investments by amending the laws regarding this issue, foreign ventures were few and far between. Faced with large balance of payments deficits, the government instituted import controls and thus the liberal phase of 1950-1953 was abandoned. While they contributed to the reduction in imports, the measures did not alleviate the foreign exchange problem. Despite all the subsidies, exports failed to increase further, reaching a peak in 1953 and declining over the course of the decade (Table 3.2). This was also due to the overvaluation of the lira as the domestic economy suffered from an unprecedented inflation. The wholesale price index, which had declined in 1950 and 1951 to 91 and 94 respectively (1948=100), by 1956 reached 145, and by 1958 had more than doubled to 205.[44]

Table 3.2: Balance of Trade 1950-1960 (millions of dollars)

Year	Imports	Exports	Trade Deficit
1950	286	263	23
1951	402	314	83
1952	556	363	193
1953	533	396	137
1954	478	335	143
1955	498	313	185
1956	407	305	102
1957	397	345	52
1958	315	247	68
1959	470	354	116
1960	468	321	147

Source: Morris Singer, *The Economic Advance of Turkey: 1938-1960* (Ankara: Turkish Economic Society, 1977), p. 392.

By 1958 the economic situation had deteriorated to such an extent that Turkey was unable to borrow any funds from abroad, and US aid, which had for the most part constituted the lion's share of all foreign aid during the fifties, had also dwindled. External pressures, paired with the rising cost of political unrest in the country, forced the Democrats to announce a stabilization program in August 1958. This program included a *de facto* devaluation, restraint on government expenditures and the liberalization of the import regime. The delay in implementing a new import regime also triggered a minor recession.[45] The Democrats did not, however, enjoy the benefit of seeing whether or not their economic program would succeed as the military intervened to remove them from power on May 27, 1960.

After years of being restrained by authoritarian — Ottoman or Etatist — state structures, it is during the Democrat Party administration that the private sector finally emerged and gained some confidence in its abilities. But as the subsequent chapters will show, this confidence was not total as this sector continuously strived to use the state to support and protect it from the vagaries of the marketplace as well as foreign competition.

Notes

[1]Max Weber, *Economy and Society*, Gunther Roth and Claus Wittich

(eds.) (Berkeley: University of California Press, 1978), pp. 1077-1079.

[2]Halil Inalcik, *The Ottoman Empire, The Classical Age 1300-1600* (New York: Weidenfeld and Nicolson, 1973), p. 110.

[3]For an overview of the Ottoman land tenure system see Halil Inalcik, *The Ottoman Empire, The Classical Age 1300-1600* and Halil Inalcik, "Land Problems in Turkish History," *Muslim World*, Vol. 45 (1955).

[4]Halil Inalcik, "Military and Fiscal Transformation in the Ottoman Empire, 1600-1700," *Archivum Ottomanicum*, Vol. 6 (1980), pp. 283-337.

[5]Bernard Lewis, *The Emergence of Modern Turkey* (New York: Oxford University Press, 1979), p. 24.

[6]Halil Inalcik, "Capital Formation in the Ottoman Empire," *Journal of Economic History*, Vol. 29, No. 1 (March 1969), p. 105.

[7]Ilkay Sunar, *State and Society in Turkey's Development* (Ankara: Siyasal Bilgiler Fakültesi Yayinlari, 1974), p. 36.

[8]Halil Inalcik, "The Ottoman Economic Mind and Aspects of the Ottoman Economy," M.A. Cook (ed.), *Studies in the Economic History of the Middle East* (London: Oxford University Press, 1970), p. 217.

[9]See also, Gilles Veinstein, "Trésor Public et Fortunes Privées dans l'Empire Ottoman (milieu XVIe - début XIX siècles)," *Actes des Journés d'études Bendor* Vol. 3-4 (1979), p. 122; Rifat A. Abou-el-Haj, "The Ottoman Vezir and Pasha Households 1683-1703: A Preliminary Report," *American Journal of Oriental Studies*, Vol. 94 (1974), p. 446 fn. 36.

[10]Lewis, *The Emergence of Modern Turkey*, p. 32.

[11]Sunar, *State and Society in Turkey's Development*, p. 38. From a comparative perspective, absentee landlords with similar tastes were also a very common feature in Latin America, Barbara Stein and Stanley Stein, *The Colonial Heritage of Latin America* (New York: Oxford University Press, 1970).

[12]Lewis, *The Emergence of Modern Turkey*, p. 36.

[13]Osman Okyar, "The Role of the State in the Economic Life of the 19th Century Ottoman Empire," *Asian and African Studies*, Vol 14 (1980), p. 147.

[14]Okyar, "The Role of the State in the Economic Life of the 19th Century Ottoman Empire," pp. 153-155.

[15]Frederick Frey, "Patterns of Elite Politics in Turkey," George Lenczowski (ed.), *Political Elites in the Middle East* (Washington, D.C.: American Research Enterprise, 1975), p. 61.

[16]Zvi Y. Hershlag, *Turkey: The Challenge of Growth* (Leiden: Brill,

1968), p. 22.

[17]Osman Okyar, "The Concept of Etatism," *Economic Journal* (March 1965), p. 99.

[18]Çağlar Keyder, *The Definition of a Peripheral Economy: Turkey 1923-1929* (Cambridge: Cambridge University Press, 1981), p. 76

[19]*Ilke* (1974), p. 70.

[20]Okyar, "The Concept of Etatism," p. 99.

[21]Okyar, "The Concept of Etatism," p. 99.

[22]Lewis, *The Emergence of Modern Turkey*, p. 291.

[23]Hershlag, *Turkey: The Challenge of Growth*, p.88.

[24]Korkut Boratav, *Türkiye'de Devletçilik* (Ankara: Savaş Yayinlari, 1982), pp. 53-59, 97-98.

[25]Thomas Skidmore, *Politics in Brazil: 1930-1964* (New York: Oxford University Press, 1986), p. 46.

[26]Boratav, *Türkiye'de Devletçilik*, p. 152.

[27]Okyar, "The Concept of Etatism," p. 100.

[28]Boratav, *Türkiye'de Devletçilik*, pp. 139-146.

[29]Hershlag, *Turkey: The Challenge of Growth*, p. 71.

[30]Hershlag, *Turkey: The Challenge of Growth*, pp. 124-125.

[31]Okyar, "The Concept of Etatism," pp. 101-102.

[32]Robert Kerwin, "Private Enterprise in Turkish Industrial Development," *Middle East Journal*, Vol. 5, No. 1 (1951), *in passim*.

[33]Kerwin, "Private Enterprise in Turkish Industrial Development," p. 27.

[34]In relation to the SEEs, the private sector was relatively small in size, and consisted mostly of small establishments and of commercial rather than industrial enterprises.

[35]A disproportionate share of the burden of the *Varlik Vergisi* fell on the minorities whose tax was estimated at levels ten times higher than their Muslim counterparts of equal stature and resources. Furthermore, these assessments were arbitrary. Once levied, sums had to be paid within thirty days and, if the individual could not pay, his and his families' assets were seized and he was sent to a forced labor camp for an unspecified period. For an insider's view of the process see Faik Ökte, *The Tragedy of the Turkish Capital Tax* (London: Croom Helm, 1987). Ökte was director of finance of Istanbul and was in charge of implementing this levy which he disliked.

[36]Çağlar Keyder, "The Political Economy of Turkish Democracy," *New Left Review*, No. 115 (May-June 1979), pp. 14-15.

[37]Lewis, *The Emergence of Modern Turkey*, pp. 303-304.

[38]Okyar, "The Concept of Etatism," p. 106.

[39]For the 1947 plan, see Ilhan Tekeli and Selim Ilkin, *Savaş Sonrasi Ortaminda 1947 Türkiye Iktisadi Kalkinma Plani* (Ankara: ÖDTÜ Yayinlari, 1974); Boratav *Türkiye'de Devletçilik*, Hershlag, *Turkey: The Challenge of Growth*. Tekeli and Ilkin, and Boratav argue that foreign pressure, especially US demands, led to the failure to fully implement the plan, as Turkey's government was seeking funds from abroad. Coincidentally, 1947 is also the year the Truman Doctrine came into effect.

[40]Morris Singer, *The Economic Advance of Turkey* (Ankara: Turkish Economic Society, 1977), p. 250.

[41]William Hale, *The Political and Economic Development of Turkey* (New York: St. Martin's Press, 1981), p. 94.

[42]Singer, *The Economic Advance of Turkey*, p. 259.

[43]Dwight Simpson, "Development as a Process: The Menderes Phase in Turkey," *Middle East Journal*, Vol. 19 (Spring 1965), p. 149. No government since then managed to reimpose the tax on agricultural income. Once abandoned, it proved politically too dangerous to reinstitute, and it is only the military government following the September 12, 1980 coup that finally resurrected it.

[44]Bill Warren, *Inflation and Wages in Underdeveloped Countries* (London: Frank Cass, 1977), p. 166.

[45]Anne Krueger, *Foreign Trade Regimes and Economic Development* (New York: National Bureau of Economic Research, 1974), pp. 63-74, 106-107.

4

Planning and Implementing ISI in Turkey

This chapter details the mechanisms by which Turkish authorities implemented ISI in the post-1960 period. Building upon the historical discussion of the previous chapter, this chapter discusses the intellectual, institutional and practical contexts of the industrialization drive. This includes the economic and political arguments advanced in favor of import substitution, the goals and expectations associated with it, the role of state institutions, most importantly, the State Planning Organization (SPO) and its five year development plans. By detailing the mechanisms of the process, this chapter also sets the stage for understanding the interplay between the economic preferences of groups and those of state institutions.

The Underpinnings of ISI in Turkey

Until the 1960s, Turkey's experience with import substitution had been limited to the Etatist Era's state-based industrialization attempts and what Hirschman would call "accidental" beginnings triggered by foreign exchange shortages of the 1950s. As a result of those efforts, Turkey had reached the same stage of industrial development attained by Latin American countries at the the dawn of their ISI drive. In other words, it possessed "a significant nucleus of non-durable consumer goods industries."[1] In this context, two sets of arguments in favor of adopting ISI emerged in the early 1960s. These can be analyzed in two clusters: political and economic.

Political Rationale

Politics provided the main impetus for ISI. The message was carried by a coalition of interests which had emerged on the eve of the 1960 coup and strongly believed that the solution to Turkey's chronic problems lay in industrialization. They also agreed on the need for ISI and its implementation through state-directed plans. The main components of this coalition included the new industrial bourgeoisie, the intelligentsia and both the civilian and military bureaucracies. Eventually the industrial working class would also be party to this coalition.

The private sector had flourished during the Democrat Party rule. What was new, however, was the emergence from the ranks of traders of a new class of industrialists.[2] Even if, by the end of the 1950s, the majority of industrial concerns were still relatively small in size and mostly family owned, the Turkish economy had developed a pool of second generation industrialists to draw upon. They owed their emergence to the haphazard beginnings of ISI and, naturally, became some of ISI's fiercest supporters. Overall, through the unrestricted access to a protected domestic market that only the state could provide, ISI offered the manufacturing sector potential for rapid growth and, both economically and politically, a means of increasing and consolidating its relative importance and position. In its 1964 recommendations for the First Five Year Development Plan, the Union of Chambers of Commerce, Industry and Commodity Exchanges (TOB), the main business organization, called on the government "to make a serious effort in the direction of import substitution."[3]

Throughout the 1960-1980 period, industrialists were most adamant in their support for ISI. They stood to gain the most and their commitment was buttressed by the economic rents and benefits they acquired from the state's interference in the market. Their commitment and support did not go unnoticed by the politicians of the period. Turkey, in the 1960s, experienced the same kind of unabashed optimism in its yet unproven domestic industry that characterized the exuberant and easy phase of import substitution in Latin America. The industrialists desire for protection coincided with the new obsession of the time: that almost everything could be manufactured in Turkey. The strong underlying nationalistic appeal of such an obsession further increased the allure of ISI,[4] and was also responsible for some of the fantastic projects proposed later, such as the manufacturing of jet aircraft and tanks. While these were quickly dismissed, the dominant political view lent itself to the consolidation of ISI as the strategy for industrialization.

ISI's strong nationalist overtones was attractive to both the military and civilian bureaucracies. In the early years of the Republic, they, as the previous chapter indicated, had been an integral part of the Republican People's Party's (RPP) plans and fortunes, such as Etatism.[5] What a planned ISI strategy offered them was a nationalist solution to Turkey's problems and the means to avoid repeating the haphazard policies of the Democrat Party. Always suspicious of the private sector, the civilian bureaucracy found itself shunned by the Democrats, who often attacked its interests and prerogatives. Therefore, for the bureaucracy, a planned strategy of import substitution promised the best of both worlds: it provided a conduit for strengthening the state's role over the unruly and untrustworthy private sector and it directed the private sector to assume a nationalist posture. The military also supported the idea of a planned growth strategy. Their motivations, while not significantly different than those of their civilian counterparts, had the added impetus of having suffered a great deal from the economic reversals of the decade.[6]

The third group supporting ISI, the intelligentsia, had become disillusioned with the Democrat Party government which, in its last years, increasingly resorted to borrowing from abroad and to repression to cover up economic mismanagement. Turkish intellectuals who had initially welcomed the new party sought ways to express their disenchantment. A number of them joined the journal, *Forum*, which played an influential role in both crystallizing their opposition and in actually shaping the issues for a future leadership. One issue which attracted a great many intellectuals' attention was planning, which was a reaction to the *ad hoc* measures that ruined an otherwise promising beginning in 1950.

Most members of the intelligentsia in their search for a political home returned to the RPP, despite its legacy of an authoritarian past. In the struggle against the dictatorial tendencies of the Democrats, the RPP regained some of its old stature and respectability as Atatürk's party. The RPP-bureaucracy-intelligentsia combination also fused well with the idea of planning. With the Democrats' economic debacle, the RPP could point to its Etatist past with a measure of pride. In fact, the party had in the last years of the fifties returned to the idea of planning as the only way out of the impending economic crisis.[7] From the RPP's perspective, there was another reason to support ISI: it could have meant the beginning of a rapprochement with some segments of the private sector and the mending of fences with others. What did emerge was a powerful coalition composed of the civilian and military bureaucracies with ideological and political support from an intellectual class and a rejuvenated RPP. This coalition was determined to rid the country of the Democrats and institute a more directed and controlled form of development. They wholeheartedly endorsed the 1960 coup and enshrined their principles in the 1961 Constitution.

Was this coalition similar to the multi-class coalitions which characterized the populist movements in Latin America, such as Peron's in Argentina? The results of the 1961 elections clearly demonstrated that the RPP banner under which the pro-planning groups had rallied failed to achieve a majority. Devoid of charismatic leadership and carrying the heavy burden of a bureaucratic past, the RPP had never before aspired to becoming a populist party. The private sector in general, and a majority of the working class sided with the newly created Justice Party (JP), which was established as a continuation of the banned Democrats. In the period between 1961 and 1965, Turkey was ruled by an uneasy alliance consisting at times of the RPP, under the leadership of Ismet Inönü, and the JP or the RPP with other center-right parties. In 1965, a rejuvenated Justice Party, under a new group of leaders, captured a majority of the votes in national elections. By 1965, the Justice Party had also embraced the idea of import substitution. Given the wide ranging support for this strategy among burgeoning industrial circles, the party may not have had much choice. The JP was, however, much less enthusiastic about planning and the SPO, fearing the latter as a RPP-inspired organization. The JP, therefore, sought to neutralize the effectiveness of SPO functionaries who, if not RPP devotees, were, in fact, "nationalist-etatist" in orientation.[8]

Despite the inclusive nature of the 1960 coup, a populist coalition with fiery leaders à la Latin America did not materialize in Turkey. Nonetheless, the 1960 intervention did represent a new beginning for labor. Through its 1961 Constitution, the new regime opened the political system and liberalized the rules governing the behavior of unions. The rights to strike and to collective bargaining were legalized for the first time, and social welfare ideas were incorporated into the new constitution, encumbering the state with new responsibilities. Not unlike their Latin American counterparts, the industrial unions wholeheartedly supported public and private attempts at enlarging the industrial sector. While the union movement would eventually split and follow different political tendencies, the labor movement, in general, provided crucial support for the state's protectionist policies.

Until the end of the seventies, this array of groups supporting import substitution remained stable. Despite complaints by some in the private sector, industrialists steadfastly supported the industrialization strategy, even when it was clearly failing. The nationalistic appeal also constrained the debate among intellectual circles by inhibiting the serious discussion of alternatives.[9]

Economic Rationale

While the political reasons for adopting an ISI-driven strategy were compelling, the economic conditions made it equally imperative. The economic argument for ISI can be traced to two reasons: (1) the lackluster growth, and (2) the chronic balance of payments deficits of the 1950s.

At the heart of both lay an unreliable agricultural sector. In 1960, Turkey was still overwhelmingly an agricultural society. Despite the efforts of the Etatist Era and the "accidental" beginnings of ISI in the fifties, both of which are detailed in the previous chapter, agriculture accounted for 75 percent of total employment compared with industry's 7.5 percent.[10] In 1962, agriculture and manufacturing accounted for 43.8 percent and 12.8 percent of GNP respectively.[11] In the same year, 62.3 percent of manufacturing sector activity was oriented towards consumer goods, whereas the relative shares of intermediate and investment goods were 27.8 percent and 9.9 percent respectively.[12] Turkey was not only overwhelmingly agrarian, but its industry was primarily involved in simple consumer goods production.

Democrats in the late fifties abandoned their efforts to rely on agricultural exports as a means of fueling growth. Their hopes and expectations, built on the experience of 1950-1953 when agricultural exports increased dramatically, were dashed as exports and agricultural incomes declined continuously after 1953.[13] This failure contributed considerably to the shortage of foreign exchange, a problem which plagued Turkey for the rest of that decade. In 1958, faced with mounting balance of payments deficits, the Democrats were forced to institute a stabilization program and devalue the currency.

This 1950s experience gave rise to an atmosphere of pessimism about the export sector's potential and viability. The SPO clearly stated, early on, that because of the low elasticity of Turkish exports, increases in exports could not be achieved without restructuring the sector as a whole.[14] On the other hand, a partially modernized agricultural sector, vulnerable to the vagaries of the weather and markets, did not offer a dependable long-term growth solution to a society with an annual population growth of 3 percent.

That left the manufacturing sector which clearly was not in a position to sustain an export-led industrialization strategy. As one of the early directors of the SPO's Economic Planning Office, Baran Tuncer argued, the development plans were based on the belief that the manufacturing sector's export potential was non-existent and, even if production was to be increased, great difficulties would be encountered in trying to market the products abroad.[15] Hence, industry as well was in need of a restructuring. Given this perceived unreliability of the exports sector and the weakness of industry, import substitution would emerge as a natural policy alternative for maximizing foreign exchange resources and assuring economic growth. SPO's calculations show that during the first five years of planned development, it expected import substitution efforts to yield $500 million in foreign exchange savings (see Table 4.4). It appeared that import substitution, especially if planned, bestowed a sense of control over powerful economic forces and currents.

One of the more compelling arguments in favor of import substitution was that it had already gotten a start in the previous decade. Even the SPO, despite its ideological and political dislike of the Democrats, acknowledged that the period under that party's rule had brought about a new degree of economic dynamism and integration.[16] However, just as in other societies, the incipient industrial sector was in need of further protection. This reasoning was clearly reflected in the SPO's goals, which promised to protect "newly established industries" "through import restrictions and customs policies until they overcome the problems of the initial years of establishment and gain international competitive strength."[17]

As Table 4.1 shows, by 1962, the share of consumer goods in Turkey's import bill had fallen to 8.8 percent. Until the effects of the oil shocks were felt, this rate continued to decline steadily, although not as dramatically as in the 1950s.[18] In fact, the relatively low rate of consumer goods imports meant that Turkey was able to manufacture a significant share of such goods. By contrast, it is in the capital and intermediate goods industries where the economy was vulnerable. Interruptions in their supplies could potentially have a disastrous impact on existing industries and the establishment of new ones. Hence, by consolidating the decline in consumer goods imports, more resources could be devoted to the procurement of intermediate and investment goods.[19]

For the SPO, as the leading state institution in charge of overseeing the implementation of the industrialization program, ISI represented more than simply a means of saving foreign exchange. "The goal of industrialization is to effect structural change in Turkish industry which is primarily composed of small units producing consumer goods with outmoded production techniques."[20] Structural change required backward and forward linkages, as well as technological innovations to

Table 4.1: Composition of Imports, (selected years, %)

Year	Investment Goods	Intermediate Goods	Consumer Goods
1950	46.0	33.0	21.0
1951	43.0	32.0	25.0
1953	52.0	28.0	25.0
1955	54.0	31.0	15.0
1958	44.0	44.0	12.0
1960-62	47.0	44.2	8.8
1963	45.8	48.8	5.4
1965	41.8	53.8	4.4
1967	47.2	47.9	4.9
1968	48.0	47.2	4.8
1970	47.1	47.9	5.0
1972	50.0	45.3	4.7
1973	48.0	47.6	4.4
1975	41.4	54.3	4.3
1977	38.9	58.0	3.1
1979	31.5	66.6	1.9
1980	37.0	60.5	2.5

Source: Memduh Yaşa, *Cumhuriyet Dönemi Türkiye Ekonomisi* (Istanbul: Akbank Yayinlari, 1980), pp. 343, 362, 374; TOB, *Iktisadi Rapor 1971* (Ankara: TOB, 1971), p. 389; TÜSIAD, *The Turkish Economy, 1981* (Istanbul: TÜSIAD, 1981), p. 131.

help reduce dependence on outside sources. To accomplish such an alteration, more importance needed to be given to investment goods and to engineering industries.[21] In effect, by the time the third plan was promulgated, the SPO and government leaders were acknowledging the importance of making a transition to the second and more difficult stage of ISI. Without such a move, Turkey would be unable to catch-up to the more advanced societies. SPO plans betrayed a great deal of optimism about Turkey's ability to reach the goals set. With these economic and political foundations in mind, we now turn to the specifics of the five year plans and how ISI was actually implemented.

Import Substitution and the Five Year Plans

The 1960 military coup symbolized a dramatic a break with the past, as had the Democrats' ascendancy to power a decade earlier. The young officers who were at the core of the intervention also sought to simultaneously quicken the pace of development and eradicate what they perceived as an increasing level of societal inequity. To them planning was the single most efficient way of achieving these goals.

The new regime differed from that of the Democrats in one other important respect: its reliance on state plans to achieve its goals. The plans had a significant impact because they *institutionalized* ISI as *the* official development strategy. There were to be four plans between 1963 and 1980, plans that were distinctly different from those of the Etatist era. During the Etatist period, the plans had concentrated solely on state activities. By contrast, the five year programs, starting in 1963, were all-encompassing, taking into account all sectors of the economy — including the private sector. This was also a reflection of the changes that had transpired in the economy: by 1963 the private sector accounted for 47.3 percent of all value added in the manufacturing sector calculated at current prices, up from 37.8 percent in 1950.[22]

The State Planning Organization, SPO,[23] was established soon after the May 1960 coup. To institutionalize their concerns for proper planning, the officers made sure that SPO would be included in the 1961 Constitution as an integral state organ. Article 41 of the new Constitution stated that it was the *duty of the state* to devise development plans which would, within the confines of democratic processes, realize the progress of society along economic, social and cultural lines.[24] Accordingly, the SPO was to formulate, execute and, when necessary, revise the development blueprints. A High Planning Council, comprised of the Prime Minister, the head of the SPO, three relevant cabinet ministers and three SPO section chiefs, was created. The SPO prepared plans were subject to the High Planning Council's approval. The final decision, therefore, rested with the Council which, by its very nature, subjected the plans to the political considerations of the time.

While the SPO could not coerce the private sector, it could suggest relevant policy directions. The public sector was a different matter. Beyond the absolute requirements outlined for it in the plans, the public sector had to respond to its private counterpart's successes and shortcomings. Through its yearly revisions, the SPO would use the public sector to compensate for private sector behavior. The guidelines, published in the First Five Year Plan (FFYDP), made it clear that the private and public sectors were not independent and autonomous entities, but rather two complementary parts of a whole.[25]

Table 4.2: Planned and Achieved Annual Growth Rates for the Four
Five Year Development Plans (%)

	First		Second		Third		Fourth	
	1963-1967		1968-1972		1973-1977		1978-1983	
	P[1]	A	P	A	P	A	P	A[2]
GNP	7	6.7	7	6.9	7.4	6.5	8	
Agriculture	4.2	3.2	4.1	3.1	3.7	3.3	5.5	
Manufacturing[3]	12.9	8.1	12.0	10.4	11.7	8.8	11.4	

[1]P = Planned; A = Achieved

[2]The Fourth Five Development Plan was overridden by the January 24, 1980 measures.

[3]Manufacturing figures do not include mining, electricity and gas production.

Source: DPT, *Yeni Strateji ve Kalkinma Plani Üçüncü Beş Yil: 1973-1977* (Ankara: DPT, 1973), p. 293; DPT, *Dördüncü Beş Yillik Kalkinma Plani: 1979-1983* (Ankara: DPT, 1979), p. 8.

Despite its relatively small share of national income, industry, specifically the manufacturing sector, was alone in offering the greatest hope of achieving the 7 percent annual growth rate targeted by the SPO. Accordingly, the organization put its emphasis on this sector (Table 4.2). Although it never fulfilled its expectations, the manufacturing sector's planned performance was expected to compensate for the slow growing agricultural sector. The planned sectoral distribution of investments also reflects this bias towards the manufacturing sector (Table 4.3). With the exception of the first plan, where the manufacturing sector was ranked third in the overall percentage distribution of all planned investments, the three subsequent five year plans allocated this sector the largest share.

The critical factor in the growth of the manufacturing sector was the emphasis on import substitution. The first plan stated that the manufacturing sector was to be protected by restructuring and even banning imports of locally produced goods. Through changes in the tax laws, the SPO would encourage assembly industries (*montaj sanayi*) to increase the domestic content of their products.[26] To avoid an escalation in the prices of domestically manufactured commodities, the plan also proposed to allow for controlled imports of selected goods.[27]

Table 4.3: Distribution of Planned Sectoral Investments (%)

	FIRST	SECOND	THIRD	FOURTH
Agriculture	17.7	15.2	11.7	12.2
Mining	5.4	3.7	5.8	6.1
Manufacturing	16.9	22.4	31.1	27.4
Energy	8.6	8.0	8.5	10.6
Transportation	13.7	16.1	14.5	16.3
Tourism	1.4	2.3	1.6	1.3
Housing	20.3	17.9	15.7	14.6
Education	7.1	6.7	5.0	4.8
Health	2.3	1.8	1.4	1.4
Other	6.6	5.9	4.7	5.5

Source: DPT, *Dördüncü Beş Yillik Kalkinma Plani: 1979-1983* (Ankara: DPT, 1979), pp. 34, 215.

This would inject an element of international competition into manufacturing. Although a far-reaching proposal in line with the theoretical ISI prescription, this objective, as we shall see later, was never realized.

The pivotal importance of import substitution in the first plan can be seen in the SPO's calculations regarding the country's import needs. The total contribution of import substitution to foreign exchange savings was expected to amount to just under 500 million dollars (Table 4.4). The ratio of import substitution was expected to increase from 7.1 percent of the net import bill in 1963, to 23.6 percent by 1967. Although in subsequent plans the specific impact of import substitution was not as carefully calculated as in the first, the emphasis on ISI remained.

SPO estimates for the Second Plan, for instance, showed that import substitution would reduce the annual rate of increase in imports from 7.4 to one lower than the national income. For that, the plan expected that import substitution efforts would concentrate on chemical fertilizers, metallurgical and petrochemical goods, as well as the machine manufacturing production.[28] The Second Plan also suggested that "the most effective utilization of scarce foreign exchange resources will be ensured by putting emphasis on import substitution in the fields considered economically suitable, and particularly in those fields based on natural resources."[29]

Table 4.4: Imports and Import Substitution Estimates for the First Plan
(million $)

	1963	1964	1965	1966	1967
Total Imports	607.0	672.0	740.0	804.9	870.0
Import Substitution (IS)	-40.0	-45.0	-110.0	-130.0	-166.0
IS as a % Total Imports	6.6	6.7	14.9	16.2	19.1
Net Imports[1]	567.0	627.0	630.0	674.9	704.9
IS as a % Net Imports	7.1	7.2	17.5	19.3	23.6

[1](Total Imports - Import Substitution)

Source: DPT, *Kalkinma Plani: Birinci Beş Yil* (Ankara: DPT, 1963), p. 519.

In the Third Plan (1973-1977), the SPO reiterated the need for increased import substitution and its faith in this method to reduce balance of payments deficits. The SPO stated that in order to induce vertical integration[30] in production and increase the country's development potential, it would encourage import substitution in iron and steel, chemical products, machinery products and transportation vehicles.[31] According to the new 15 year perspective that was published along with the third plan, by 1987 Turkey was expected to realize $3.5 billion worth of import substitution a year.[32]

By the time the fourth plan — delayed by a year — came into effect in 1979, Turkey was experiencing one of its worst economic crises. The oil price rise was finally being felt with a devastating impact. With extremely large trade deficits looming on the horizon, the SPO emphasized the need for exports as opposed to import substitution. In theory, this emphasis was not altogether new. All previous plans had mentioned the need to export and that an industrial structure willing and able to export was import substitution's ultimate goal.

The emphasis on exports in the fourth plan was deceptive. Despite the absence of direct allusions to import substitution, much of the plan's designs for manufacturing revolved around classical import substitution methods. The SPO blamed the rapid rise in imports during the third plan on lagging substitution efforts in the iron and steel, electrical and non-electrical equipment, and automotive sectors.[33] "In the manufacturing sector," the fourth plan stated, "in order to enhance the self-sufficiency and strength of the national economy, investments would be primarily directed at machinery producing, metallurgical, electronic and chemical industries."[34] This did not constitute a change from the stated objectives of the previous plan. Similarly, in consumer goods producing industries, if investments were to be channelled "to exporting sectors and sectors which would *reduce scarcity and the bottlenecks in the economy*,"[35] the SPO was simply repeating previously stated objectives.

What this reflected was a change in the structure of ISI. Whereas, the first two plans dealt with the first and easy phase of import substitution, the third and fourth plans had to come to terms with a more complex economy and the need to move into the more difficult and advanced stage of substitution.

The plans, as the discussion above indicated, were, for the most part, guiding documents. The mechanisms for implementing ISI while influenced by the plans, were contained in other government policies.

Implementing ISI

The Import Regime

The import regime, which establishes the guidelines of what can or cannot be brought into the country, constitutes a country's single most important mechanism for the implementation of import substitution. One basic principle guided the Turkish import regime of this era: all available foreign exchange resources were to be spent and distributed among the different sectors of the economy in accordance with the government's and SPO's development programs and goals. Through the import regime, the government controlled both the quantity and nature of imports, and attempted to strike a balance between the private and public sector requirements.

Until 1980, when major revisions were made to the system, the import regime distinguished among three categories of commodities. (1) The first included freely imported goods. These consisted of *necessary* items, such as medicine, for which no domestic substitute existed. Goods crucial to the realization of the development plans were to be given priority in the import regime.[36] (2) The second category encompassed goods which were subject to quantity restrictions because local production partially satisfied domestic demand. Usually imported in quantities that, when added to the local supply, total availability would not exceed total demand. This was achieved through a permit system. Permits were issued in accordance with developmental priorities and foreign exchange availabilities. (3) Finally, the third category included those goods which were banned because local production satisfied demand, or because they were judged to be unnecessary luxury items.

Reflecting the categorization above, imports into Turkey were organized along four "lists." (1) The Liberalized List, which dealt with goods that could be imported freely (category 1);[37] (2) the Quota List, which determined quantities in which category 2 goods above could be imported; (3) bilateral trade imports, which referred to goods purchased from countries with which Turkey had special trade arrangements.[38] (4) self-financed imports, which included "capital goods imported in connection with investments made under project aid."[39]

Import programs, published semi-annually until 1969 and then annually, were issued by the Ministry of Commerce with the SPO's active participation. They were formulated in four stages. "(1) The SPO projects import requirements; (2) those requirements are allocated globally among lists and financing sources; (3) a determination is made of which imported commodities are to be of each list; and (4) negotiations are carried out to determine the value of each quota list item."[40]

The first stage involved the estimation of imports by use, that is, the distribution of imports according to three broad categories: investment, intermediate and consumer goods. As far as the SPO was concerned, this distribution represented a target goal if the development plans were to be successful.[41] The next two stages allocated the three kinds of goods among the import lists discussed above. In phase 2, officials determined the share of investment goods to be imported under the liberalized list. In stage 3, they assigned individual commodities to specific lists. Goods not classified in the Liberalized or the Bilateral Trade List were assigned to the Quota List. Finally, in stage 4, officials set the specific quantities to be imported, "by adding up the estimated import requirements of the public and private sectors commodity by commodity, and then cutting them back to the expected availabilities of foreign exchange by a process of 'negotiation' whose ultimate logic is not easy to perceive."[42]

In fact, the whole import program was subject to foreign exchange availabilities. The SPO used import requirement estimates and projected foreign exchange availabilities to bargain for foreign aid with institutions like the OECD Consortium on Turkey. With changing foreign exchange availabilities, the mix of commodities included in different lists changed from year to year. A commodity which was included in the Liberalized List in one import program could be shifted to the Quota List, or even banned altogether depending on locally produced quantities and existing demand. This, in essence, was the main mechanism through which the state could enforce and/or monitor the level of import substitution. This is one of the primary mechanisms targeted by the different segments of the private sector in their zeal to maximize their share of "economic rents."

In addition to the state, two types of groups were allowed to import: commercial importers and industrialists. Commercial importers were wholesalers who acted as intermediaries by buying goods abroad and distributing them nationally. Industrialists, on the other hand, imported goods exclusively for their own use. Reflecting this difference, the Quota List deliberately favored industrialists over commercial importers. In order to procure import permits in either of these categories, the government required a firm or an individual to obtain an "importer's license." These were issued by local chambers of commerce to commercial importers and by local chambers of industry to industrialists. If no separate chamber of industry existed in a certain locality, then industrialists addressed themselves to the chamber of commerce *and* industry.[43]

Other features of the import regime included guarantee deposits. A guarantee deposit was a percentage of the cost of a good deposited with the Central Bank upon applying for an import permit. Held until the goods cleared customs, the amount of these deposits varied from import list to list and sometimes by commodity. In view of the chronic delays in importing, these funds remained blocked at the Central Bank for long periods of time further reducing incentives to import. Here too, manufacturers were the beneficiaries of preferential treatment: guarantee deposit rates for commercial importers were set at considerably higher ratios than those for industrialists importing the same item. As Table 4.5 shows, this difference could be as great as fourfold or, as in the case of 1979, even higher. In general, these rates were a function of foreign exchange availabilities: the higher the foreign exchange reserves, the lower were the guarantee deposit rates.

Custom duties were the primary means through which tariffs were applied. In addition to custom duties, other taxes such as municipality, port and stamp taxes were also levied. Although these taxes increased the cost of imported goods, like all such levies, they also contributed significantly to government revenues. These rates were reduced and even eliminated if the government thought it was necessary to support a specific industry or enterprise.

Table 4.5: Guarantee Deposit Requirements for Imports
(selected years, %)

Year	Liberalized List		Quota List	
	List 1	List 2	Importer	Industrialist
1963	23-30	-	10-20	10
1965	70	100	30	10
1967	70	100-125	30	10
1969	90	120-150	50	20
1971	50	40	25	10
1973	50	20	20	5
1975	20	10	10	2.5
1977	20	10	10	2.5
1979	25-40	25-40	40	2.5
1980	15-30	10-20	20	10

Source: Halil Seyidoğlu, *Türkiye'de Sanayileşme ve Dış Ticaret Politikasi* (Ankara: Turhan Kitabevi, 1982), p. 54.

Non-import Regime Measures

The most significant non-import regime measure was the overvalued exchange rate policy. During this period, with the exception of intervals immediately following devaluations, the Turkish Lira was constantly maintained at a higher level than its international free market value. Predictably, this lowered the cost of imports while overpricing exports. The resulting natural tendency of imports to rise dramatically was kept in check by the constraints imposed through the import regime outlined above, and by the availability of foreign exchange reserves. Since the SPO limited consumer good imports while offering incentives for investment goods, the overvalued exchange rate was designed specifically to benefit import substituting industrialists.

This was especially instrumental in developing what came to be known as the assembly industries, or *montaj sanayi*. Despite their high foreign content, assembly industry products were marketed as Turkish made. In 1964 in order to encourage these industries to augment their products' locally manufactured contents, the SPO, in conjunction with the government, introduced the Assembly Industries Guidelines (*Montaj Sanayi Talimatnamesi*). Accordingly, these industries were obliged to conform to the increasing domestic content requirements established by the Ministry of Industry[44] which, in theory, would contribute to the conservation of foreign exchange. The economic and political problems associated with assembly industries will be discussed in detail in a later chapter.

Other measures included incentive mechanisms aimed at increasing overall investments in import substituting industries. Table 4.3 demonstrated how investments were skewed in favor of manufacturing. Since the SPO could only make recommendations to the private sector, various tax rebate schemes were devised to channel investments. The government also regulated interest rates charged by banks. In general, interest rates were maintained at levels lower than prevailing inflation rates, thus providing industrialists with access to inexpensive funds. For instance, from March 1978 to March 1980, when time deposits earned between 6 and 22 percent, the interest rate for medium term bank credit to industry was fixed at 16 percent.[45] The inflation rate at the time was much higher. In short, borrowers were subsidized by the saving public: a fact which was not conducive to raising aggregate savings levels.

This explains the rationale and main features of the Turkish ISI policies: the import regime, with its complicated "lists," overvalued exchange rates, and low interest rates for industry. These features were of great importance to all participants. They represented the source of the "economic rents" over which private sector groups struggled. What remains to be analyzed are the overall results and, more importantly, the policies' contribution to the emergence of the political-economic crisis at the end of the seventies.

Notes

[1]Celso Furtado, *Economic Development of Latin America* (London: Cambridge University Press, 1970), p. 90.

[2]Alec P. Alexander, "Industrial Entrepreneurship in Turkey: Origins and Growth," *Economic Development and Cultural Change* (July), 1960, pp. 355, 358.

[3]TOB, *Beş Yillik Kalkinma Planinin Uygulanmasi ve Hazirlanacak 1965 Yili Programi Hakkinda Özel Sektörün Görüş ve Teklifleri* (Ankara: TOB, 1964). It categorically stated that imports of industrial goods ought to be banned if local manufacturers could produce them. Given the tensions between industrialists and commercial groups, which would soon develop inside this organization (see Chapters 6 and 7), this declaration attests the general acceptance given to ISI at the time.

[4]Osman Okyar, "Development Background of the Turkish Economy: 1923-1973," *International Journal of Middle East Studies*, Vol. 10 (1979), pp. 336-339.

[5]There were, of course, some officers who, in the late forties, supported a transition to a multi-party system. Therefore, not all of them ought to be portrayed as solidly behind the RPP. In fact, disenchantment in the army ranks at that time probably helped speed up the process of change.

[6]The ruling officers, however, were divided between those who saw themselves as reformists and those inclined to push for more radical economic measures. Whereas the first group wanted to tax agricultural estates and thus generate necessary investment funds, the second group was disposed to a complete takeover of the economy by the state. In the ensuing power struggle the reformists won and forced 14 radical officers into exile in November 1960.

[7]Gencay Şaylan, "Planlama ve Bürokrasi," *ODTÜ Gelişme Dergisi*, Special Issue, 1981, p. 200.

[8]Çağlar Keyder, "The Political Economy of Turkish Democracy," *New Left Review* No. 115, (May June), 1979, p. 27.

[9]There was severe criticism by the intelligentsia regarding the conduct of the private sector. These criticisms, however, were primarily directed at the perceived fact that not enough substitution was taking place.

[10]William Hale, *The Political and Economic Development of Turkey* (New York: St. Martin's Press, 1981), p. 213.

[11]Devlet Planlama Teşkilati, *Kalkinma Plani: Birinci Beş Yil* (Ankara: Devlet Planlama Teşkilati, 1963), p. 141.

[12]Devlet Planlama Teşkilati, *Yeni Strateji ve Kalkinma Plani: Üçüncü Beş Yil 1973-1977* (Ankara: Devlet Planlama Teşkilati, 1973), p. 13.

[13]Tuncer Bulutay, "Türkiye'nin 1950-1980 Dönemindeki Iktisadi Büyümesi Üzerine Düşünceler," *ODTÜ, Gelişme Dergisi*, Special Issue (1981), p. 502.

[14]Devlet Planlama Teşkilati, *Kalkinma Plani: Birinci Beş Yil*, p. 514.

[15]Baran Tuncer, "Türkiye'nin Sanayileşmesi ve Sanayi Politikalari," Ekonomik ve Sosyal Etüdler Konferans Heyeti, *Diş Ticaret ve Ekonomik Gelişme* (Istanbul: Ekonomik ve Sosyal Etüdler Konferans Heyeti, 1979), p. 179.

[16]Devlet Planlama Teşkilati, *Kalkinma Plani: Birinci Beş Yil*, p.

24.

[17]Devlet Planlama Teşkilati, *Second Five Year Development Plan: 1968-1972,* (Ankara: Devlet Planlama Teşkilati, 1969), p. 404.

[18]One deceptive aspect of this table regards the nature of the investment goods category. As assembly industries expanded in the late sixties, inputs for such industries, ranging from automobiles to washing machines, were imported under this import category.

[19]Devlet Planlama Teşkilati, *Second Five Year Development Plan: 1968-1972,* p. 47.

[20]Devlet Planlama Teşkilati, *Yeni Strateji ve Kalkinma Plani: Üçüncü Beş Yil 1973-1977,* p. 120.

[21]Devlet Planlama Teşkilati, *Yeni Strateji ve Kalkinma Plani: Üçüncü Beş Yil 1973-1977,* p. 120.

[22]Uğur Korum, "The Structure and Interdependence of the Public and Private Sectors in Turkish Manufacturing Industry," in Mükerrem Hiç (ed.), *Turkey's and Other Countries' Experience with the Mixed Economy* (Istanbul: Istanbul University Faculty of Economics, 1979), p. 469.

[23]In Turkish, *Devlet Planlama Teşkilati,* (DPT).

[24]Suna Kili, *Türk Anayasalari* (Istanbul: Tekin Yayinevi, 1982), p. 86.

[25]Devlet Planlama Teşkilati, *Kalkinma Plani: Birinci Beş Yil,* p. 59.

[26]Devlet Planlama Teşkilati, *Kalkinma Plani: Birinci Beş Yil,* pp. 205, 206. Assembly industries refer to industries, mostly in consumer durable production, which import their component parts and simply assemble them domestically. Their contribution to value added and import substitution is, therefore, minimal.

[27]Devlet Planlama Teşkilati, *Kalkinma Plani: Birinci Beş Yil,* p. 206.

[28]Devlet Planlama Teşkilati, *Second Five Year Development Plan: 1968-1972,* p. 100.

[29]Devlet Planlama Teşkilati, *Second Five Year Development Plan: 1968-1972,* p. 132.

[30]By vertical integration, the SPO meant the development of intermediate and capital goods industries to compliment the existing consumer goods indiustries.

[31]Devlet Planlama Teşkilati, *Yeni Strateji ve Kalkinma Plani: 1973-1977,* p. 893.

[32]Devlet Planlama Teşkilati, *Yeni Strateji ve Kalkinma Plani:*

1973-1977, p. 142.

[33]Devlet Planlama Teşkilati, *Dördüncü Beş Yillik Kalkinma Plani: 1979-1983* (Ankara: Devlet Planlama Teşkilati, 1979), p. 65. This was mostly true; as foreign exchange reserves became abundant in the post 1970 devaluation era, substitution efforts slackened.

[34]Devlet Planlama Teşkilati, *Dördüncü Beş Yillik Kalkinma Plani: 1979-1983* p. 273.

[35]Devlet Planlama Teşkilati, *Dördüncü Beş Yillik Kalkinma Plani: 1979-1983* p. 273, *emphasis added.*

[36]Devlet Planlama Teşkilati, *Kalkinma Plani: Birinci Beş Yil,* p. 522.

[37]The liberalized list itself was sub-divided into two lists with the second entailing some restrictions, such as, requiring prior ministerial approval.

[38]However, imports under this list were still subject to the same constraints that operated in the liberalized and quota lists. In other words, if a commodity did not appear on either of these lists, it could not be imported.

[39]Anne Krueger, *Foreign Trade Regimes and Economic Development: Turkey* (New York: National Bureau of Economic Research, 1974), p. 138. US imports under PL-480 and other items, such as automobiles etc. brought back by Turkish workers living abroad.

[40]Krueger, *Foreign Trade Regimes and Economic Development: Turkey,* p. 139.

[41]H. Lubell, D. Mathieson, R. Smith and B. Viraph, *The Turkish Import Regime* (Ankara: AID, 1968), p. 11.

[42]Lubell et al., *The Turkish Import Regime,* p. 16.

[43]As it will be shown later, this seemingly minor issue was, in fact, of critical importance. Because it gave the Union of Chambers of Commerce, Industry and Commodity Exchanges — the umbrella organization to which all local chambers belonged — a direct role in the process of bargaining over the allocation of foreign exchange; this practice continued until the military backed government of 1971 abolished it and consolidated the license disbursement within the Ministry of Commerce.

[44]Mükerrem Hiç (ed.), *Montaj Sanayi: Gelişmesi, Sorunlari ve Ekonomimizdeki Yeri,* (Istanbul: Ekonomik ve Sosyal Etüdler Konferans Heyeti, 1973), pp. 15-22.

[45]William Hale, *The Political and Economic Development of Turkey,* pp. 156-157.

5

Successes and Failures of ISI
in Turkey

By 1980 Turkey had not achieved the industrial status its planners and politicians had visualized at the beginning of the sixties. ISI had, however, clearly energized the manufacturing sector and spawned its development. This vigor, however, had its price, one which increased daily for the two decades the policies were in effect. By the end of the seventies, the cost of import substitution had reached crisis proportions.

This chapter analyzes the results of twenty years of "planned" import substitution. How did the Turkish economy change? What were the economic shortcomings of the period? By dissociating the economic explanations of the crisis from the political ones, this chapter focuses on the ISI-related determinants of the ultimate crisis. The political components are explored in later chapters.

There are three parts to this chapter. The first discusses the impact of ISI on the manufacturing sector. The second explores those internal and external factors which aggravated existing trends toward disequilibrium and ultimately helped bring about the crisis. In the final segment, the economic dimensions of the crisis are analyzed.

Twenty Years Later: ISI and the Manufacturing Sector

Significance of the Manufacturing Sector

The manufacturing sector's output grew and became increasingly sophisticated during the planned period and, correspondingly, its share of the GNP continuously rose.

Table 5.1: Composition of GNP (selected years, %)

	1962	1965	1970	1975	1977	1978	1979	1980
Agriculture	35.28	31.10	26.21	21.87	20.74	20.70	21.37	21.97
Industry	14.19	19.65	22.35	19.64	21.22	21.99	20.84	19.92
of which								
Mining	1.40	1.96	1.73	1.66	2.17	2.67	2.25	2.06
Manufacturing	12.27	16.52	19.34	16.63	17.48	17.60	16.74	16.04
Energy	0.51	1.17	1.29	1.34	1.57	1.71	1.86	1.82
Construction	5.27	6.36	6.62	5.68	5.79	5.87	6.14	6.25
Commerce	6.78	10.06	11.38	12.66	12.99	13.12	12.87	12.44
Transportation	6.43	7.02	8.05	8.98	9.35	9.32	8.95	8.72
Banking	2.43	2.35	3.65	2.12	2.25	2.29	2.37	2.44
Ownership Dwelling	4.50	5.69	5.18	4.13	4.34	4.39	4.57	4.81
Private Services	4.17	5.07	5.10	4.57	4.54	4.56	4.54	4.54
Government Services	8.04	9.22	9.18	8.53	8.63	8.91	9.32	9.97
GNP	100.00	100.00	100.00	100.00	100.00	100.00	100.00	100.00

Source: World Bank, *Turkey: Industrialization and Trade Strategy* (Washington, D.C.: World Bank, 1982), p. 408; Memduh Yaşa, *Cumhuriyet Dönemi Türkiye Ekonomisi* (Istanbul: Akbank Yayinlari, 1980), pp. 46-47; TOB, *Iktisadi Rapor* (Ankara: TOB, various years).

By 1980, the industrial sector[1] in general accounted for a larger share of GNP than it did in 1962, and in 1978 it supplanted agriculture as the largest sector in economy. The steady gains achieved by the manufacturing sector, from 12 percent of GNP in 1962 to 17.6 percent in 1978, came at the expense of agriculture. Industry was not the only one to expand at agriculture's expense: the services sector scored impressive gains as well.

The employment picture, however, offers another perspective as demonstrated by Table 5.2. While the percentage of the economically active population in agriculture declined from 77.2 percent in 1962 to 61.9 percent in 1981, the fact remains that, despite the relatively reduced share of this sector in GNP figures, over three fifths of the population in 1981 was still involved in it. Table 5.2 also shows that services in general accounted for the largest share in absorbing the labor force released by agriculture. Industry, as a whole, and manufacturing were a poor second and third. Manufacturing's share in GNP during this period had increased by more than 64 percent, while its share in total employment only rose by 2.8 percent. The manufacturing sector's failure to make significant advances in employment is primarily the result of the increase in the capital output ratios and the tendency to invest in capital intensive industries fostered by ISI.

Table 5.2: Percentage Distribution of the Economically Active Population

	1962	1981	(1981-1962) Change	
Agriculture	77.2	61.9	-15.3	
			Absorbed by	Relative Share of Absorption
Industry	8.3	11.8	3.5	22.9
Mining	0.5	0.8	0.3	2.0
Manufacturing	7.5	10.3	2.8	18.3
Energy-Water	0.3	0.7	0.4	2.6
Construction	2.1	3.8	1.7	11.1
Transportation	2.0	3.2	1.2	7.8
Commerce	2.4	4.2	1.8	11.8
Banking	0.4	1.4	4.0	6.5
Services	7.5	13.6	6.1	39.9
Total	100.0	100.0	15.3	100.0

Source: TÜSIAD, *The Turkish Economy, 1982* (Istanbul: TÜSIAD, 1982).

As Table 4.1 of the previous chapter demonstrates, the trend toward lowering the share of consumer goods among imports, established well before the advent of planned development, continued. While the change in the composition of imports can generally be attributed to import substitution, some studies have shown that during the 1963-1968 and the 1968-1973 periods the contribution of ISI to the growth of manufacturing has been minimal, and even negative at times.

Derviş and Robinson's study demonstrates that between 1963 and 1968, ISI's contribution to the aggregate growth rate was 8.3 percent, while export expansion and domestic demand expansion accounted for 4.9 percent and 83.6 percent, respectively. In the following period, 1968-1973, the role of ISI was -1.4 percent, while the two others accounted for 16.3 percent and 81.8 percent. For the 1973-1977 period,

Derviş and Robinson speculated that while domestic demand was expected to account for 100.4 percent and exports for -1 percent, ISI's contribution would have been of the order of 0.6 percent.[2]

In another study, Uğur Korum has argued that during the 1963-1968 period, domestic demand and export growth accounted for 91 percent and 2 percent of total growth, while ISI's share was only 7 percent. In the subsequent 1968-1973 period, he estimates the ratios to be 95.9 percent, 10 percent, and -2.3 percent, respectively.[3] These studies indicate that, as the easy phase of substitution ended in the late 1960s, ISI's contribution became negative, reflecting the difficulties encountered by the manufacturing sector in making a transition from the first and easy phase of import substitution to the more demanding second one.

These difficulties are also affirmed by the stagnant distribution of the manufacturing sector's output. The share of intermediate goods not only failed to increase significantly as expected, but this ratio in 1980 was almost indistinguishable from its 1972 level (Table 5.3). More alarming perhaps was the trend in investment goods figures, which in Turkey include consumer durables. After a rapid rise, between 1962 and 1972, this ratio declined. The capital goods figures also point to the limited potential of the durable industries: as Turkish manufacturing shifted to consumer durables, the share of investment goods, instead of increasing, decreased.

Table 5.3: Composition of Output in the Manufacturing Sector (%)

	1962	1967	1972	1977 planned	1977 realized	1980
Consumer	62.3	52.9	46.6	38.3	49.3	48.5
Intermediate	27.8	35.4	39.4	44.2	35.7	40.2
Investment[1]	9.9	11.7	14.0	17.5	15.0	11.3
Total	100.0	100.0	100.0	100.0	100.0	100.0

[1]Investment figures include consumer durables.

Source: Memduh Yaşa, *Cumhuriyet Dönemi Türkiye Ekonomisi* (Istanbul: Akbank Yayinlari, 1980), p. 196; DPT, *Yeni Strateji ve Kalkinma Plani: Üçüncü Beş Yil 1973-1977* (Ankara: DPT, 1973), pp. 138, 289; DPT, *1982 Yili Programi* (Ankara: DPT, 1982), p. 139.

Import Dependency and Contribution to Exports

How dependent was Turkey's industrial sector on imports? Table 4.1 showed how the share of consumer goods among all imports had declined over time. Table 5.4, on the other hand, estimates the changes in the import needs of Turkish industry and its sub-sectors. This table calculates the percentage share in national demand and production that is satisfied by imports, as well as the percentage share of production that is exported. Two results are immediately apparent: (1) in 1980, imports still constituted a significant proportion of domestic demand in all categories except consumer goods where the share of imports, in the total demand increased slightly from 0.7 percent in 1967 to 1.5 percent in 1980. With respect to intermediate goods, imports accounted for 15.1 percent of demand in 1967, and 15.3 and 16.8 percent in 1977 and 1980, respectively. However, in the critical categories of import substitution such as chemicals, iron and steel, petrochemicals and fertilizers, the share of imports in demand and production is considerably higher than the corresponding sector averages.

(2) By contrast, there has been a perceptible decline in the levels of import dependence of capital goods. The difference in trend can, for the most part, be explained by the inclusion in the investment goods figures of consumer durables, the mainstay of the manufacturing sector in the seventies. The SPO points out that, in 1976, 24 percent of non-electrical machinery category's output consisted of consumer durables.[4] Exact figures, however, are difficult to come by for other such categories. In an import substituting sector such as metal products which, in turn, supplies other categories, one can discern a trend in favor of increased dependence. Therefore, with respect to all three sectors, consumer, intermediate and investment goods, import dependence ratios cannot be said to have declined dramatically. Progress, in other words, has been made in very selective areas.

More significant, however, is the export picture. As Table 5.4 demonstrates, the Turkish manufacturing sector did not achieve any significant gains in exports. In fact, after registering a decline, the relative increase in exports was barely sufficient to return to the levels of the late 1960s and early 1970s. In the intermediate goods category, exports fluctuated between 2 and 2.6 percent, with 1972 being the one exception.

Table 5.4: Import and Export Dependency Figures for the Manufacturing Sector (selected years, %)

	1967			1972		
	M/D[1]	M/P[1]	X/P[1]	M/D	M/P	X/P
CONSUMER	0.7	0.7	9.5	0.5	0.6	9.2
Food	0.4	0.4	9.0	0.2	0.2	9.7
Beverages	0.4	0.5	0.6	0.5	0.8	1.3
Tobacco	0.0	0.0	52.7	0.0	0.0	33.1
Textiles	1.3	1.3	0.2	1.2	1.1	3.2
INTERMEDIATE	15.2	17.2	2.0	15.4	16.1	4.0
Forestry Prod.	0.0	0.0	0.3	0.0	0.0	1.9
Paper	27.0	37.0	0.0	9.7	10.6	1.9
Printing	4.4	4.6	0.2	28.6	4.7	0.4
Leather	3.9	3.9	3.9	1.3	1.2	11.2
Rubber	7.2	7.8	0.0	4.0	4.1	0.9
Plastics	0.8	0.8	0.0	0.5	0.5	0.5
Chemicals	30.7	43.5	1.8	18.8	22.5	2.4
Petro-Chemical	78.0	354.5	0.0	62.0	161.8	0.8
Petroleum Prod	5.3	6.3	1.4	3.4	3.4	1.8
Fertilizers	76.9	251.2	0.0	49.5	98.1	0.0
Cement	0.0	0.0	8.6	0.0	0.0	4.3
Clay	2.7	0.9	0.0	17.0	5.9	0.4
Glass	12.2	13.8	0.4	2.1	2.1	4.7
Ceramics	2.8	9.3	0.0	1.9	6.4	0.0
Iron-Steel	16.9	15.2	9.3	33.4	33.3	1.0
Non-Ferrous	28.4	26.7	25.9	22.4	24.9	8.2
INVESTMENT	53.1	90.1	0.1	37.2	57.5	0.8
Metal Products	10.9	12.2	0.1	10.0	11.0	0.6
Non-Electrical	58.7	195.5	0.1	58.3	138.6	0.8
Instruments	n.a.	n.a.	n.a.	n.a.	n.a.	n.a.
Electrical Mach.	42.2	73.0	0.1	35.9	55.5	0.9
Electronics	68.9	221.1	0.0	36.4	56.8	0.6
Vehicles	74.5	100.0	0.0	15.1	17.7	0.2
Railroad vehicle	92.5	100.0	0.0	16.5	18.5	6.5
Shipbuilding	61.8	155.6	3.1	62.7	164.2	2.4
Aircraft	n.a.	n.a.	n.a.	n.a.	n.a.	n.a.
TOTAL	14.3	17.0	7.1	12.7	14.7	5.4

Table 5.4: (continued)

	1977 M/D	M/P	X/P	1980 M/D	M/P	X/P
CONSUMER	1.2	1.1	6.1	1.5	1.5	8.7
Food	1.3	1.3	4.9	1.7	1.6	6.7
Beverages	0.3	0.3	1.4	0.0	0.0	0.8
Tobacco	0.0	0.0	14.9	0.0	0.0	17.7
Textiles	1.4	1.3	7.3	2.1	1.9	14.1
INTERMEDIATE	15.3	18.0	1.8	16.8	19.1	2.4
Forestry Prod.	0.1	0.1	0.1	0.2	0.2	0.6
Paper	11.2	12.6	0.1	18.7	22.9	0.6
Printing	1.3	1.3	0.1	0.5	0.5	0.1
Leather	0.1	0.1	6.7	0.1	0.1	7.1
Rubber	29.0	40.7	0.0	1.7	1.7	3.4
Plastics	2.3	2.4	1.4	0.7	0.7	1.6
Chemicals	24.6	31.9	3.0	27.0	35.7	3.7
Petro-Chemical	30.2	48.5	2.6	27.9	37.5	3.2
Petroleum Prod	11.3	13.0	0.0	15.7	18.4	1.2
Fertilizers	54.7	120.8	0.0	60.5	73.2	0.0
Cement	0.0	0.0	6.2	0.0	0.0	8.0
Clay	4.0	4.2	0.1	9.7	9.5	0.4
Glass	2.0	1.8	12.2	3.4	3.0	17.4
Ceramics	1.7	1.7	0.1	0.6	0.6	3.7
Iron-Steel	23.9	30.6	0.3	20.7	24.6	1.0
Non-Ferrous	14.4	18.1	3.6	12.7	14.6	6.0
INVESTMENT	33.0	48.8	0.7	29.0	39.8	2.6
Metal Products	12.8	14.6	1.1	20.4	25.1	1.9
Non-Electrical	53.5	114.3	0.5	38.6	62.0	1.5
Instruments	78.0	351.9	0.5	69.7	228.4	0.8
Electrical Mach.	24.7	32.8	0.1	32.1	46.5	1.6
Electronics	34.5	52.4	0.7	37.1	57.6	2.1
Vehicles	20.6	25.8	0.5	18.0	20.8	4.9
Railroad vehicle	23.9	30.4	3.4	21.3	27.0	0.0
Shipbuilding	31.4	45.7	0.3	41.1	64.1	8.1
Aircraft	4.9	5.2	0.0	34.3	51.4	0.0
TOTAL	13.0	14.2	3.8	11.9	12.9	5.4

[1]M/D = Imports/Domestic Demand; M/P = Imports/Domestic Production; X/P = Exports/Domestic Production.
Source: DPT, *Annual Reports* (selected Years); Memduh Yaşa, *Cumhuriyet Dönemi Türkiye Ekonomisi* (Istanbul: Akbank Yayinlari, 1980).

Correspondingly, in the investment goods sector, the level of exports has remained below the one percent mark, with 1980 representing the exception. Since durable goods are also part of these figures, the implication is that only an insignificant share of durable production — where import substitution efforts were claimed by industrialists to be strong — has found its way abroad.[5]

Similarly, consumer good exports fell below expectations. This group's exports increased from 8.8 percent of production to 9.3 percent in 1972, in large measure as a response to the 1970 devaluation, but declined to 6.1 percent in 1977 to edge up again in 1980. The textiles sector is the only sub-group that consistently increased its share of exports.

The foregoing analysis further demonstrates the insular nature of Turkish industry and its reliance on the domestic market for expansion and growth. A rigorous analysis undertaken through the use of input-output matrices shows that between 1968 and 1973[6] the import dependence of the economy and the manufacturing sector had increased considerably.[7] Therefore, ISI's application in Turkey contributed to neither a more independent industrial sector, nor a more confident one capable of penetrating foreign markets.[8]

The paradoxical nature of the import substitution efforts are further illustrated in Table 5.5, which lists the various sub-sectors of the manufacturing sector in a descending order of contribution to backward and forward linkages.[9] Four sub-sectors — transportation (vehicles and accessories), electrical machinery, non-electrical machinery and petroleum/coal — account for 84.6 percent of the share of import substitution. However, the table clearly shows that these have had a limited impact on the economy in general. From the perspective of backward and forward linkages, they all represent weak sub-sectors and their contribution to employment has lagged behind those with higher linkage potential. These sub-sectors also have an inordinate share in the rate of increase of imports: almost 45 percent. Therefore, the results are somewhat surprising: the sectors with the highest rates of contribution to ISI are also those with the highest rates of import dependence. Overall, sub-sectors which accounted for 90 percent of the import substitution efforts were also responsible for 63 percent of the increases in imports. The accelerating growth of assembly industries is, in large measure, to blame for this development.

Table 5.5: The Manufacturing Sector's Contributions:
According to Backward and Forward Linkages (1965-1975), %

Sectors according to strength of linkage contributions	Share in value-added increase	Share in production increase	Share in intra-sectoral IS increase	Share in employment increase	Share in export increase	share in imports increse
STRONG						
Iron & Steel	19.70	5.38	-	16.46	-	21.88
Food	4.85	11.38	-	6.35	4.99	7.89
Textiles	13.70	13.32	2.35	12.02	30.24	1.07
Forestry Products	1.36	1.17	0.30	1.45	0.47	0.05
Leather	0.12	0.34	-	1.26	0.12	0.01
Metal Products	3.84	3.05	-	-	3.47	2.29
6 SUBSECTORS	**25.34**	**34.64**	**2.65**	**37.54**	**39.29**	**33.19**
MEDIUM						
Furniture	0.26	0.37	0.02	0.49	0.02	-
Paper & Printing	3.41	2.94	2.45	4.01	1.08	0.6
Clothing	4.52	3.32	0.02	1.05	24.68	-
Others	-	1.90	2.12	3.31	1.80	-
Non-ferrous Metal	3.77	3.53	1.45	9.34	11.86	1.12
Chemicals	4.06	6.38	6.67	7.43	3.33	18.50
6 SUBSECTORS	**16.02**	**18.44**	**12.73**	**25.63**	**42.77**	**20.91**

Table 5.5 (continued)

Sectors according to strength of linkage contributions	Share in value-added increase	Share in production increase	Share in intra-sectoral IS increase	Share in employment increase	Share in export increase	Share in imports increse
WEAK						
Vehicle Production	14.08	12.88	38.54	12.41	2.32	6.73
Tobacco	18.88	6.99	-	-	-	-
Electrical Machines	7.63	6.57	15.84	7.53	0.70	8.52
Beverages	1.53	1.04	-	2.18	0.35	0.06
Petroleum & Coal	14.31	-	6.16	1.05	11.39	0.70
Rubber	1.82	1.31	-	1.15	0.66	0.75
Machinery	5.02	5.93	24.09	12.52	2.53	29.14
7 SUBSECTORS	**58.27**	**46.93**	**24.09**	**12.52**	**2.53**	**29.14**

Source: Zafer Tunca, "Türk Sanayinde İthal İkamesi ve Yapisal İlişkiler," in 2. *Türkiye Iktisat Kongresi* (Ankara: Devlet Planlama Teşkilati, 1981), Vol. 6.

Concentration of Capital

During the 1960-1980 period, the manufacturing sector experienced a significant increase in the degree of capital concentration. This concentration occurred along two lines: size and geographic distribution. The exact role of import substitution in this development is difficult to discern and a variety of other factors, including the lack of an organized capital market which reinforced the family-owned nature of a great many industrial concerns, are also to blame. However, the quota system, which encouraged oligopolistic practices, the relative small size of the market, the lack of export opportunities and the increasing capital intensive nature of the manufacturing process all contributed to this concentration.

In 1980, the 500 largest industrial concerns in Turkey accounted for 49.4 percent of all manufacturing sales.[10] Of the 500, 79 were government/public enterprises. In fact, the 12 largest were state owned.[11] Of the 421 privately owned companies, 253 were organized in the Istanbul region, and these accounted for 61.5 percent of the sales realized by the private sector and 62.4 percent of its capital.[12] The Istanbul region was followed by the Aegean with 59 enterprises, 10.9 percent of private sector sales, and 8.6 percent of its capital. Istanbul and Izmir, therefore, accounted for more than 70 percent of private sector sales and private capital. In the following year, 431 private corporations represented almost a quarter of the manufacturing sector's total sales.[13] In 1981, of the 6,000 members of the Istanbul Chamber of Industry, 251 accounted for 14.5 percent of the total manufacturing sales. In 1981, the top ten firms within this chamber were credited with 20.6 percent of total manufacturing sales of the 251, 6.34 percent of the sales of the 500 largest and 12.4 percent of the private sector's share of the 500 largest.

Still, the Istanbul Chamber of Industry figures underestimate the degree of concentration because holding companies are de-aggregated so that each subsidiary, even if wholly owned, is tabulated separately. Conducted at approximately the same time, another study of the largest holding corporations in Turkey reveals that, in 1979, 57.4 percent of these were controlled by a single person or a single family (Table 5.6). Abdurrahman Ariman's analysis of 34 holding companies[14] show that the top three account for 41.3 percent of combined capital, while the top five and ten enterprises' shares are 55.2 and 72.6 percent, respectively.[15] The first, third and fifth holding corporations are family owned, the second is a banking conglomerate (the Iş Bank), and the fourth is OYAK, the Army Mutual Assistance Corporation. This concentration of capital, as well as its regional distribution is one of the sources of tension within the Turkish political economy whose implications will be further discussed in Chapter 6.

Table 5.6: Distribution of the Holding Corporations by Shareholders

	Number	%
Controlled by one person	54	30.7
Controlled by one family	47	26.7
Controlled by one corporation	4	2.3
Controlled by two persons or families	15	8.5
Controlled by 10 or less persons	19	10.8
Holding holdings or bank holdings	6	3.4
Holdings with > 10 shareholders	31	17.6
Total	176	100.00

Source: Abdurrahman Ariman, *Türkiye'de Sermaye Yoğunlaşmasi ve Sermaye Gruplarinin Oluşumu* (Istanbul: Istanbul Technical University, Unpublished Dissertation Thesis, 1981), p. 36.

Building Towards a Crisis: The Internal and External Factors

Two sets of economic conditions aggravated ISI's inherent trend toward exhaustion: (1) Internal factors resulting from domestic conditions and policy choices, which included excessive rates of protection and overvalued exchange rates; and (2) External factors resulting from worldwide economic changes, the most significant of which was the oil price increases.

Internal Factors

Protectionism. Both tariffs and quotas were used haphazardly — with little regard for the principles of economic rationality — to ensure the protection of the domestic market. This resulted in economy-wide distortions and misallocations of resources.

Ad valorem tariffs, first instituted in 1954, were combined with non-tariff import levies (see the example in Table 5.7) to inflate the cost of imports and allow domestic producers the latitude needed to set their prices. This affected all levels of production.[16] The tariff structure, which varied from -11 percent to almost 2,000 percent, had "no discernible economic rationale." "Overprotection has led to overcrowding in many industries with uneconomic size of plants and with prices and profits remaining high."[17]

Table 5.7: Illustrative Tariff and Non-Tariff Levies on Imported Manufactures, 1973

Machinery Import	25% Custom Duty (%)	50% Custom Duty (%)
1. Import Price c.i.f.	100.00	100.00
2. Customs Duty [25 or 50% of 1]	125.00	150.00
3. Municipal Tax [15% of 2]	128.75	172.50
4. Wharf Duty [5% of (1 + 3)]	135.18	181.11
5. Production Tax [10% of (1+2+3+4)]	148.69	199.22
6. Stamp Duty [10% of 1]	158.69	209.22
7. Total duties and levies; [2+3+4+5+6]	58.69	109.22
of which: custom duties	25.00	50.00
other levies	33.69	59.22

Source: World Bank, *Turkey: Prospects and Problems for an Expanding Economy* (Washington, D.C.: World Bank, 1975), p. 243.

The quota determination process in general enhanced the misallocation of resources and contributed to the building of excess capacity in manufacturing. At any given time, allocations of foreign exchange in any one category were based solely on considerations of capacity and foreign exchange availability to the exclusion of all other considerations. Understandably, therefore, manufacturers maximized their capacity so that in times of foreign exchange shortages, which was almost always the case, they could assure themselves a minimum or sufficient supply of inputs. A firm could demand no more foreign exchange than what its capacity figures prescribed. If total capacity in any segment of the manufacturing sector was $100,000 and the total state allocation consisted of $10,000, then each firm requesting an import permit was be allocated only one tenth of their initial requisition. Therefore, if a firm, could (in fiction or in reality) demonstrate increased capacity, its share of the total allocation increased. It also followed that any firm by receiving a percentage of the total foreign exchange allocation was automatically guaranteed a share of the domestic market.[18] To limit the inflation in capacity figures, the government asked the local quasi-public chambers of commerce and industry to monitor capacity figures. Despite such monitoring, excess capacity was created by industrialists seeking to improve their chances when allocation decisions were made. This led the World Bank to recommend that,

> more generally it would be desirable, even in the absence of general foreign exchange rationing, for a system of protection of domestic industry to be based to a much greater extent on tariffs and similar charges. The present system of commodity-specific quotas and prohibitions, by providing unlimited protection, makes it hard to discriminate systematically between industries in accordance with governmental priorities and preferences. It also permits undesirable wide variations in efficiency among enterprises within particular industries, since even very inefficient producers are completely shielded from foreign competition.[19]

Foreign Exchange Rates. Overvalued exchange rates were among the industrial sector's favorite methods of encouraging growth. As Table 5.6 demonstrates, for most of the period in question, the value of the Turkish lira was sustained at a level much higher than its international value relative to the U.S. $ and the currencies of Turkey's principal trading partners. By the end of the fourth quarter of 1978, the Turkish lira's value had appreciated by 25 percent vis à vis the dollar when compared to 1973. Caused by the high rates of domestic inflation, the lira's continuous appreciation had two basic effects: (1) it further exacerbated the inward orientation of the economy, and (2) it biased the industrialization process in favor of capital intensive processes.

(1) In the first case, the manufacturing sector realized higher rates of return in Turkey than abroad because as the prices of manufactured products increased, the overvalued exchange rate cushioned Turkish producers from increases in the cost of foreign inputs. In addition, the overvalued exchange rate priced Turkish goods out of foreign markets, and hence limited the revenues of those who managed to export. Had the lira been periodically adjusted to reflect its real value, the Istanbul Chamber of Industry estimated the losses in immediately realizable extra revenue to have been quite substantial (Table 5.9). In the seven-year period, therefore, the private sector alone lost 1,472 billion TL,

Table 5.8: Real Exchange Rates in Turkey, 1967-1979.

Year	Exchange Rate; Lira/U.S.$	Index of Real Exchange Rate vis à vis U.S.$	Index of Real Exchange Rate vis à vis Trading Partners
1967	9.00	93.3	79.2
1968	9.00	95.5	78.2
1969	9.00	91.6	74.7
1970	11.50	110.0	92.7
1971	14.92	126.7	110.5
1972	14.15	106.5	98.7
1973	14.15	100.0	100.0
1974	13.93	92.2	92.3
1976	16.05	93.4	90.5
1977	18.00	86.8	86.8
Q1	17.00	89.8	88.5
Q2	17.68	91.6	90.2
Q3	17.89	86.6	86.9
Q4	19.44	83.1	85.2
1978	24.28	82.0	88.1
Q1	21.38	83.7	89.4
Q2	25.25	90.1	94.4
Q3	25.25	83.1	89.9
Q4	25.25	75.0	83.3
1979	31.09	67.3	74.6
Q1	25.25	68.7	76.1
Q2	31.02	71.8	77.6
Q3[1]	47.10	97.3	109.2
Q4[1]	47.10	88.6	99.2
1980	76.04	100.0	108.7
Q1	61.60	93.4	103.9
Q2	75.53	101.3	111.3
Q3	80.10	104.5	114.8
Q4	86.93	100.7	105.0

[1]My calculations; based on June 10, 1979 devaluation.

Source: Bela Balassa, *Growth Policies and the Exchange Rate in Turkey* (Washington, D.C.: World Bank, 1981), p. 27; World Bank, *Turkey: Industrialization and Trade Strategy* (Washington, D.C.: World Bank, 1982), p. 44.

Table 5.9: Export Losses and the Exchange Rate Policy

	(1)	(2)	(3)	(4)	(5)	(6)	(7)	(8)	(9)	(10)
		Private Sector	Purchasing Power Parity,	Nominal		Total Export	Price	Adjusted Total Export	GNP (current	6/9, %
Year	Exports $	Exports $	$1=1TL	Rate	3 - 4	Loss	Index	Losses	prices)	
1973	1317	1119	21.02	14.15	6.87	9.0	240.1	115.7	309.8	2.9
1974	1532	1302	23.94	15.99	7.95	12.2	311.8	120.0	427.1	2.9
1975	1401	1191	29.18	15.15	14.03	19.7	343.2	175.9	535.8	3.7
1976	1960	1661	36.12	16.16	19.96	39.1	396.6	302.9	675.0	5.8
1977	1753	1490	42.43	19.44	22.99	40.3	492.1	251.5	872.9	4.6
1978	2288	1945	59.2	25.25	33.95	77.7	750.8	317.7	1290.7	6.0
1979	2261	1922	69.5	36.05	33.45	75.6	1230.7	188.7	2199.5	3.4
1980	2910	2473	169.62	79.62	90.0	261.9	3071.0	261.9	4435.2	5.9
Total						535.5		1734.4		

Source: Tabulated from Istanbul Sanayi Odasi, *Türkiye'nin Dişa Açilma Stratejisi İçinde İhracat Sorunu ve Sinai Ürünlerin İhracatini Arttirma Imkânlari* (Istanbul: ISO, 1981), p. 47; OECD, *Turkey: Country Report* (Washington, D.C.: OECD, 1981).

and the economy as a whole was deprived of an extra 1,723 billion TL in potential additional revenues. These calculations do not include the possibility of additional exports that could have been generated from lower prices. The significance of these losses can be seen in the proportion of GNP they represented, which ranged from 2.9 percent in 1974 to as high as 6 percent in 1978.

Table 5.10: Exports, Imports, Trade Balance, and Worker Remittances 1960-1980, (millions of dollars)

Year	Exports (X)	Manufac -turing Exports	Imports (M)	Trade Balance (X-M)	X/M (%)	Worker Remit- tances	Overall Balance
1960	321		468	-147	68.6		-10
1961	347		510	-163	68.0		11
1962	381		622	-241	61.3		-43
1963	368	65	688	-320	53.5		-30
1964	411	76	537	-126	76.5	9	40
1965	464	82	572	-108	81.2	70	82
1966	490	79	718	-228	68.2	115	8
1967	523	75	685	-162	76.4	93	55
1968	496	66	764	-268	64.9	107	-16
1969	537	99	801	-264	67.0	141	28
1970	588	109	948	-360	62.0	273	144
1971	677	149	1171	-494	57.8	471	223
1972	885	243	1563	-678	56.6	740	267
1973	1317	443	2086	-769	63.1	1133	917
1974	1532	600	3777	-2245	40.6	1462	-461
1975	1401	503	4730	-3329	29.6	1312	-1301
1976	1960	596	5129	-3169	38.2	· 982	-1766
1977	1753	586	5797	-4044	30.2	982	-1908
1978	2288	621	4599	-2311	49.7	983	-388
1979	2261	785	5069	-2808	44.6	1694	-963
1980	2910	1047	7909	-4999	36.8	2071	-1338

Source: William Hale, *The Political and Economic Development of Modern Turkey* (New York: St. Martin's Press, 1981), p. 230; OECD, *Economic Survey: Turkey* (Washington, D.C.: OECD, 1983), p. 69.

Despite the saturation of the market, what was remarkable about the durable industries was that these industries had not made any moves to export. For instance, TÜSIAD estimated that by 1981, 88 percent of households had domestically manufactured television sets, yet this industry's exports to date had been negligible.[20]

There were also opportunity costs best seen after the 1970 devaluation, when Turkish exports boomed. Most significantly, it is the manufacturing sector which experienced the dramatic increases, proving that, with proper currency valuation, its products could effectively compete abroad (Table 5.10). Until the lira became overvalued again in 1974, manufacturing exports, led by textiles, jumped from $109 million to $600 million. Textiles alone increased from $25.8 million to $147 million in the same period. Substantial increases were also experienced in other sub-sectors of the economy, including many import substituting ones. However, as the Turkish lira appreciated again, the value of manufacturing exports declined and the $600 million mark established in 1974 was not exceeded until 1978.

The devaluation of 1970 also affected the flow of workers' remittances which increased from $273 million in 1970 to $1,426 million in 1974 (Table 5.10). Just as with exports, worker remittances declined when the lira became overvalued. It took five years to surpass the high reached in 1974. The 1979 increase was due to the government's decision on April 10, 1979 to adjust the exchange rate and offer a premium of 20.6 TL for each dollar sent back by Turkish workers.[21] In effect the 1970 devaluation, with its impact on both exports and workers' remittances, replenished the foreign exchange reserves and allowed for the expansion of the country's import capacity.

(2) In addition to exacerbating the inward-orientation of the economy, the overvalued exchange rate also biased investment decisions, capital utilization and product selection. The overvalued exchange rate encouraged the movement towards *montaj* or assembly industries which further increased the economy's dependence on imports. Component parts for the domestic assembly of consumer durables were cheaper to import because they would fall under the category of investment and/or intermediate goods in the import regime.

Concurrently, the appreciation of the lira significantly altered the nature of production in the manufacturing sector. Bela Balassa shows how the capital intensity of the manufacturing sector associated with import substitution increased; ". . . the incremental capital output ratio in manufacturing rose from 1.6 in 1963-67 to .4 in 1968-72 and 4.7 in 1973-77. Parallel with these changes, the amount of investment per job created,. . . expressed in 1976 prices, increased from 267 thousand TL to

363 thousand TL and, finally, to 572 thousand TL."[22] In the same vein, the amount of capital per worker employed in the manufacturing sector increased considerably between 1965 and 1975 (Table 5.11). While the public and private sectors experienced approximately the same rate of increase in the 1965-1970 period, the private sector in the subsequent period outpaced its public counterpart by more than 2:1.[23]

Table 5.11: Capital per Worker in the Manufacturing Sector (1000's TL. at 1965 Prices)

	1965	1970	% increase	1975	% increase
Public Sector	49.72	72.01	44.8	92.6	28.6
Private Sector	26.05	38.72	48.6	65.9	70.2
Total	36.52	51.01	39.7	75.54	48.1

Source: DPT, *Dördüncü Beş Yillik Kalkinma Plani: 1979-1983* (Ankara: DPT, 1979), p. 20.

ISI's inherently "imitative" nature also contributed to the capital intensity of the manufacturing sector. Hence, despite its primarily labor-intensive origins, the drive to emulate "modern" methods of manufacturing quickly transformed it into a capital-intensive process. The acceleration of capital-intensive production processes in societies with abundant labor supplies creates stresses which ISI was initially designed to remedy. Also, the imitative quality of the process means that the life span of some industries is not as long as it had been in the developed world. Obsolescence arrives sooner in the late-late industrializers.[24] Overvalued exchange rate policy aggravates the trend towards obsolescence by suppressing the real cost of foreign technology and, consequently, further deepening the dependence on such foreign technological inputs.

These were, in essence, the internal policies and their consequences on the economy. We now turn to the external determinants.

External Factors

From the beginning, attempts at industrialization were guided by one constraint: foreign exchange availability. While there were periods of relative "plenty," this external restraining factor was ever-present during much of the two decades in question. Hence, the dramatic increases in the price of oil of the 1970s had a serious impact on Turkish balance of payments. Ironically, the first oil price hike occurred at a time when Turkey had bountiful supplies of foreign exchange. By the time the second oil crisis hit, the Turkish economy was deeply immersed in its own crisis, and the new round of price increases just served to aggravate an already difficult, if not desperate situation.

In 1974, Turkish foreign exchange reserves stood at an all-time high. This was mainly due to the mini-export boom triggered by the 1970 devaluation and the beginnings of the flow of remittances from the ever-increasing number of Turkish nationals seeking work in the industrial heartland of Western Europe. Unlike the rest of the world, Turkey did not make the painful adjustments necessary to overcome the impact of the oil price increases; instead, it used its reserves to cushion the blow and thus avoid such politically difficult choices as raising domestic fuel prices. Even when the mini-export boom came to an end — mainly because of the revaluation of the lira and, to a lesser extent, the emerging recession in the West — the continuing steady flow of worker remittances represented a source of extra income in dollars. These became a source of economic rents, used to delay any type of adjustment policies. The absence of any serious attempts at devaluing the currency from 1970 through 1979 can be attributed to this phenomenon. In other words, the Turkish economy became addicted to these remittances, without which, as Table 5.10 showed, its trade balance could have become unmanageable. Despite the efforts at cushioning, Table 5.12 shows that by the end of the decade the structure of imports had been profoundly affected by the changes in the oil trade.

Table 5.12: Oil and Non-Oil Import Prices and Volume Indices

Year	Oil Imports		Non-Oil Imports		All Imports	
	Price	Volume	Price	Volume	Price	Volume
1977	100	100	100	100	100	100
1978	119	96	102	61	113	70
1979	136	81	145	57	140	62
1980	156	85	249	56	197	65

Source: TÜSIAD, *The Turkish Economy, 1981* (Istanbul: TÜSIAD, 1981), p. 138.

While the price of all imports doubled between 1977 and 1980, the volume of imports declined by 35 percent. Not all of the blame can be directly ascribed to petroleum prices. As oil price hikes worked themselves through the international economy, these increases directly affected Turkey's other imports, specifically imports of finished goods. Although oil prices in this period rose by one half, the price paid by Turkey for its non-oil imports jumped by two and a half times. In the general inflationary atmosphere at the end of the decade, every country was responding to the higher oil prices by increasing the prices of their own exports. For Turkey, the sharp contraction in the volume of imports — by more than 40 percent for the non-oil category — affected all sectors of the economy, the worst and most dependent of all being manufacturing.

Finally, the 1974 Cyprus invasion was economically an unwelcome event. In addition to the cost of the operation, the continued maintenance of large numbers of troops on the island and the subsidization of the Turkish Cypriot administration, the invasion also provoked the U.S. Congress to impose an arms embargo on Turkey. The embargo proved to be an expensive punishment because it forced Turkey to use valuable foreign exchange resources to buy arms which, otherwise, would have been received under such favorable conditions as grants and the like.

It is the confluence of external transformations with domestic policies which ultimately ignited the crisis.

Analyzing The Crisis

The crisis of the late seventies, which culminated in the January 24, 1980 stabilization program and the September 12, 1980 military intervention, was the most acute of recent Turkish history. It was an amalgamation of difficult economic conditions and a tense political atmosphere, punctuated by violence and a great deal of uncertainty. It did not materialize overnight and, as the previous sections implied, its economic facets were long in the making. If there was one single event which pinpoints the beginnings of the crisis, it would be the February 1977 indefinite suspension of transfers of currency abroad. From then on, with each passing day, Turkey's foreign exchange constraint became progressively more severe and debilitating.

Accustomed to consistent growth rates, higher than those of Latin American and OECD countries, Turkey's economy experienced a decline for the first time since the 1960 coup. This was followed by another deterioration. Hardest hit was the industrial sector which fell by 5.7 percent at 1982 prices and 5.5 percent in 1979 and 1980, respectively.[25] In other words, in two years the loss in industrial production amounted to 10.9 percent of its 1978 value. Within the industrial sector, the manufacturing sector's output declined by 6.1 and 3.9 percent, respectively.[26] As a result, manufacturing's growth rate was reduced from an average of 9.3 percent per annum during the 1970-1975 period, to 1.9 percent from 1975 to 1980.[27]

Foreign trade deficits, as Table 5.10 indicated, continued to grow at a fairly rapid rate. Following the oil price increases in the early 1970s, the trade deficit jumped from $769 million in 1973, to $2,245 million in 1974. Exports, which previously could on the average finance 65 to 70 percent of imports, were sufficient at their lowest point in 1975 to cover only 30 percent of this bill. This ratio did not improve significantly during the remainder of the decade. Not surprisingly, foreign exchange reserves were rapidly depleted. The Central Bank suspended payments abroad for an indefinite time, although it did not acknowledge the suspension's duration publicly. Instead, it devoted all its precious foreign exchange receipts to the acquisition of necessary resources, mostly oil. This left local importers and industrialists at the mercy of foreign creditors. By 1977, the situation had become so desperate that, to dramatize the problem, the Prime Minister announced that the country was in need of 70 cents, as a Central Bank check for this amount had bounced abroad.[28] When the last Demirel government took over, it found that the Central Bank's disposable cash reserves to finance all imports stood at $30 million,[29] or just enough for two days. This lack of foreign exchange forced manufacturers and importers to resort to the black market and other illegal schemes or to sharply reduce their production.

In the mid-seventies, the Turkish authorities' response to the increasing foreign exchange requirements was to borrow, and borrow at unfavorable conditions. Turkey's "cautious" debt policy gave way to one which caused the external debt to rise from $8 billion in 1975 to $15 billion in 1978; short-term debt component to rose from less than a quarter to more than a half; debt service ratios increasing from 42 percent in 1975 to 97 and 231 percent in 1976 and 1977, respectively.[30] Not surprisingly, in the 1979 surveys done by the State Institute of Statistics, foreign exchange shortages were blamed for the low capacity utilization in the manufacturing sector.[31]   In turn, the low capacity utilization translated into substantial declines in manufacturing sector investments. Whereas the annual increase in private sector investments in manufacturing during the 1963-1977 period was of the order of 7.5 percent, during the 1977-80 period they declined at the rate of 10.2 percent (Table 5.13). The decline in investments was global.   Only the housing and energy sectors escaped this predicament.[32] On the other hand, manufacturing investments fell victim to a variety of problems, ranging from inflation to the lack of imported inputs and, finally, to what the Turkish Union of Chambers called "ideologically motivated strike activity."[33]

Table 5.13: Average Annual Increase in Total Fixed Capital Investments (%)

	Total		Public		Private	
	1963/77	1977/80	1963/77	1977/80	1963/77	1977/80
Agriculture	10.4	-21.7	8.4	-17.2	12.9	-25.6
Manufacturing	10.8	-2.4	17.7	4.7	7.5	-10.2
Energy	12.8	9.1	13.5	9.1	2.4	6.7
Transportation	12.5	-16.8	10.4	-14.8	20.3	-20.0
Housing	7.1	8.5	8.2	-6.6	7.0	9.6
Total	10.2	-5.2	11.1	-4.5	9.3	-6.0

Source: TÜSIAD, *The Turkish Economy, 1982* (Istanbul: TÜSIAD, 1982), p. 13.

Table 5.14: Indicators of Inflation (%)

Year	Wholesale Price Index	Istanbul Cost of Living Index	Implicit GNP Deflator
1970	6.7	7.9	11.9
1971	15.9	19.0	18.3
1972	18.0	15.4	16.4
1973	20.5	14.0	22.1
1974	29.9	23.9	28.3
1975	10.1	21.2	16.1
1976	15.6	17.4	16.2
1977	24.1	26.0	25.0
1978	52.6	61.9	44.0
1979	63.9	63.5	69.6
1980	107.2	94.3	10.3

Source: TÜSIAD, *The Turkish Economy 1983* (Istanbul: TÜSIAD, 1983), p. 67.

Concurrently, inflationary pressures got out of hand (Table 5.14) and the inflation rate reached a high of 107.2 percent in 1980. Budget deficits increased at a rapid rate, from 20 billion TL in 1978 to 52 billion

TL in 1979, and 122 billion in 1980 as the share of the deficits in the GNP increased accordingly from 1.6 to 2.3 and 2.7 percent, respectively.[34]

Table 5.15: Strike Activity (1960-1982)

Year	Number of Strikes	Number of Workers Participating	Number of Workdays Lost
1972	48	14,879	659,362
1973	55	12,286	671,135
1974	110	25,546	1,109,401
1975	116	13,708	668,797
1976	58	7,240	325,830
1977	59	15,682	1,397,124
1978	87	9,748	426,127
1979	176	24,920	1,432,078
1980[1]	220	33,832	4,298,413

[1]January-September 1980; strikes were banned by the military government.

Sources: TÜSIAD, *The Turkish Economy, 1981* (Istanbul: TÜSIAD, 1981), p.12; TÜSIAD, *The Turkish Economy, 1982* (Istanbul: TÜSIAD, 1982), p. 57.

Table 5.16: Average Real Daily Wages of Insured Workers (1975=100)

Year	Gross	Net
1976	98.21	64.21
1977	99.06	62.25
1978	86.81	50.94
1979	75.13	40.93
1980	57.16	28.47

Source: TÜSIAD, *The Turkish Economy, 1981* (Istanbul: TÜSIAD, 1981), p. 104.

In the period leading to the military intervention, strike activity increased considerably (Table 5.15) as worker management disputes intensified. This was accompanied by a significant increase in lockouts.

The number of workdays lost due to lockouts increased from 53 thousand in 1978 to 653 thousand in the first nine months of 1980. Similarly, in the first nine months of 1980, the number of days lost to strikes tripled in comparison to the entire previous year. Underlying the above trend was the steady decrease in real wage rates from 1976 onwards (Table 5.16). During this period the net average daily wage of insured workers was reduced by one half. This erosion was also reflected in minimum wage rates, which were established by the government. In 1976 the minimum wage stood at 13.97 TL at 1963 prices, and by 1981 it had declined to 10.15 TL.

The crisis atmosphere was not helped by the absence of any discussion of solutions. While the reasons for the political deadlock will be explored in the next chapters, suffice it to say here that the paralysis engendered by the lack of options contributed to the sharp decline in business confidence and even to the fear of violent political change.

Averting the Crisis

Could the crisis have been averted? From an economic standpoint there were solutions. Most, however, entailed abandoning some, if not all, of the practices associated with import substitution.

Clearly, the opportunity costs of Turkey's developmental policy were high. While outward-oriented newly industrializing countries (NICs) also suffered from the oil price hikes (in some ways the shocks to their systems were considerably greater), they nevertheless succeeded in maintaining higher growth rates. Whereas Turkey grew at an annual rate of 2.1 percent between 1976-79, the performance of NICs with 9.7 percent was considerably better.[35] As Anne Krueger demonstrated, alternative or modified import substitution tracks would have allowed Turkey to realize much bigger gains in employment, exports and industrial production. Under policy options she called "moderate import substitution" and "balanced export promotion and import substitution," the Second Five Year Development Plan, for instance, would have yielded significantly better results.[36] The experience of 1970 alone — with the dramatic rise in export earnings — was a clear indication of the capabilities of the Turkish economy.

Instead ISI's implementation in Turkey was characterized by a certain degree of rigidity. This rigidity manifested itself in the exorbitant levels of protection and in the reluctance to open the domestic market to competition from abroad — even after the infant industries had achieved a significant level of maturity. This, combined with an unwillingness to seek exports markets also limited the range and availability of products and, as Şevket Pamuk demonstrates, put the substitution drive completely at the mercy of foreign exchange availabilities. [37]

Why were policies, as this chapter indicated, which accentuated ISI's inherent faults, continued despite overwhelming evidence that they were not working? The economic case against pursuing these policies was strong and compelling. So the answer must lie in the unwillingness to change and in the state's inability to act decisively to counteract domestic distortions. Therefore, the answer is a political one. It is the absence of political leadership which, combined with the external pressures, spiraled Turkey into the crisis. As we will see in later chapters, the state's reluctance to alter strategies or make corrections to them was reinforced by private sector fears of foreign markets and competition, but also by that sector's comfortable and profitable position behind all the state erected barriers.

Notes

[1]The industrial sector is composed of manufacturing, mining and energy production.

[2]Kemal Derviş and Sherman Robinson, "Structure of Income Inequality in Turkey," in Ergun Özbudun and Aydin Ulusan (eds.), *The Political Economy of Income Distribution in Turkey* (New York: Holmes and Meier, 1980), pp. 128-135.

[3]Uğur Korum, "The Structure of Interdependence of the Public and Private Sectors in the Turkish Manufacturing Industry," in Mükerrem Hiç (ed.), *Turkey's and Other Countries' Experience with the Mixed Economy* (Istanbul: Istanbul University Faculty of Economics, 1979), pp. 99-109.

[4]Devlet Planlama Teşkilati, *Dördüncü Beş Yillik Kalkinma Plani: 1979-1983* (Ankara: Devlet Planlama Teşkilati, 1979), pp. 606-607.

[5]The 1980 increase represents the response to the January devaluation of that year and the government's decision to deflate the domestic economy. In order to get rid of their stocks, industrialists had to literally dump them on Middle Eastern markets at prices considerably lower than what their costs.

[6]Studies using input-output matrices are limited to 1968 and 1973 because these are the only two years for which such figures are available.

[7]Uğur Korum, *Türk Imalat Sanayi ve Ithal Ikamesi: Bir Değer-*

lendirme (Ankara: Siyasal Bilgiler Fakültesi Yayini, 1977), pp. 80-82.

[8]For a discussion of how worker remittances flowing in during the 1970s discouraged exports see Şevket Pamuk, "Ithal Ikamesi, Döviz Darboğazlari ve Türkiye 1947-1979," in Korkut Boratav, Çağlar Keyder and Şevket Pamuk, *Krizin Gelişimi ve Türkiye'nin Alternatif Sorunu* (Istanbul: Kaynak Yayinlari, 1984), pp. 58-64.

[9]Backward linkages refer to a sub-sector's use of domestic inputs. Forward linkages, by contrast, refer to the use of a sub-sector's product as an input in other sectors' output.

[10]*Istanbul Sanayi Odasi Dergisi* No. 188 (October 15, 1981). See Table 6.2 in the next chapter for a regional distribution of the firms.

[11]These figures refer to individual companies. A significant number of private sector companies are wholly owned subsidiaries of larger holding corporations, but in the study quoted they appear as separate entities and therefore the state enterprises occupy the first twelve rankings.

[12]*Istanbul Sanayi Odasi Dergisi*, Vol. 16, No. 188 (October 15, 1981).

[13]*Istanbul Sanayi Odasi Dergisi*, Vol. 17, No. 198 (August 15, 1982). The change in year in the text is the result of the inconsistency of the data: some of the information was available only for 1980 and other only for 1981.

[14]Of the largest eighteen, only one; of the largest 25, five are missing from this study.

[15]Abdurrahman Ariman, *Türkiye'de Sermaye Yoğunlaşmasi ve Sermaye Gruplarinin Oluşumu*, (Istanbul: Istanbul, Technical University, unpublished dissertation thesis, 1981), pp. 54-55.

[16]For instance, caustic soda, a vital intermediate type of good, sold internationally for 32-37 Deutsche marks, whereas its domestic cost was 90, *Rapor*, September 28, 1981.

[17]World Bank, *Turkey: Prospects and Problems for an Expanding Economy* (Washington, D.C.: World Bank, 1975), p. 245.

[18]The absurdity of the situation was exemplified by numerous cases where a firm, based on its capacity, would requisition $100,000 to purchase an intermediate product from abroad only be allocated only $1,000. If the $1,000 was not enough to start production, as it invariably would be, an industrialist had two choices: try to purchase similar licenses elsewhere at a premium and, thus, try to raise the total amount to a realistic level, or sell his license elsewhere on the market at a premium. In either case, economic rents are earned by the various participants who benefit from the manipulation of foreign exchange

shortages.

[19]World Bank, *Turkey: Industrialization and Trade Strategy* (Washington, D.C.: World Bank, 1982), pp. 95-96.

[20]*Görüş*, (TÜSIAD publication) April 1982.

[21]OECD, *Country Report: Turkey* (Washington, D.C.: OECD, 1981), p. 67. This is what explains the dramatic increase in worker remittances from $55.7 million in March to $639 million in May.

[22]Bela Balassa, *Growth Policies and the Exchange Rate in Turkey* (Washington, D.C.: World Bank, 1981), p. 21.

[23]This does not mean that the public sector was more frugal in its expenditures on capital. Rather, it was the result of its more liberal employment policies, that is, state enterprises were more likely to have surplus labor.

[24] The Turkish radio industry is a particularly telling example of the kind of rapid changes which cause havoc in significant parts of the manufacturing sector. In 1968, the production of radio receivers stood at an all time high of 271,000 units manufactured by 27 different companies. This was remarkable since most assembly industry was dominated by a few large firms. By 1980, with the introduction of TV receivers and their widespread distribution, only four companies continued to produce radios with a combined annual production of 41,655 units, an 85 per cent drop. This industry like other assembly industries had insignificant exports which could have cushioned it against changes in the domestic market. The same fate has also befallen the black and white TV industry which had reached a peak of 740,000 units in 1977 but then saw its output decline to 326,541 by 1980 as the country geared itself for color transmission. Jak Kamhi, "Dayanikli Tüketim Mallari Sanayi," in *2. Türkiye Iktisat Kongresi* (Ankara: DPT, 1981), Vol. 6, p. 105.

[25]OECD, *Country Report: Turkey* (Washington, D.C.: OECD, 1982), p. 54.

[26]TÜSIAD, *The Turkish Economy, 1980* (Istanbul: TÜSIAD, 1980), p. 157; TÜSIAD, *The Turkish Economy, 1981* (Istanbul: TÜSIAD, 1981), p. 39.

[27]OECD, *Country Report: Turkey*, p. 38.

[28]Emin Çölaşan, *Bir Dönemin Perde Arkasi* (Istanbul: Milliyet Yayinlari, 1983), pp. 73-74.

[29]Çölaşan, *Bir Dönemin Perde Arkasi*, pp. 25-27.

[30]Peter Wolff, *Stabilization Policy and Structural Adjustment in Turkey, 1980-1985* (Berlin: German Development Institute, 1987), pp.

58-59.

[31]For instance, in the chemicals sector, most firms operated at 60 percent and a third at less than 40 percent of capacity. Devlet İstatistik Enstitüsü, *Imalat Sanayii: Istihdam, Üretim, Eğilim, 1978 (III) - 1979 (III)* (Ankara: DPT, 1980), pp. 18-102.

[32]This was mainly because the state's interests in energy were hightened by the oil crisis, and housing prices rise quickly in a highly inflationary atmosphere.

[33]TOB, *Iktisadi Rapor, 1981* (Ankara: TOB, 1981), p. 308.

[34]TÜSIAD, *The Turkish Economy, 1981*, p. 172.

[35]World Bank, *Turkey: Industrialization and Trade Strategy*, p. 46.

[36]Anne Krueger, *Foreign Trade Regimes and Economic Development: Turkey* (New York: National Bureau for Economic Research, 1974), pp. 249-265.

[37]Şevket Pamuk, "Ithal Ikamesi, Döviz Darboğazlari ve Türkiye 1947-1979."

6

Private Sector Cleavages

As put forth in Chapter 2, it was private sector cleavages — and not ISI's inherent tendencies — that crippled the Turkish state and rendered it incapable of formulating and implementing policies to correct the deficiencies of import substitution. The previous chapter focused on the debacle of the Turkish industrialization drive. The next two chapters, by contrast, look at the consequences of import substitution from a different perspective. Here, the focus is on private sector groups and on their interaction with the state and its institutions.

Private sector cleavages in Turkey gave rise to a bewildering array of alliances and a myriad of conflicts which spelled the demise of ISI. The primary motivation for the struggles was the state's policies from which economic rents were generated. Therefore, influencing policy choices was of great importance to rent seekers. As the different factions of the private sector, deeply suspicious of each other, maneuvered to maximize their respective share of economic rents, they pulled and pushed in a variety of directions. Their pursuit of rents and short-term goals hampered their ability to coalesce, and consequently their ability to present and accept long-term solutions to Turkey's worsening economic crisis. The result: competing pressures on the state which led to its ultimate paralysis. While the latter will be discussed in Chapter 7, this chapter provides an overview of the structure of the private sector and its organizations by focusing, in detail, on three different arenas of competition and discord within the private sector: policy issues, regional questions, and representational conflicts. In the final analysis, all three are, in one way or another, linked to and influenced by one another.

This chapter is for the dedicated: it provides intricate details that constitute the proof of the arguments advanced in the earlier segments of the book.

The Structure of the Private Sector and its Organizations

The Turkish private sector of the 1960s and 1970s was comprised of five major groups: (1) agricultural interests, (2) commercial interests, (3) commodity brokers, (4) industrialists, and (5) small artisans and shopkeepers. The state organized these groups into three "quasi-public organizations:" representative institutions that were sanctioned by the state and designed to ascertain private sector attitudes to policy questions and other matters. Commercial groups, commodity brokers and industrialists were made members of the Turkish Union of Chambers, or *Türkiye Odalar Birliği* (TOB). Agricultural groups were organized within the Union of Agricultural Chambers, or *Ziraat Odalari Birliği*; while artisans, shopkeepers and some of the self-employed were represented within the Confederation of Tradesmen and Artisans, *Türkiye Esnaf ve Sanatkârlar Dernekleri Konfederasyonu.*[1]

There were also non-quasi-public organizations, the most important of which were TÜSIAD and TISK. TÜSIAD, the Turkish Industrialists and Businessmen's Association (*Türk Sanayicileri ve İş Adamlari Derneği*) represented the largest of the commercial and industrial interests; and TISK, the Turkish Confederation of Employers' Unions (*Türkiye İşverenler Sendikalari Konfederasyonu*), was designed to primarily offer a common employers' front in industry-wide collective bargaining negotiations with labor unions.

Of the organizations mentioned above, the ones most directly relevant to this study were the Union of Chambers and TÜSIAD.

Turkish Union of Chambers (TOB)

The state created the TOB, which stood for the Union of Chambers of Commerce, Industry and Commodity Exchanges,[2] just as the private sector was emerging from the restrictive conditions of the Etatist era. Two months before its resounding 1950 defeat to the Democrat Party, the Republican People's Party implemented Law 5590 which set the guidelines for uniting the 90 existing chambers of commerce. This law also allowed for the formation of separate chambers of industry, which were not only distinct from the chambers of commerce, but were envisaged to become members of the overarching union.[3] But it is not until 1952 that the Türkiye Odalar Birliği, hereafter referred to as the TOB, came officially into being with the prodding of the Ministry of Commerce.[4]

The TOB, which quickly became the most important private sector organization, was primarily designed for the government to exercise control over the private sector and respond to its demands. Membership in the subsidiary chambers, and hence in the Union itself, was mandated by law, providing the TOB with a vast network and access to funds through compulsory dues. While the Union's importance waned for industrialists after 1980, for other groups it remained the single most effective organization for representation, as demonstrated by the 1982 amendment to Law 5590 which allowed for the inclusion of a new sub-group: the maritime chambers of commerce.

Structure. The structure of the TOB and its subsidiary chambers has often shaped the intra-sectoral and inter-regional conflicts. The primary basis of the TOB is regional: its principal constituents are regionally organized chambers. Disregarding the maritime chambers of commerce, which are of recent origin, the TOB consists of the following types of local chambers: (1) chambers of commerce *and* industry, (2) chambers of commerce, (3 chambers of industry, and (4) commodity exchanges.[5] Of the four categories listed, the chambers of commerce and industry are the most numerous, followed by commodity exchanges, commercial chambers and, finally, industrial chambers.[6] Whether or not a region possesses a separate industrial chamber depends largely on the relationship between its industrialists and commercial interests and the industrialists' strength in numbers and finances.

In terms of membership and resources, the Istanbul and Izmir[7] industrial chambers are the two oldest and most powerful of the eight such organizations. However, when compared to their commercial counterparts, the industrial chambers do not have large memberships. For instance, the Istanbul Chamber of Industry (*Istanbul Sanayi Odasi*, ISO) had a total membership of 6,600 in 1982, while its regional commercial equivalent, the Istanbul Chamber of Commerce (*Istanbul Ticaret Odasi*, ITO) could claim over 100,000 members.

Functions. In addition to acting as the official representative of industrialists, commercial interests and commodity brokers, the TOB was also accorded some administrative functions. Until 1971, when the military-backed government suspended the practice, the most important such task related to distributing government-set import quota allocations among industrialists and commercial importers. The quota allocations were based on the capacity figures of individual enterprises. In turn, these capacity figures had to be certified by the local chambers. From 1971 onwards, quota allocations were dispensed by the Ministry of Commerce, although the practice regarding capacity reports continued to be in the hands of the chambers. As part of its functions, the TOB was also responsible for monitoring the veracity of import prices claimed by importers as a safeguard against over-invoicing and other irregularities. This practice, which dated back to 1958, was abolished in 1962, only to be returned to the organization in 1971.[8] All these administrative tasks provided the TOB with considerable powers.

TÜSIAD and TISK

Since membership in the TOB was compulsory, the organization did not distinguish between large and small members, as both sets enjoyed the same rights. In 1971, frustrations resulting from differences over size and other issues compelled some of the largest industrialists and commercial interests to form the Turkish Industrialists and Businessmen's Association, TÜSIAD. Unlike the chambers, TÜSIAD was *not* a quasi-public organization, so the state was not obliged to consult with it on policy matters. However, since its membership consisted of the richest business enterprises, no government could ignore it. And as a wholly private organization, TÜSIAD enjoyed greater freedom to publicize private sector concerns.[9]

Similarly, the employers' confederation, TISK, was free of government constraints. Unlike TÜSIAD and the TOB, the TISK defined its role more narrowly and limited itself to questions of labor management relations. While its interactions with the state focused primarily on these same issues, its aggressive leadership frequently caused the TISK to supersede its mandate. However, in the cases of both TÜSIAD and TISK, their members individually belonged to the quasi-public chambers, often giving rise to divided loyalties.

Policy-Based Cleavages

The policy issues that divided private sector interests ranged from industrialization policies to interest rates and quota allocations. These can be divided into five broad categories (1) protectionism and import substituting industrialization, (2) foreign trade and exchange rate policy, (3) banks and bank credits, (4) direct foreign investments, and (5) land and tax reform. While the saliency of these issues varied at different times, the intensity of conflict was determined by the availability of foreign exchange. In an economy as dependent as Turkey on foreign exchange receipts, shortages in such foreign exchange resources simultaneously restricted and increased opportunities for gains. This was the case because foreign exchange represented the primary source of economic rents. Therefore, it is not surprising that some import substituting businesses performed extremely well at the height of the economic crisis by manipulating this scarce resource.

The private sector achieved a modicum of cohesiveness only at the end of 1979 when confronted with a complete collapse of the economy. Until then, groups pursued their own interests with little regard for the long-term ramifications of their actions; any appearance of collaboration between them was due to the similarity in short-term interests and not to conscious attempts at restructuring industrial policies.

Protectionism and Import Substituting Industrialization

During the 1960s and 1970s, continued protection and import substitution were the single most important issues on which industrialists could, by and large, agree. However, the manufacturing community itself was not unanimous on all the underlying issues relating to ISI's implementation. Not surprisingly, the industrialists' main antagonists on these issues were their sectoral competitors: the commercial and agricultural interests. Of these sectoral competitors, the commercial groups posed the greatest threat since they shared such representative institutions as the TOB, and since they were in direct competition with each other. Not all commercial groups were equally opposed to import substitution. Importers were most threatened by the industrialization strategy because as industrialists diversified their product lines under the protective arm of the state, they increasingly intruded into the importers' domain.

Importers, mostly concentrated in cities such as Istanbul and Izmir, strenuously objected to the restrictive import provisions associated with import substitution. As the number of goods placed on the government's "prohibited list" increased in response to claims of local manufacturing, importers were continuously forced to make adjustments. To protect themselves, some importers became importer-industrialists. Without abandoning their primary importing activities, they also engaged in the local manufacturing of products they previously imported. Importer-industrialists had to wear two hats, that of importer and that of industrialist. Where there were separate local chambers of commerce and industry, importer-industrialists, by virtue of their dual activities, would belong to both.

Since the Istanbul Chamber of Commerce (ITO) contained the largest concentration of importers, opposition to ISI was centered there. Commercial chambers in the Anatolian countryside had a more ambiguous position. Independent of the foreign trade sector, they welcomed the nationalistic overtones of import substitution. On the other hand, they expressed reservations about the concentration of industry and resources in the Western regions of the country and the lack of improvement in the domestic content of local manufactures.

ITO's criticism of ISI emanated from two concerns. First, by emphasizing industrial production at the perceived expense of other forms of economic activity, ISI threatened the predominance of commercial chambers. It is this fear that fueled tensions in the representative institutions, the impact of which is to be discussed later in this chapter. Second, ITO criticized the inefficiencies that resulted from ISI: the high cost of domestically produced goods and their poor quality. These inefficiencies directly impacted the commercial sector which was obliged to coexist with its industrial counterpart and serve as the latter's national distribution network. In addition, as ITO's president pointed out, no industry which surrounded itself with protective customs barriers of the magnitude of 150 percent could ever hope to export its output.[10]

Nowhere was the issue of protectionism more tested than with assembly industries. To import substituting industrialists, support for the assembly industries became a question of faith, especially in the politically charged atmosphere of the late sixties and seventies. In 1964, the government instituted guidelines for the assembly industry in anticipation of ISI's take-off. The Assembly Industry Guidelines (*Montaj Sanayi Talimatnamesi*)[11] were formulated in response to these industries' tendency to degenerate into "disguised importation."[12] Proponents who favored this form of industrialization published many studies purporting to show that, by 1970, in a great number of consumer durable products, the share of the domestically produced components had increased dramatically. One such study found that 95 percent of refrigerator components were of Turkish origin, as well as some 89 percent of the vacuum cleaner components.[13] In 1970, in the automotive industry, with only one company in production and two others just getting ready to go, it was claimed that 70 percent of the components used were of domestic origin.[14] Despite such claims of successes, from 1965 onwards, industrialists persistently asked for the downward revision of domestic content requirements in the Assembly Industry Guidelines on the basis that their stringency was adversely affecting the quality of the final products.[15]

Critics charged that the figures provided by assembly industries proponents were exaggerated and self-serving. It was relatively easy to overestimate the content ratio if one assembly industry made use of another's output. Thus the 1964 guidelines gave rise to auxiliary industries designed to provide the main industries with domestically assembled inputs, which allowed for these exaggerated claims. With the proliferation of such sub-sectors, state authorities, specifically the SPO, found it impossible to control and enforce the 1964 guidelines.[16] The SPO's own calculations found the overall actual domestic content figure to be closer to 23 percent.

The automobile sector, more than any durable product, came to represent the frivolity of such industries. In 1979, the Automotive Industrialists Association estimated that this industry alone needed $195 million in direct imports and another $100 million for the production of the inputs, for a total of $295 million. Government estimates put this number at $700 million, while total automotive exports did not exceed $7 million.[17] In 1978, $700 million represented over 20 percent of Turkey's non-oil imports: a figure inordinately high for such a nascent industry.[18]

Conservative Justice Party leader and Prime Minister Süleyman Demirel found himself in the middle of a political storm in 1970 when, as part of the August 10, 1970 stabilization program, he also introduced new taxes, including some on assembly industry products. The government was immediately and bitterly denounced by the TOB. Ironically, these accusations were leveled at a government which had been instrumental in the establishment of the automobile industry, over the objections of the State Planning Organization.[19] In the final analysis, this industry's long term stability and success was assured with the direct involvement of the armed forces. The Army Mutual Assistance Fund, OYAK, the fourth largest holding corporation in Turkey, was induced by this industry's champions to buy into a Renault car assembly plant.[20]

In general, industrialists were very protective of ISI, and therefore quick to criticize the government for any action that could hurt import substitution. For instance, in 1975, when Prime Minister Demirel criticized industrialists for hiding behind protectionist barriers, it was the Eskişehir Chamber of Industry that pointedly responded by stating that Turkish industry was incapable of surviving without barriers.[21] Some went even further by lending their support to those advocating increased state planning to achieve desired objectives.[22]

While support for ISI was universal within the manufacturing sector, there was no unanimity over its implementation. Some industrialists were as critical of their colleagues as were ISI's external detractors. The move to consumer durable production in the 1970s, at the expense of intermediate and capital goods production, was severely criticized by the Eskişehir Chamber of Industry.[23] In 1970, this chamber published what it called the "Socially Conscious

Industrialist's Manifesto," in which it argued for a different type of import substituting industrialization strategy. The manifesto argued that industrial production ought to be geared toward the "whole economy," not just the higher income levels,[24] in other words, away from the preoccupation with consumer durables. It also called for reduced consumption levels and increased outlays of intermediate and capital goods investments, specifically in the iron-steel, industrial chemicals and machinery producing sectors.

Despite their expansion into Anatolia in the 1970s, the vast majority of consumer durable production facilities were located in a few selected regions in the West. This concentration of industries constituted one of the most important reason for Anatolian industrialists' objections to the way ISI was being implemented. In 1970, all 9 firms involved in the production of refrigerators, washing machines, and vacuum cleaners were located in the Marmara region, which encompassed Istanbul (home to 8 of these) and surrounding provinces. Similarly, of the 12 enterprises producing electric and electronic goods, 11 were situated in Istanbul and 1 in Izmir.[25] The three passenger car manufacturers were also situated in the Marmara region.

Hence, the outward manifestation of support for ISI did not mean that all industrialists were oblivious to ISI's shortcomings in Turkey.[26] Nevertheless, they rarely publicized their criticisms of each other for fear of endangering governmental and/or public support. As a result, industrialists were reluctant to suggest policy choices which would have pitted member against member. Instead, they articulated their priorities in the most general fashion and expected the government to go along with them.[27] Thus, when it came to advising the government on the forthcoming Fourth Five Year Development Plan, for instance, the Union of Chambers of Industry drafted a set of proposals which simply suggested that, in view of the few industries capable of competing internationally, the new plan ought to continue the state's past protective policies. This, at a time when the economy was about to face serious economic difficulties, was typical of the kinds of compromises they had been accustomed to formulating. Ironically, this particular one was drafted by the severest of the industrial critics, Eskişehir's Mümtaz Zeytinoğlu.[28] Such compromises implied that the lowest common denominator, "protection for the sake of protection," would be the only acceptable outcome.

Foreign exchange supplies were the overriding constraint on ISI. As long as foreign exchange reserves were sufficient, import substituting industrialists showed little concern for the dislocations created. This was typified by Vehbi Koç the leading import substituting industrialist. When asked in a 1976 interview what his family of companies did to earn foreign exchange to pay for their imports, he simply argued that their contribution was limited to import substituting efforts, and that "exporting was a completely different [type of] activity." He further pointed out that KOÇ Holding "saves a lot of foreign exchange by producing FIAT cars in the country."[29] He could just as easily have added refrigerators, washing machines, office equipment etc. as activities in which his companies "saved" foreign exchange.

The reaping of economic rents cushioned everyone, especially industrialists, from the vagaries of international competition and prevented the formulation of new ideas in favor of maintaining the status quo. The import regime itself meant that, "since a producer had installed industrial capacity, he would generally request that the government remove the items produced from the list of permitted imports, and expect that his request be granted. Thus, the Turkish trade regime of the 1960s, especially after about 1965, was one in which prohibitive protection was automatically granted to a new industry."[30]

It took the desperate economic conditions of 1979 to convince some industrialists to take a second look at ISI. TÜSIAD was at the forefront of this move when in 1979 its president declared that the past policy of trying to manufacture everything domestically was the real source of the difficulties facing the country.[31] ISO, by contrast, defended ISI until the bitter end. Ironically, when the time came to acknowledge ISI's failures some ISO members chose to ignore their own steadfast support for the strategy, preferring instead to blame the government for having imposed it on them; "since the fifties, all governments knowingly or unknowingly have over protected us. The more we asked for a market economy, the more protection they offered us. It is with custom barriers, quotas and cheap credits that we have reached our present state of affairs. . ."[32]

By mid-1979, under pressure from other chambers and organizations, ISO appeared convinced of the futility of its resistance to change. It decided to support moves toward liberalization which were finally ushered in by the January 24, 1980 stabilization plan. Even then, however, this support was tempered by its fear of competition. Its executive committee informed the SPO that they wholeheartedly supported the new government's attempted transformation of the political economy, but also warned that "the economy *should not* under any circumstances be opened up to free competition without first achieving a desired level of strength."[33] Little seemed to have changed from previous positions.

By 1980, the once superficially united industrialists were divided among themselves with one segment backing the government's moves away from ISI and another, while pretending to support the changes, actively fighting the new measures and bitterly complaining of the hardships endured. As Chapter 8 will demonstrate, these divisions could have led to the unraveling of the 1980 rescue operations.

Foreign Trade and Exchange Rate Policy

Foreign Trade. As ISI progressed, causing Turkey to become increasingly dependent on imports of intermediate and investment goods, the struggle for control over imports intensified with each group, industrialists and commercial importers, maneuvering behind-the-scenes.

The control and licensing of imports, a partial TOB function until 1971, was one source of contention dividing industrialists from commercial groups. In general, industrialists found the whole notion of having to cooperate with what one ISO leader called "opportunistic merchants (*tüccar*)" to be thoroughly repelling.[34] Industrialists had no faith in their competitors' motives either, and blamed the looming 1977 crisis on commercial groups and their appetite for imports.[35] Therefore, in 1971 industrialists strongly supported the government's removal of the TOB's power to allocate and distribute quotas. Moreover, they stressed their opposition to any return to the *status quo ante* when another administration made inquiries over this very same question.[36]

A logical solution for industrialists was to gain control of the import trade from commercial interests. Politically this was an unrealistic option. Instead, they settled for gradual gains at the expense of commercial groups. First, they sought a division of the quota lists: one for each group. Once that was accomplished, they demanded preferential treatment by pointing out that satisfying their quota requirements was of vital national importance, whereas the commercial sector's similar needs were of much less significance.[37] This was coupled with the discriminatory practice of requiring higher guarantee deposits on importers' quota items compared to those of industrialists' (Table 4.6).

These behind-the-scenes manipulations were quite successful as industrialists managed to have the lion's share of imports allocated to themselves. In the 1978 import regime, for example, importers received an allocation of $331 million, in contrast to industrialists who received

$769 million.[38]

Foreign Exchange Rates and Devaluations. As with many other import substituting countries, Turkey failed to adhere to realistic exchange rates, thus aggravating the dislocations created by ISI. Until 1979, this failure to correct exchange rate imbalances can be traced to the private sector which systematically struggled against devaluations and attempted to limit adjustments to the currency. This unified private sector front, with the exception of the agricultural interests, continued to paralyze the governmental attempts to remedy the situation. Again, the crucial variable was the availability of foreign exchange, since as soon as it became apparent in 1979 that the country had simply ran out of this resource, the consensus disintegrated.

As far as the private sector was concerned, the state was responsible for maintaining the flow of imports. Devaluations represented one of many different options available to achieve this goal. However, because devaluations increased the cost of imports (and hence of inputs), it was viewed by importers and industrialists alike as a last resort measure.

It was, therefore, not surprising that industrialists vigorously resisted devaluations. For instance, four months before the August 10, 1970 devaluation, World Bank representatives visited Turkey's industrial chambers to solicit comments and views regarding a possible devaluation which, at the time, seemed inevitable. Industrialists responded by asserting that, "a devaluation would not bring any relief. Turkey has previously tried such a measure, and such a move would be to the detriment of producers, industrialists, consumers and investments. As in the past, a devaluation would have only a limited effect and its sole beneficiaries would be the middlemen."[39] Instead, they proposed what they termed "an export-oriented adjustment of the exchange rate, with some further customs adjustments," a proposal meant to vaguely suggest export and tax rebates,[40] or another source of rents for themselves.

Because of this across-the-board opposition, the 1960s and 1970s saw but a few minor currency adjustments and just two major devaluations: 1970 and 1979.

In 1970, despite the shortages in imported commodities, delays in import licenses and lack of foreign exchange,[41] industrialists resisted the devaluation fearing their highly import-dependent industries would be severely hurt by cost increases. These would result from import price increases and the expectation that labor unions would use the occasion to demand wage increases to compensate their members for the price hikes. In turn, such wage increments would fuel inflationary pressures. The loudest voices in opposition came from the weakest: the assembly industries.

The 1970 devaluation lived up to the government's expectations. Export earnings and increased workers' remittances flowing into Turkish coffers created an abundance of foreign exchange reserves, which reached an all time high of $917 million in 1973.

Whereas industrialists grudgingly conceded that Demirel had been right about the potential effects of a devaluation,[42] commercial groups, which had also opposed the devaluation, remained unrepentant. ITO blamed the 1970 devaluation for destabilizing the economy and for leading to a reduction in the growth rate.[43] Moreover, in a memorandum published in 1973, it also charged that the devaluation had led to the importation of "foreign inflation," and had created extra sources of income for industrialists who had benefited from their monopolistic position.[44]

The lesson of 1970 — that timely devaluations could substantially improve the country's foreign exchange position — was never learned. In March 1976, under pressure from industrialists, the Demirel government vowed that it would not implement a new devaluation.[45] Despite such promises, industrialists remained suspicious of such promises on the eve of the 1977 elections and when pressures were building up in international financial circles for adjustments to the currency.[46] In fact, this pressure was mounting with every passing day. In January 1977, Turkey defaulted on a Wells Fargo bank loan, an event the government managed to suppress[47] and in February all currency transfers were stopped for an indeterminate period of time. Industrialists were right to suspect the government's motives since, in response to the IMF's pressure and reluctance to release any funds, the Minister of Finance, in secret negotiations with that organization, had promised to implement a devaluation soon after the elections.[48]

The 1977 elections were inconclusive. Demirel's main rivals, Ecevit and his RPP, garnered a plurality, but were unable to muster the parliamentary majority needed to survive the first vote of confidence. As a result, Demirel returned to power with the second National Front coalition. Burdened with internal tensions,[49] this government had to confront the prior devaluation promise. A timid 10 percent downward adjustment of the currency in September 1977, primarily designed to satisfy the IMF, went largely unnoticed and made no impact on the real exchange rate of the lira (Table 5.10). On the other hand, the private sector, itself in disarray, had no concrete solutions to offer to end the foreign exchange shortage. The best it could contribute was a suggestion to increase the price of gasoline to reflect the real cost of imported oil and encourage foreign exchange savings.[50] This was one suggestion that no government could accept for fear of alienating the public at large.

In the meantime, with the country's foreign exchange position deteriorating, another government crisis ensued which led to Demirel's fall and Ecevit's return. It was now Ecevit's turn to try his hand at stabilization. In March 1978, the lira was devalued by 29 percent. Just as the previous effort, this too was half-hearted; even energy prices were not adjusted to reflect their true cost.

Again, the government was caught between the implacable demands of the private sector and the exigencies of the economic situation. When IMF and European Community officials visited Turkey to convince government and private sector representatives to take further action they were, once again, met by determined opposition. In a replay of 1970, ISO leaders told them in no uncertain terms that they were opposed to any kind of devaluation and argued that, because of the previous March 1978 devaluation, the inflation rate had jumped to 60 percent.[51] ISO maintained a devaluation ought not be attempted without adequate reserves of foreign currency. In other words, ISO wanted to see a commitment to new funds before agreeing to a devaluation, and this was not what the visitors were prepared to make any concessions on. Some influential members of the Ecevit's government were also in theoretic agreement with this position of forcing the hand of the donor group to commit itself to funds in advance.[52] ISO's adamant stand notwithstanding, movement could be detected in the other chambers and groups' positions. The February 1977 halt in the foreign currency transfers was finally forcing some to concede that, without a serious devaluation, no new loans or aid packages would be forthcoming. The Eskişehir Chamber of Industry typified the new emerging consensus outside of ISO. "Once foreign exchange sources are guaranteed from abroad," its leader argued, "a devaluation ought not be delayed."[53]

The difficulties of operating under severe foreign exchange constraints spawned bizarre practices, which contributed to the change in the private sector's attitudes. Among these was a government procedure called *kur farki* or exchange rate difference. This practice, which forced importers — commercial or industrial — to make payments to the state long after they had dispensed with their imported merchandise, resulted in large financial losses and a great deal of uncertainty.[54]

In January 1979, amidst the foreign exchange crisis, the Ecevit government invited the industrial chambers of Istanbul, Ankara, Aegean and Eskişehir and the chambers of commerce of Istanbul and

Izmir, to discuss new proposed stabilization measures. In preparation for the meeting these six chambers first met among themselves to consider their recommendations to the government. ISO consented to everything except a devaluation,[55] which the others argued was the only means of obtaining new sources of desperately needed foreign exchange. At ISO's insistence, it was decided that each chamber would independently present its views to government.

At the joint meeting with Ecevit, ISO, in a minority of one, vigorously argued against the devaluation[56] and carried the day. Ecevit, convinced that the IMF was not prepared to support him with an injection of funds, went along with the Istanbul industrialists by declining to implement the devaluation.

Instead, the government instituted another flawed austerity package which pleased no one except ISO. New provisions designed to increase the flow of workers' remittances were introduced. The government offered to buy their dollars at a premium rate of 47.10 TL, instead of the official 26.50 TL to the dollar.[57] Additional measures included permission for exporters to spend up to 50 percent of the foreign exchange they earned for their own use, and government controls on gold sales in an effort to stem illegal exports. By maintaining two different exchange rates, the government created explicit economic rents: it purchased dollars from workers at a rate which was higher (47.10 TL) than the one at which it sold them to importers (26.50 TL). Not surprisingly ISO welcomed the measures.

These meetings and measures represented a turning point. As TÜSIAD and others attacked the measures, ISO found itself isolated. TÜSIAD called the measures amateurish and charged that, to avoid a devaluation, the government was sacrificing the economy as a whole.[58] The Union of Industrial Chambers criticized the new measures for being too weak and simply inflationary.[59] Sezai Diblan, TOB leader, argued that Turkey had nothing to gain by antagonizing the IMF, as the government seemed intent on doing, and was particularly irritated by the controls on domestic gold sales.[60] Even within ISO, discordant voices were raised as Halit Narin, leader of the employers' confederation and a leading ISO member, predicted that the government's policy of multiple exchange rates would not work and urged the implementation of a realistic exchange rate policy.[61] Only the president of ISO's executive committee, Nurullah Gezgin, was supportive of the government's measures and even of the gold controls.

ISO's isolation, as we shall see in the next chapter, did not last long as the atmosphere between Ecevit's government and the private sector got poisoned, in large measure, because of TÜSIAD's active campaign against the government. However, even if ISO's isolation proved to be temporary, the organization and its members continued to believe that devaluations had to be resisted. The change of heart among most business groups, ISO notwithstanding, meant that most of them were finally reconciled with the notion that, in order to obtain the necessary foreign exchange, they would have to give into measures such as devaluations.[62] This realization would finally pave the way for the January 24, 1980 stabilization program.

Banks and Bank Credits

One of the major impediments to the accumulation of capital in Turkey had been the absence of an organized and well developed capital market. Commercial interests and industrialists had basically one source of financing: banks. The limited sources of capital often led to conflicts among and within the two groups. During the 1960s, the main divisions were centered around the sectoral and regional distribution of bank credits. From the mid-seventies onwards, the main concern shifted to the emergence of large holding corporations intent on buying banks to finance their acquisitions process and growth.

The main source of tension between these groups emanated from the banking sector's natural business practices. By maintaining low interest rates on individual deposits, government policy encouraged and forced banks to offer funds to the commercial and industrial sectors at below-market rates. This system not only facilitated the transfer of funds from agricultural to urban areas, mostly in the form of mercantile and industrial credits, but it also induced banks to aggressively seek savings from individual depositors, thus leading to an unprecedented expansion in bank branches.[63]

As satisfactory as this arrangement seemed to industrialists,[64] they were still uncomfortable with the sizeable share of credits that commercial groups received. Banks favored commercial interests because manufacturers, facing longer gestation periods, insisted on long-term low interest loans. On the other hand, banks could obtain much higher rates of return from money loaned to commercial groups, which typically worked with shorter turnover periods. An Eskişehir Chamber of Industry sponsored study in 1971 found that, while the commercial sector accounted for 9.8 percent of GNP in 1969, it obtained 24 percent of all bank credits.[65] In 1972, ISO argued that of the 36 billion TL in savings deposited in banks, the public and private industrial sectors' share amounted to only 14 billion TL, or 39 percent, and that this amount was being loaned at exorbitantly high interest rates.[66] In effect, the artificially low interest rates, another of the government-created rents, were generating a bitter dispute between the two groups. From a regional perspective, the largest consumer of bank credits, whether commercial or industrial was, of course, the Marmara region.[67] In turn, this fueled the existing antagonisms between the Istanbul-based business groups and those of the Anatolian hinterland.

In the 1970s, a new phenomenon appeared: that of the holding corporation. It was a response to credit scarcities and banking laws which prohibited banks from lending more than 10 percent of their capital to a single concern. By contrast, a bank was allowed to lend unlimited sums to the firm if it owned more than 25 percent of that firm's equity.[68] Hence, in their need to tap the public's deposits in the banking sector, industrial companies organized holding corporations which included one or more banks. By 1980, all the major holding corporations owned or controlled at least one bank. This development added a new wrinkle to the intra-business strife because it effectively reduced the access of small and medium sized companies to bank credits. The holding corporation had thus gained an unfair competitive advantage since, in scarce credit markets, it could cripple the competition by further limiting their access to funds. With most of the holding corporations belonging to TÜSIAD, this issue pitted it against all others. There were numerous calls from ISO for the banking industry's regulation and for restrictions on such practices as bank acquisitions.[69]

The degree of concentration in the banking industry can be seen in the fact that, of the existing 24 private banks in 1980, 19 were controlled by individual holding corporations or families, and, in the case of the twentieth largest bank, it was owned by another: the İş Bank. In 1982, the top 10 banks in the country accounted for 90 percent of savings deposits (Table 6.1). If we take into consideration that the Ziraat Bankasi, the second largest in the country, is primarily involved with the agricultural sector, then the significance of the private holding corporations is that much increased.

The increased concentration in the banking industry erupted into the political arena with the rising inflation rates of the late 1970s. Industrialists found that while banks owned by holding corporations had unlimited funds to lend to concerns that were part of their own family of companies, they were unwilling to lend to others.[70] With

Table 6.1: The Ten Largest Banks, Share of Total
Deposits and Ownership, 1982

Rank	Bank Name	% of Deposits	Ownership
1	Türkiye İş Bankasi	24	Itself a holding company
2	T.C. Ziraat Bankasi	23	State
3	Akbank	12	Sabanci Holding
4	Yapi ve Kredi Bankasi	10	Çukurova Holding
5	Pamukbank	4	Çukurova Holding
6	Türk Ticaret Bankasi	4	Ercan Holding (20%)
7	Türk Emlâk Kredi Bankasi	4	State
8	Türk Halk Bankasi	3	State
9	Türk Vakiflar Bankasi	3	State
10	Türk Garanti Bankasi	3	Koç Holding

Source: *Ekonomik Mesaj* (weekly) June 15-30, 1983, supplement.

some holding corporations controlling as many as three banks,[71] ISO alarmed by this trend and officially proposed a set of reforms for the banking industry. These included (1) a prohibition on bank ownerships by industrial firms, (2) the elimination of restrictions and regulations on the establishment of new banks, (3) increasing interest rates on non-time deposits, and (4) the reorganization of the capital markets.[72]

Industrialists were not the only ones alarmed by the increased concentration in the banking sector. Commercial interests were also apprehensive about this trend. The president of the Istanbul Chamber of Commerce deplored what he called the phenomenon of banks becoming family companies.[73] ITO and other commercial groups linked this to the monopolization of Turkish industry: a danger they had warned against as early as 1971.[74]

In 1979, in reaction to these concerns, the TOB decided to back changes in the laws governing the banks and asked for limits on the amount, as a percentage of paid capital plus reserves, that a bank could lend to one of its companies.[75] Again, changes in banking regulations would have to await the 1980 stabilization program.

Direct Foreign Investments

Turkey's record on attracting foreign investment had never been a good one. First, the bureaucratic and legal barriers were considered insurmountable for foreign investors. These were remnants of Etatism and the "mind set" that had been created then toward both domestic and foreign capital. Second, with the abundant flow of foreign exchange from Turkish workers employed abroad, direct foreign investments were not perceived as an important source of foreign exchange receipts.

On the surface, the private sector, with some notable exceptions represented by quasi-nationalistic small entrepreneurs, welcomed direct foreign private investments. However, underlying this welcome, it had serious misgivings regarding the role of foreign capital in Turkey.

Two factors were responsible for the foreign investors' attraction to the import substituting sector: (1) its higher profit margins, and (2) the strong demand previously initiated by imports. The pattern established in Latin America and elsewhere by capital migrating to less developed countries as export markets were lost to protectionism was replicated in Turkey. This was the conclusion of a 1975 TÜSIAD report, which also found that foreign investment was attracted to the economy's capital intensive sectors.[76] The bulk of these investments occurred in sectors which, according to Table 5.14, had weak backward and forward linkages to the rest of the economy. By the beginning of 1978, the automotive, electrical machinery, rubber products, each listed in the weak category with respect to the linkage effects they possessed, received 27.2, 12.7 and 9 percent of foreign investments, respectively, representing 48.9 percent of the total. The chemical industry, listed as having moderate linkage effect, obtained 18.9 percent and the metal products, listed as a strong sector, received only 4 percent of foreign investments.[77] In the case of the chemical sector, a disproportionate share of foreign investments flowed into the pharmaceutical industry.

Foreign direct investment was also a politically sensitive issue in the turbulent times of the seventies. The opposition to foreign capital was nestled in the left-wing of the political spectrum, as well as in the forces representing society's fundamentalist segments. The Turkish private sector was of two minds on this issue. On the one hand, it viewed support for foreign investment as a litmus test of the loyalty of political groups, especially of the Republican People's Party, to the principles of free enterprise. On the other hand, because of the fear of foreign competition, the Turkish private sector sought limits on foreign investments. In 1966, the TOB outlined four basic principles. Direct foreign investments had to first provide *additional* funding for investment projects. Second, they had to introduce to Turkey new techniques and production methods. Third, foreign capital was expected to collaborate with domestic firms and decision makers, and, in the absence of domestic capital, to undertake only what could not be done by domestic capital. Finally, foreign capital was expected to contribute to foreign exchange receipts through exports and/or import substitution.[78] Of the above principles, the third is the most interesting since it dealt with the fear of foreign capital. The only industry in which foreign capital achieved a significant, if not commanding position, was the pharmaceutical sector.

Two sources of opposition existed within the mainstream of the private sector. The first, a nationalistic one, expressed by such Anatolian chambers as Eskişehir's industrial representatives, objected to the obvious ties existing between foreign capital and the more cosmopolitan areas of the country, and to its orientation towards consumer durables.[79]

The second and more surprising source of opposition came from ISO. It was not overt, but rather discreet. ISO stood to lose the most by the unrestricted penetration of foreign capital. While outwardly the leaders of Istanbul based industry were strong advocates of foreign investments, the "plight of the pharmaceutical industry" was a major source of consternation for them. ISO, in general, and Turkish-owned pharmaceuticals corporations, in particular, believed that foreign-owned drug companies were using their superior resources to deliberately undercut local manufacturers by incurring losses with the expectation that domestic competitors would eventually falter. Simply stated, local producers were afraid of the financially more powerful foreigners.

Industrialists accused foreign capital of a myriad of ills, including the delays, reductions and cancellations in government promotion certificates, and even blamed foreign capital for the internecine conflict among themselves.[80] Similarly, local industrialists viewed the behavior of foreign capital in labor negotiations as irresponsible and contrary to the standards they were trying to establish. In 1975, for instance, a collective bargaining agreement negotiated by a foreign owned petroleum company allowed its workers' wages to reach levels that ISO members contended could not be matched by them for another ten years.[81] This ability of foreign corporations to upset and disrupt labor's domestic price structure was a continuous source of worry and problem for local producers. At an earlier date, when General Electric had signed a contract doubling the minimum wage it would pay over the next two years, industrialists had asked the government to intervene and initiate some kind of understanding and guidelines.[82]

The industrialists' ambivalence towards foreign capital diminished considerably at the end of the seventies when the economic crisis — and the ensuing shortage of foreign exchange — became acute. Then, direct foreign investments came to be perceived as one means out of the impasse. Starting in 1979, some private sector organizations called on the state to relax its restrictions on the infusion of foreign capital. Specifically they wanted the state to alter the provisions of the 1954 Law 6224 which regulated direct foreign investments. Both the TOB and ISO asked for amendments to the law that would facilitate the inflow of foreign money.[83] This change, like all the others, would also have to await the January 24, 1980 measures.

Land and Tax Reform and Agricultural Support Prices

Land reform is an explosive political issue in most industrializing countries. Turkey was not an exception (see Chapter 3). With the industrialization drive picking up steam in the post-1960 period, the need to transfer resources from the dominant agricultural sector to the industrial one became an important consideration. Hungry for funds, Turkish industrialists demanded the government explore ways to improve the flow of surplus capital from agriculture to industry.

Two factors mitigated against this. First, for political reasons, the agricultural sector had been favorably treated in the pre-1960 period, a treatment which included exemptions from paying taxes. Second, land distribution patterns were not conducive to increased production and capital accumulation. Nicholas Kaldor, a British economist brought in to advise the State Planning Organization on the first of the five year development plans, recommended a wide-ranging reform plan for the agricultural sector, which included provisions for new agricultural taxation.[84] Although the Kaldor plan was aborted by the political storm it created, the issue of agricultural taxation remained a powerful reminder of the industrial groups' inability to control or dictate the economic agenda of the country. The Kaldor report also revealed the intricacies in the alliance patterns within the business communities. In 1961, ITO, the largest commercial chamber in the country, joined Anatolian agricultural groups' denunciations of Kaldor, accusing him, among other things, of being a communist for having suggested the taxation of agricultural incomes.[85]

In general, tax reform — agricultural and non-agricultural — was a politically sensitive issue. Industrialists believed that the burden of taxation had fallen unfairly on them, the salaried classes, and on workers. They also accused commercial groups of tax evasion and cheating. Such accusations led to natural coalitions of interests between shopkeepers, artisans, commercial and agricultural groups, as well as to bitter disputes. In 1979, there was even an attempted secession by some of the Anatolian commercial chambers which claimed they were being unfairly maligned by industrialists for tax evasion. Since the TOB was proving inadequate in their defense, they called for a separate Union of Chambers of Commerce.[86]

State attempts at instituting land and tax reforms were often defeated and never managed to get off the ground. Elected governments shied away from these issues. The one government which tried its hand at it was the first of the military backed post-1971 administrations. It was responding to the officers' demands for reform. The industrial chambers immediately joined in support of the government's new agenda. Soon thereafter, ITO and TÜSIAD also added their voices of support to these aims. Feyyaz Berker, president of TÜSIAD, stated that "starting with agricultural and fiscal reforms," they would back the government's policies.[87] Despite such calls, no taxation of land was successfully introduced until the 1980 military intervention. Ironically, the question of land reform became a moot point in the 1970s as an unwritten pact emerged between the large landowners and industrialists, "when during the elections of 1977, the notables of Konya threatened the industrialists that if land ownership was made an electoral issue, then they would reciprocate by making factory ownership a political question."[88] In other words, by clearly linking the fate of land holdings with those of factories, landowners managed to demonstrate the manufacturing sector's weakness during a period of considerable political uncertainty and turmoil.[89]

Closely associated with the issue of land and tax reform was the question of agricultural support prices, the mechanism through which successive governments tried to arrest the deterioration in the agricultural sector's terms of trade by determining the price at which the state would buy different crops. In fact, the state offered such generous prices that the terms of trade, which had remained stable until 1969, began to deteriorate at manufacturing's expense.[90] Agricultural support prices not only denied industry needed funds, but also fueled inflation because they caused sudden expansions in the money supply. Even the few industrialists who were not altogether opposed to support prices questioned the magnitude of the transfer that was taking place.[91] Nonetheless, arguments about the inflationary character of support prices were viewed by agricultural groups as politically motivated and without any economic merit.[92] Ultimately, industrialist opposition to support prices was determined by the aggregate shifts towards agriculture produced by this policy, and by what they perceived to be a race among politicians to pander to the agricultural community's demands.[93] This was another example of the state's attempts to mollify all sides by distributing rents to potential losers in the industrialization struggle. Again, tackling the question of support prices was left to the post-1980 era.

These differences over policy further intensified regional cleavages and, more importantly, representational conflicts as the different groups sought to control those organizations with access to the state. It is to these regional and representational conflicts that we turn in the next two sections of this chapter.

Regional Cleavages

In Turkey, the question of regionalism can best be characterized as the struggle between Anatolia-based groups on the one side, versus those based in Istanbul and, to a lesser extent, in Izmir. This regional issue is intimately linked to the question of size: the size of individual business concerns, as well as that of individual chambers.

Table 6.2: Distribution by Region of the 421[1] Largest
Private Industrial Corporations in 1980

Region	No of Firms	% of Firms	% of Turnover
Marmara	283	67.2	70.3
of which Istanbul	253	60.1	61.7
Aegean	65	15.4	11.6
Mediterranean	29	6.9	10.3
North Central	34	8.1	6.5
South Central	9	2.1	1.4
Black Sea	1	0.2	0.0
East Central	-	-	-
Northeast	-	-	-
Southeast	-	-	-

[1]This list is derived from the list of the 500 largest industrial concerns in Turkey, of which 79 were in the public sector.

Source: *Istanbul Sanayi Odasi Dergisi*, No. 188 (October 15, 1981).

Because Istanbul has traditionally been home to the largest concentration of industrial and commercial activity, the rest of the country has perceived it as the primary beneficiary of the government's preferential treatment. Istanbul and Izmir were at the forefront of import substituting industrialization; consumer goods production commenced there, *and* the shift to consumer durable production almost exclusively took place in these regions. If the chambers of industry, and specifically ISO, continuously found themselves outvoted at TOB meetings by their Anatolian counterparts, it was because of the latter's resentment of the perceived intrusion of large Istanbul and Izmir based capital. Anatolian groups felt they had no means of competing with this onslaught.

Table 6.2 depicts the regional distribution of the 421 largest private industrial concerns in the country. The regions are listed in descending order of development with the Marmara region, the most developed, ranked first.[94] As the table shows, the Marmara region, in which Istanbul, Bursa and Izmit fall,[95] accounts for the lion's share of the 421 corporations. While the Marmara region accounts for as much as 67.2 percent of the firms and 70.3 percent of the total turnover, Istanbul's wealth in these categories exemplifies the lopsided nature of the distribution, especially given that the city's population represented only 10.7 percent of the nationwide total.

Istanbul's privileged position was also reflected in other areas, most notably in commerce. The allocation of bank credits and public sector investments revealed the inherent advantages of the Marmara and Aegean regions. This skewed distribution of manufacturing enterprises even caught the military's attention. On the eve of the 1980 military intervention, the National Security Council — a body consisting of the top military commanders, some cabinet officers and the president — decided to prevent further manufacturing investments in the Istanbul-Izmit corridor.[96]

The regional disparities and antagonisms erupted when Necmettin Erbakan, a Justice Party renegade who would later form the Islamic fundamentalist National Salvation Party, was elected to the TOB's leadership. Erbakan's election took everybody by surprise. As a past secretary general of this union of chambers, Erbakan had developed extensive contacts among the rank and file and, by appealing to the Anatolian petite bourgeoisie's fear of the more industrialized regions of the country, he was able to build a significant coalition. Erbakan had taken advantage of the uncertainty in the leadership of the TOB when Sirri Enver Batur's, the current president and member of the Istanbul Chamber of Commerce, decided not to seek reelection. Batur was particularly bitter about a movement afoot within the Union to banish the two Istanbul-based chambers, those of industry and commerce, as well as the Istanbul Commodity Exchange from the TOB.[97] Erbakan's accession spelled victory for these forces.

In the ensuing struggle to rid the Union of Erbakan, the regional cleavages were further crystallized, with some chambers refusing to recognize the authority of the Union.   After a period of difficult negotiations, Erbakan was finally removed from the Union presidency, but not without, in the words of one industrialist, "having made a national hero of himself."[98] Erbakan and his followers were not ready to give up. Soon after, a bid to have his followers elected to the Executive Committee of ITO was soundly defeated in 1969.[99] Four days later, however, his followers captured its Ankara counterpart,[100] thus proving that he continued to enjoy considerable support.

In his 1969 bid for election, Erbakan argued that the TOB had become an instrument of a "comprador-masonic minority." "The whole organization is under the complete control of the compradorial commercial and industrial interests."[101] Explaining his previous participation in the TOB, Erbakan maintained that he had tried to reform the organization, but "these [compradorial commercial and industrial interests] do not want to see the development of the Anatolian merchant. . . To their twenty factories they would like to add another, a twenty first."[102] The clear and direct targets of these attacks were the Istanbul and Izmir business groups.

Erbakan forcefully articulated other grievances: quota allocations and Anatolian bank savings and deposits, he argued, were being channelled into the big city merchants at the expense of other areas.[103] Before it was banned, his first political party, the National Order Party, called for a more equitable development and industrialization policy to ensure a fairer distribution of investments.[104] The lack of equity extended to state funds as well. As Table 6.3 demonstrates, the 40 less-developed provinces[105] which, according to the 1970 census comprised 43.3 percent of the total population,[106] were allocated less than one third of the total planned investments. For manufacturing, the share of the 40 was even smaller and, during the Second Five Year Development Plan (1968-1972), only 12.1 percent of all public manufacturing investments were contemplated for this group of provinces. These years also coincide with Erbakan's political rise. Not surprisingly, an analysis of the 1973 election results shows that Erbakan derived his electoral strength primarily from regions with low levels of urban and rural development and, to a lesser extent, from regions at an intermediate stage of development.[107]

Table 6.3: Regional Distribution of Planned Public Investments for the
Four Five Year Development Plans (%)

	Manufacturing		Total	
	40 provs.	27 provs.	40 provs.	27 provs.
FIRST FYDP	18.0	82.0	34.7	65.3
SECOND FYDP	12.1	87.9	28.6	71.4
THIRD FYDP	24.1	75.9	33.0	67.0
FOURTH FYDP	21.9	78.1	33.2	66.8

Sources: Memduh Yaşa, *Cumhuriyet Dönemi Türkiye Ekonomisi* (Istanbul: Akbank Yayinlari, 1980), p. 68; DPT, *Kamu Yatirimlarinin Kalkinmada Öncelikli Yöreler ve Diğer Iller Itibariyla Dağilimi* (Ankara: DPT, 1982), pp. 24, 32.

There were other regional divisions among industrial chambers, cleavages that were independent of the Erbakan phenomenon. The predominance of the Istanbul chamber and its linkages to foreign interests in both Western Europe and, to a lesser extent the U.S., were sources of concern for the smaller and more inward looking chambers, such as the Eskişehir Chamber of Industry. The president and main driving force behind the Eskişehir chamber, Zeytinoğlu, attributed the differences between Istanbul and Izmir's industrial make-up on the one hand, and that of Anatolia on the other, to the former's close and direct relations with the West. Devoid of such connections, Anatolian industry had to rely on the "non-Muslim merchants of Istanbul or Izmir" to link up with the West. Hence, with respect to production methods and consumption patterns, Anatolian industry did not develop the dependence on the West exhibited by the two cities.[108] While disguised in a somewhat chauvinistic explanation, this articulation tries to conceal a fear of the larger cities which are, by his own admission, much stronger in marketing and other fields than their Anatolian counterparts.[109]

Erbakan's temporary tenure at the TOB had wide-ranging consequences. First, it challenged Justice Party's — and consequently Demirel's — control over the Union, thus endangering the party's confidence in obtaining the majority, if not the totality, of the private sector support in national elections. This point will be further explored in the next chapter. Second, it led to the realignment of certain groups, specifically the Istanbul Chamber of Commerce (ITO). Whereas ITO had always sided with other commercial chambers against industrialists, including its Istanbul counterpart, after 1969 it adopted a more defensive strategy. Having realized the depth of antipathy to Istanbul in Anatolia, ITO adopted a more populist tone, often criticizing "monopoly conditions in industry." Yet, despite the rhetoric against industrial enterprises, ITO sought to improve its cooperation with other Istanbul interests and even align itself with the industrialists of its region. By the late 1970s, this had been achieved as ITO's president joined ISO's governing council.

These regional cleavages figured significantly in the disintegration of the Justice Party. In turn, this development, as the Chapter 7 will argue contributed to the loss of cohesiveness in industrial policies.

Representational Cleavages

Private sector cleavages over policy and regional differences gave rise to conflicts over representation. Since the TOB was the quasi-public organization empowered by the state to represent private sector interests, its control, which provided access to the state, was a much coveted prize. The numerically superior mercantile interests had traditionally dominated the TOB. As the manufacturing sector came of age, industrial elites, feeling neglected, fought hard for better representation. This struggle, which pitted industrialists against commercial groups became increasingly bitter during the 1960-1980 period.

From early on, industrialists lobbied for an independent organization to better represent their interests. In 1973, a typical year, the TOB encompassed 7 chambers of industry,[110] 40 chambers of commerce, 112 chambers of commerce and industry and 53 commodity exchanges.[111] With such a distribution, industrialists believed that the chambers of commerce and commodity brokers had a natural advantage in the TOB's executive and general councils.[112] In the early 1960s, Ismet Inönü's government looked favorably upon this request, and the Ministry of Industry and the State Planning Organization backed the demand for an independent organization of industrialists.

Fearing a secession and the development of a rival institution, the TOB argued that a split would divide the private sector and thus weaken it in its dealings with the state.[113] To placate industrialists' doubts, the TOB even agreed to form of a "confederation" that would give industrialists, commercial groups and commodity exchanges five votes each, thus assuring all groups equal power in the running of the Union. However, the TOB leadership had no intention of being accommodating. These proposals were simply delaying tactics since, in a clandestine proposal to the government, the TOB reduced the manufacturing sector's representation in the so-called confederation from five to three.[114]

By 1964, having failed to get a single representative elected to the TOB's executive council, the three existing chambers of Industry, Ankara, Aegean and Istanbul, concluded an agreement to establish an independent union.[115] Yet in 1968, five years after the initial discussions on breaking away, the chambers of industry, now numbering six, were still far from their elusive goal. The main bottleneck to their demands — in addition to the TOB — was the government which had changed hands. Led by Demirel and carrying the mantle of the banned Democrat Party of the 1950s, the conservative Justice Party government was reluctant to antagonize the numerous voters represented by the small commercial establishments throughout the country. In fact, the party had developed a very strong relationship with the Union, at times even dominating it by succeeding to get its sympathizers elected to key positions. Since government support was required to change the law regulating the Union, the Justice Party's reluctance effectively negated the industrialists' efforts. Still, they persisted. In 1968, these efforts were again sidetracked by the TOB which, after seeming to concede again, postponed the promised action for a year and then had its legal department veto it on a technicality.[116]

This issue was particularly important to the Istanbul Chamber of Industry which, as the largest such chamber, provided the leadership and vigorously campaigned for the changes. This vigor was in large measure due to ISO's inability to gain a seat on the TOB executive council throughout the 1960s. Furthermore, ISO's membership was frustrated by the less-than-genuine support extended by its sister organizations in Istanbul, namely the local chambers of commerce and the commodity exchange. Time after time, the two Istanbul-based chambers failed to support either ISO's positions or its candidacy at the TOB meetings.[117]

The desire to secede from the TOB was fueled by the increasing self-confidence of the manufacturing sector. In the view of ISO's members, the "age of industry had arrived," and hence manufacturing no longer needed to play a secondary role to commercial groups.[118] Not unexpectedly, industrialists harbored a degree of contempt for the other groups. One future head of ISO would argue in 1964, "of Turkey's 50 billion TL GNP, we [industrialists] account for 9 billion. How much does commerce produce? All commerce provides is 'services' and transport; 3 billion worth. . . We are the producers. . . And, when we seek to advance our rights, we are relegated to a position inferior to that of the *middlemen*."[119]

The TOB resisted industrialist demands to break away fearing that, without its monopoly on representation, its effectiveness and importance would diminish considerably. In addition, a separate organization of industrialists would mean significant revenue losses for the Union at both the local and national levels.[120] In 1969, of the TOB's 370,000 members, fewer than 18,000 were industrialists and of these, 2,000 accounted for an estimated 80 percent of the country's manufacturing capability.[121] Thus, an even smaller group of industrialists was in effect responsible for a large segment of the national output. Hence, the secession of this group would have meant a major setback for the TOB. In this respect, the legislation establishing these quasi-private sector organizations, Law 5590, worked to the TOB's advantage by effectively "imprisoning" all of the private sector within the confines of one overarching unit.[122]

The chambers of industry, therefore, tried to get the law amended. In fact, this was one aspect of a two-pronged strategy adopted in 1964. The other element consisted of increasing the number of chartered chambers of industry across the country.[123] From 1964 to 1969 they managed to increase the number from three to six. Despite the addition of two industrial chambers in the following six years, they were unable to make much progress along this line. Not surprisingly, industrialists also realized that changing the law was a more effective way of accomplishing their ends than maximizing the number of chambers.

Table 6.4: Associational Breakdown of Delegates at the 28th General Convention of the Union of Chambers (TOB) in 1973.

Organization	Number	Percentage
Chambers of Commerce and Industry	437	46.6
Chambers of Commerce	168	17.9
Chambers of Industry	53	5.6
Commodity Exchanges	281	29.9
Total	939	100.0

Source: Tabulated from the list of delegates provided by the TOB. TOB, *XXVIII. Genel Kurulu* (Ankara: TOB, 1973).

Table 6.4 gives the breakdown of delegates at the TOB's 1973 28th General Convention. The seven industrial chambers of industry had a combined share of 5.6 percent of the delegates. By contrast, the chambers of commerce *and* industry, and the chambers of commerce controlled 46.6 percent and 17.9 percent of the delegates, respectively, for a combined percentage of 64.5.[124] Since the general convention elects the Union's executive council, the lopsided distribution in the share of delegates is also reflected in the composition of the executive council.

The 1972-73 Executive Council was comprised of nine members: four from the chambers of commerce and industry; one — the TOB's president — from a chamber of commerce; two from commodity exchanges; two from industrial chambers, one each from ISO and the Aegean Chamber of Industry.[125] This represented a major improvement from the preceding years when industrialists had no representation on the board. The following year, with the addition of the Kayseri Chamber of Industry, industrial representation was increased to three, only to be reduced again to two.[126]

Despite these improvements, the TOB remained under the control of the more numerous mercantile groups. The industrialists realized that their own ability to influence TOB affairs would be severely restricted so long as the organization's general council was dominated by mercantile groups. In 1969, the chambers of industry managed to create the short-lived Turkish Organization of Cooperating Chambers of Industry (*Türkiye Sanayi Odalari Işbirliği i Teşkilati*). This organization, which was semi-officially recognized by the government,[127] was, by contrast, ignored by the TOB. Little progress could be achieved so long as the TOB continued to control the allocation of import quotas — the lifeblood of Turkish industry which, when used politically was enough to subdue the most rebellious of the industrial chambers.

The already complex relationship between the TOB and industrialists took a turn for the worse in 1969, as Erbakan's election triggered a crisis at the heart of the Union. The new TOB leader had built his reputation and coalition at the expense of Istanbul-based business interests, and he was hostile to the government's industrialization policies. Therefore, Erbakan represented a far worse alternative than the TOB's traditional leadership, and his election was particularly unwelcome to Istanbul's industrialists.[128] To complicate matters further, Demirel decided to punish the TOB and its new "renegade" leadership by freezing some of the quota distributions. The Ministry of Commerce, which was withholding the quota allocations, openly told the ISO leadership that they would only be released if Erbakan resigned.[129]

Despite the fact that Erbakan had offered his support to industrial chambers during his tenure as TOB's secretary general,[130] his election represented another affront to the industrialists and their hopes of increasing their influence. Although the Erbakan problem was eventually resolved through a series of confrontations and negotiations, the increased and overt politicization of the intra-TOB relations convinced the largest of the Turkish industrialists to create an organization of their own. Thus, in August 1971, the Turkish Industrialists and Businessmen's Association, TÜSIAD, came into being. Unlike the chambers of industry, TÜSIAD was not a quasi-public organization whose behavior was subject to the stipulations of Law 5590. As such, TÜSIAD was free to pursue or advocate any course of action it deemed desirable and, by the end of the 1970s, it emerged as a powerful and influential business organization.

The birth of TÜSIAD was initially received with skepticism and bitterness by that segment of ISO which represented those corporations that were too small to be included in the new organization. In the words of one ISO General Council member, TÜSIAD was nothing more than an "association for the protection of property."[131] For some in ISO, TÜSIAD represented a small clique of industrialists who, for a variety of reasons, could not get elected to responsible positions within ISO.[132] There is no question that the creation of TÜSIAD posed a difficult problem for the chambers of industry, and specifically the Istanbul chamber since most of TÜSIAD's members came from within its ranks. However, membership in TÜSIAD did not preclude membership in other organizations. In any case, participation in the local chambers was mandated by law. Some of ISO's most influential constituents were founding members of TÜSIAD, including the former's president Ertuğrul Soysal, and the country's leading businessman, Vehbi Koç.[133]

Ultimately TÜSIAD grew to complement existing quasi-public organizations. Many of its aims and endeavors, in the long run, helped smooth the differences between the industrial chambers. It assumed an activist role by arguing that "industrialists are the leading power of the development process,"[134] by attempting to influence public opinion at a time when the private sector felt much maligned, and by financing research activities. While success was not immediate, and conflict between ISO and TÜSIAD was periodically revived, some ISO members came to value TÜSIAD's existence, especially since it compensated for the deficiencies of quasi-public organizations and their state-imposed restrictions.[135] The complementarity had its limits. As Robert Bianchi argues, in the 1970s, TÜSIAD's position on labor relations was distinctly more conciliatory than that of the main employers' confederation, TISK.[136]

Interestingly enough, TÜSIAD relieved some of the tensions over the representation issue. In part because TÜSIAD quickly emerged as an activist organization, as well as a potential a harbinger of other organizations, the TOB finally acquiesced to the rise of an organization of industrial chambers within its midst. In 1974, the *Sanayi Odalari Birliği* (Union of Industrial Chambers), SOB, was born. In May 1979, the head of the Ankara industrial chamber was elected president of the TOB, the first industrialist to assume this position. While long overdue, this radical change coincided with with the most serious economic crisis ever experienced by Turkey.

Conclusion

As this chapter demonstrated, the private sector's pursuit of economic rents gave rise to cleavages and conflict. The suspicions engendered by this activity made it very difficult for the different groups to chart long-term goals. Because rent seeking in Turkey was a zero-sum game, incentives for cooperation were few. Therefore, even when there were periods of consensus among groups, as in the opposition to devaluations, this did not translate into cooperation but simply the pursuit of similar policies with respect to specific issues. The consensus was a function of foreign exchange availabilities: when such reserves disappeared, the consensus also disintegrated. The spilling over policy difficulties into regional and representational differences only served to heighten mutual suspicions and make cooperation more difficult to contemplate.

If relations among the groups were characterized by acrimony and hostility, it was not surprising to see state-business relations also reflect the same tensions. If rent maximization necessarily implied denying another group a share and rents were ultimately derived from state intervention in the economy, then rent maximization required influencing state behavior and, therefore, political activity. The divisions and conflicts within the private sector made a decisive contribution to the political-economic stalemate by contaminating the state with the same affliction. The next chapter explores this relationship in view of these cleavages explored here.

Notes

[1]For more information on the tradesmen, or *esnaf* as they are generally called, see, Robert Bianchi, *Interest Groups and Political Development in Turkey* (Princeton: Princeton University Press, 1984), pp. 134-138.

[2]The full name of the organization in Turkish is *Türkiye Ticaret Odalari, Sanayi Odalari ve Ticaret Borsalari Birliği*. Most people refer to the organization as Türkiye Odalar Birliği, which is the shortened version that means the Turkish Union of Chambers.

[3]Ayşe Öncü, "Chambers of Industry in Turkey: An Inquiry into State-Industry Relations as a Distributive Domain," in Ergun Özbudun and Aydin Ulusan (eds.) *The Political Economy of Income Distribution in Turkey* (New York: Holmes and Meier, 1980), p. 465.

[4]Kemal Saybaşili, "Türkiye'de Özel Teşebbüs ve Ekonomi Politikasi," *ODTÜ Gelişme Dergisi* (METU, Studies in Development) No. 13 (Fall 1976), p. 86.

[5]Any region can have both a chamber of commerce and a separate chamber of industry. However, where there are no separate chambers of industry, the chamber of commerce is known as chamber of commerce *and* industry. A new regional chamber of industry can only come into existence as a separate entity if its creation is requested, in writing, by at least 60 percent of all the industrialists in that region, which should represent no fewer than 30 people. If a chamber of industry separates from the existing chamber of commerce and industry, then the latter chamber simply reverts to being a chamber of commerce. In other words, the creation of chambers of industry represents a secession from the fold of the chambers of commerce. Öncü, "Chambers of Industry in Turkey," p. 460.

[6]For instance, in 1977 there were 8 chambers of industry, 50 chambers of commerce, 131 chambers of commerce and industry and 52 commodity exchanges, Öncü, "Chambers of Industry in Turkey," p. 458.

[7]The Izmir Chamber of Industry later adopted the name Aegean Chamber of Industry (*Ege Sanayi Odasi*) as it gained the right to represent the whole region.

[8]Saybaşili, "Türkiye'de Özel Teşebbüs ve Ekonomi Politikasi," pp. 86-87.

[9]After the September 1980 coup, TÜSIAD was accorded the quasi-public status it had been seeking.

[10]TOB, *Ödemeler Dengesi Sorunlari* (Ankara: TOB, 1978), p. 75.

[11]See Chapter 4 for more details on the guidelines as well as assembly industries.

[12]Critics contended that since the foreign trade regime banned the importation of durables, their assembly in Turkey with imported components was tantamount to importing them.

[13]Mükerrem Hiç et al., *Montaj Sanayi: Gelişmesi, Sorunlari ve Ekonomimizdeki Yeri* (Istanbul: Ekonomik ve Sosyal Etüdler Konferans

Heyeti, 1973), p. 167.

[14]TOB, *Devalüasyon — Yeni Vergiler ve Otomotiv Sanayi* (Ankara: TOB, 1971), p. 13. Another study published two years later was slightly less generous in its estimate and claimed that 65 percent was of domestic origin, Hiç et al., *Montaj Sanayi: Gelişmesi, Sorunlari ve Ekonomimizdeki Yeri*, p. 52.

[15] Istanbul Sanayi Odasi *Minutes*, 3/17/1965. These refer to the minutes of the joint monthly meetings of the Istanbul Chamber of Industry's executive and general councils. Hereafter these references will be denoted simply as *Minutes*, followed by the date of the meeting. Also, Hiç et al., *Montaj Sanayi: Gelişmesi, Sorunlari ve Ekonomimizdeki Yeri*, p. 351.

[16]Interview with a former Minister of Finance, Istanbul, June 29, 1982. I conducted a number of interviews with former officials on the condition of anonymity. Therefore, interviews are referred to by date, location and wherever possible by some general and relevant description of the personality involved.

[17]*Cumhuriyet*, May 3, 1979.

[18]This industry only produced 44,600 cars, 14,000 trucks, 7,500 pickups and fewer than 6,000 medium and regular sized buses, Devlet Planlama Teşkilati, *1980 Yili Programi* (Ankara: DPT, 1980), p. 398.

[19]Interview with former SPO official and Cabinet member, Ankara, November 9, 1982.

[20]Interview with a former Minister of Finance, Istanbul, June 29, 1982. OYAK (Ordu Yardimlaşma Kurumu) was "aimed originally at creating a pension program that would rescue career officers from economic insecurity they had suffered. . ." Bianchi, *Interest Groups and Political Development in Turkey*, p. 70.

[21]Eskişehir Sanayi Odasi, *Eskişehir Sanayi Odasinin 10. Yili ve Mümtaz Zeytinoğlu*, (Istanbul: Eskişehir Sanayi Odasi Yayinlari, 1981), pp. 233-34. Eskişehir's reaction to Demirel is noteworthy because, of all the industrial chambers, it was the most critical of both the methods used in implementing import substitution, and of its Aegean and Istanbul counterparts' dependence on imports.

[22]One such suggestion came early on from Şinasi Ertan, president of the Aegean Chamber of Industry, Iktisadi Araştirmalar Vakfi, *Ortak Pazar Karşisinda Türk Sanayiinin Durumu* (Istanbul: Iktisadi Araştirmalar Vakfi, 1970), p. 49.

[23]Mümtaz Zeytinoğlu, *Ulusal Sanayi* (Istanbul: Çağdaş Yayinlari, 1981), p. 31.

[24] Eskişehir Sanayi Odasi, *Eskişehir Sanayi Odasinin 10. Yili ve*

Mümtaz Zeytinoğlu, pp. 21-34, see also Ali Gevgilili, *Türkiye'de 1971 Rejimi* (Istanbul: Milliyet Yayinlari, 1973), pp. 180-85.

[25]Hiç et al., *Montaj Sanayi: Gelişmesi, Sorunlari ve Ekonomimizdeki Yeri*, pp. 180, 121.

[26]*Minutes*, 11/20/1968.

[27]*Minutes*, 8/16/1972 and 1/17/1979.

[28]Sanayi Odalari Birliği, *IV üncü Beş Yillik Plan Için Sanayileşme Stratejisi'ne Ilişkin Görüş ve Öneriler* (Ankara: Sanayi Odalari Birliği, 1976), p. 26.

[29]Kutlay Ebiri, "Turkish Apertura, Part I," *ODTÜ, Gelişme Dergisi* Vol 7, No 3-4, p. 229n.

[30]Anne Krueger and Baran Tuncer, "Estimating Total Factor Productivity Growth in a Developing Country," *World Bank Staff Working Paper, No. 422* (Washington, D.C.: World Bank, 1980), p. 7.

[31]Gürel Tüzün, "Bunalim, Ekonomi Politikalari, Planlama ve Devlet: Bir Yaklaşim Önerisi," *ODTÜ, Gelişme Dergisi* Special Issue. 1981, p. 13.

[32]*Minutes*, 7/15/1981.

[33]*Minutes*, 3/19/80, emphasis added. The desired level acceptable for opening was, of course, not specified, and the request was in complete opposition to government efforts. The government's 1980 plan will be discussed in chapter 8.

[34]*Minutes*, 1/19/1977.

[35]*Minutes*, 1/19/1977.

[36]*Minutes*, 12/29/1971. This was because the TOB was firmly in the grasp of commercial groups. This issue is explored later in this chapter.

[37]*Minutes*, 7/16/1969.

[38]Of the $769 million, only $120 million were to be used for public sector investments, $300 million were destined to private sector investments, and $225 million were specifically earmarked for assembly industries, *Resmi Gazete* (Official Gazette), January 28, 1979, pp. 84-112.

[39]*Minutes*, 4/15/1970.

[40]In fact, the opposition was so obstinate that when the government sought to justify the 66 percent devaluation of the lira in August of 1970, the Central Bank governor tried to convince industrialists by arguing that "contrary to the accepted notion that a devaluation is designed to reduce imports and increase exports, this particular devaluation was done *to increase imports*," *Minutes*, 8/19/1970, emphasis added.

[41]Anne Krueger, *Foreign Trade Regimes and Economic Development* (New York: National Bureau of Economic Research, 1974), p. 311.

[42]*Minutes,* 6/21/1972.

[43] *Cumhuriyet,* March 8, 1971.

[44]Ali Gevgilili, *Yükseliş ve Düşüş* (Istanbul: Altin Kitaplar Matbaasi, 1981), pp. 622-623.

[45]*Minutes,* 3/17/1976.

[46]*Minutes,* 1/19/1977.

[47]Interview with an ex-Minister of Finance, Istanbul November 5, 1982.

[48]Interview with an ex-Minister of Finance, Istanbul November 5, 1982.

[49]Demirel's National Front coalitions were composed of the Justice Party, his party; the Islamicist National Salvation Party of his old enemy Necmettin Erbakan; and the neo-fascist National Action Party of Alparslan Türkeş. The first such coalition had one other member: the National Reliance Party. These coalitions will be discussed in greater detail in chapter 7.

[50]*Minutes,* 8/17/1977.

[51]*Minutes,* 1/17/1979.

[52] Interview with a member of that government, Ankara, November 9, 1982.

[53]Eskişehir Sanayi Odasi, *Eskişehir Sanayi Odasinin 10. Yili ve Mümtaz Zeytinoğlu,* p. 317.

[54]The *ex post facto* payments demanded by the state were to compensate the Central Bank for any exchange rate depreciation that occurred in the months (or years) intervening between the arrival of the goods and the time it took for this bank to transfer needed currency to the suppliers abroad.

[55]Eskişehir Sanayi Odasi, *Eskişehir Sanayi Odasinin 10. Yili ve Mümtaz Zeytinoğlu,* p. 315.

[56]ISO even blamed the rumors of an impending devaluation for the spiralling inflation rate, *Minutes,* 2/21/79.

[57]The 47.10 rate was calculated in the following manner; a 10 TL premium was added to a 40 percent premium on the official exchange rate. The 10 TL was reduced to 5 TL a month later, so that the rate was lowered to 42.10 TL to the dollar.

[58]*Cumhuriyet,* April 11, 1979.

[59] *Cumhuriyet,* April 8, 1979.

[60]*Cumhuriyet,* April 19, 1979.

[61]*Cumhuriyet,* April 11, 1979.

[62]Finally, in June of that year, Ecevit had to devalue the currency to 47.10 TL to the dollar, the rate at which Turkish workers in Europe

were exchanging their foreign currency. Again, the devaluation was late as the Turkish Lira had, by then, further depreciated in value.

[63]While there were 29 branches per banking concern in 1960, by 1980 this figure had climbed to 135. More significantly, the number of persons served by one branch declined from 16,488 in 1962, to 7,590 in 1980, Arslan Yüzgün, *Cumhuriyet Dönemi Türk Banka Sistemi 1923-1981* (Istanbul: Der Yayinevi,1982), p. 49.

[64]How could they complain, remarked one ISO member, at a time when inflation was at 110 percent, they paid back their loans at interest rates which never exceeded 35 percent, *Minutes*, 7/15/1981. Not all industrialists were happy with this arrangement. Some Anatolians argued that the banking system discouraged savings and encouraged consumption, at the expense of long-term investments in intermediate and capital industries, Zeytinoğlu, *Ulusal Sanayi*, p. 54.

[65]Hayri Sevimay, *Bankalar Sistemi ve Kredi Düzeninin Eleştirisi* (Eskişehir: Eskişehir Sanayi Odasi Yayinlari, 1971), p. 54.

[66]Gevgilili, *Türkiye'de 1971 Rejimi*, p. 462.

[67]Yüzgün, *Cumhuriyet Dönemi Türk Banka Sistemi 1923-1981*, p. 245.

[68]Öncü, "Chambers of Industry in Turkey," p. 472.

[69]*Minutes*, 9/15/1976. Despite the crisscrossing memberships between ISO and TÜSIAD, the former's leadership reflected the more numerous and vocal smaller enterprises.

[70] *Minutes*, 3/19/1980.

[71]Çukurova Holding acquired both Pamukbank and Yapi ve Kredi Bankasi, which together disposed of 14 percent of savings deposits (Table 6.1). In addition, it owned the Uluslararasi Endüstri ve Ticaret Bankasi, a smaller (seventh overall among private banks) internationally specialized bank.

[72]*Minutes,,* 3/19/1980.

[73]*Minutes*, 2/21/1981.

[74]Gevgilili, *Türkiye'de 1971 Rejimi*, p. 274.

[75]TOB, *Bankalar Kanunundaki Değişikliklere Ilişkin Görüşler ve Öneriler* (Ankara: TOB, 1979), p. 20.

[76]TÜSIAD, *The Turkish Economy, 1975* (Istanbul: TÜSIAD, 1975), p. 131.

[77]Güngör Uras, *Türkiye'de Yabanci Sermaye Yatirimlari* (Istanbul Formül Matbaasi, 1979), p. 147.

[78]TOB, *Özel Sektörün Yabanci Sermaye Hakkinda Görüşü* (Ankara: TOB, 1966), p. 78.

[79]Zeytinoğlu, *Ulusal Sanayi*, p. 92.

[80]*Minutes*, 7/18/1973.

[81]*Minutes*, 10/15/1975.

[82]*Minutes*, 8/19/1970.

[83]TOB, *Türk Hür Teşebbüs Konseyi: I. Genel Kurul* (Ankara: TOB, 1979).

[84]Nicholas Kaldor, "Türk Vergi Sistemi Üzerine Rapor," *Toplum ve Bilim*, No. 15-16 (Autumn-Winter) 1981-1982, p. 88.

[85]By 1969, however, ITO switched sides and joined the industrialists in their demands for the taxation of agriculture, Gevgilili, *Türkiye'de 1971 Rejimi*, pp. 43-45. ITO's conversion was prompted by the increasing hostility of Anatolian business interests towards all Istanbul-based groups.

[86]*Cumhuriyet*, April 28, 1979. In reality, this attempted secession had more to do with the upcoming election of Ankara Chamber of Industry's president as head of the TOB than with the accusations.

[87]Gevgilili, *Türkiye'de 1971 Rejimi*, p. 404.

[88]Interview with an ex-Minister of Finance, Istanbul November 5, 1982.

[89] The same issue resurfaced, albeit in a completely different political setting, when a member of the post-1980 Constituent Assembly, known for his pro-Justice Party leanings, objected to a military-sponsored agricultural reform bill by pointing out that, "while this bill is taking away land from some large landowners, what would happen to those with winter and summer residences, automobiles and factories? Should not one also take their possessions away?" *Nokta* (weekly) August 22-28, 1983.

[90]Ismail Bulmuş, "Türkiye'de Tarimsal Taban Fiyat Politikasi ve Etkileri," *ODTÜ Gelişme Dergisi* 1981 Special Issue, p. 556.

[91]Zeytinoğlu, *Ulusal Sanayi*, p. 49.

[92]Ekonomik ve Sosyal Etüdler Konferans Heyeti, *1972 Sonbaharinda Türkiye'nin Iktisadi Durumu* (Istanbul: Ekonomik ve Sosyal Etüdler Konferans Heyeti, 1973), n.p.

[93]*Minutes*, 7/18/1978.

[94]This ordering of regions is based on Özbudun's rank ordering, Ergun Özbudun, *Social Change and Political Participation in Turkey* (Princeton: Princeton University Press, 1976), pp. 100-101.

[95]In Bursa and Izmit there are no independent chambers of industry, hence their chambers are classified as chambers of commerce *and* industry. These two regions also ranked as the fourth and sixth largest chambers in the country, based on the distribution of the largest 500 industrial concerns.

[96]*Minutes*, 3/19/1980. Izmit is an industrial town east of Istanbul.

At a time of increased societal polarization, the National Security Council decision was influenced, if not prompted, by the high concentration of mobilized workers engaged in industrial action in this area.

[97]*Minutes*, 5/21/1969.

[98]*Minutes*, 6/18/1969. The political controversy surrounding Erbakan will be further discussed in the next section and also in the following chapter.

[99]*Cumhuriyet*, November 30, 1969.

[100]*Cumhuriyet*, December 4, 1969.

[101]Quoted in Ismail Cem, *12 Mart* (Istanbul: Cem Yayinevi, 1978), p. 359. Erbakan also made a practice of couching his accusations in anti-semitic terms.

[102]Cem, *12 Mart*, p. 359.

[103]Muzaffer Sencer, *Türkiye'de Siyasal Partilerin Sosyal Temelleri* (Istanbul: May Yayinlari, 1974), p. 365.

[104]Sencer, *Türkiye'de Siyasal Partilerin Sosyal Temelleri*, pp. 370-371.

[105]Of Turkey's 67 provinces, 42 were initially designated by the state as priority areas for developmental assistance and incentives. Their geographic distribution depicts the unevenness of development; all of the provinces of the Northeastern and Southeastern regions were deemed backward. For further information, see Devlet Planlama Teşkilati, *Kamu Yatirimlarinin Kalkinmada Öncelikli Yöreler ve Diğer Iller Itibariyla Dağilimi* (Ankara: Devlet Planlama Teşkilati, 1982).

[106]Memduh Yaşa, *Cumhuriyet Dönemi Türkiye Ekonomisi* (Istanbul: Akbank Yayinlari, 1980), p. 67.

[107]Ergun Özbudun and Frank Tachau, "Social Change and Electoral Behavior in Turkey: Toward a 'Critical Realignment,'" *International Journal of Middle East Studies*. Vol. 6 (1975), pp. 460-480.

[108]Zeytinoğlu, *Ulusal Sanayi*, p. 121; Eskişehir Sanayi Odasi, *Eskişehir Sanayi Odasinin 10. Yili ve Mümtaz Zeytinoğlu*, pp. 359-360.

[109]Zeytinoğlu, *Ulusal Sanayi*, p. 121.

[110]The seven are, Istanbul, Aegean (Izmir), Ankara, Adana, Eskişehir, Kayseri and Denizli. By the end of the decade, another industrial chamber, in Konya, would be formed without altering the basic distribution of power within the TOB.

[111]TOB, *XXVIII TOB Genel Kurulu* (Ankara: TOB, 1973).

[112]*Minutes*, 10/18/1963.

[113]*Minutes*, 10/18/1963.

[114]*Minutes*, 6/24/1964.

[115]*Minutes*, 6/24/1964.

[116]*Minutes*, 9/18/1968.

[117]*Minutes*, 11/20/1968. What infuriated industrialists more was that a formal agreement to coordinate their voting at a TOB convention was, at the last minute, repudiated by the commodity brokers, *Minutes*, 2/25/1970.

[118]*Minutes*, 6/24/1964.

[119]Minutes, 6/24/64, emphasis added.

[120]Öncü, "Chambers of Industry in Turkey," p. 460.

[121]*Minutes*, 11/25/1969.

[122]Gevgilili, *Türkiye'de 1971 Rejimi*, p. 42.

[123]*Minutes*, 6/18/1964 and 6/24/1964.

[124]Since commercial interests dominate at the local level, a chamber of commerce and industry would also be controlled by commercial interests, irrespective of the presence of the industrialists.

[125]TOB, *XXVIII. TOB Genel Kurulu*.

[126]By contrast, all nine substitute members were non-industrialists. TOB, *XXIX. TOB Genel Kurulu* (Ankara: TOB, 1974).

[127]With semi-official recognition, the Organization of Cooperating Chambers of Industry could send representatives to meetings between the government and the private sector, but was not entitled to much more.

[128]Erbakan's relationship with industrialists, and its subsequent impact on state-business relations, will be further explored in Chapter 7.

[129]*Minutes*, 7/16/1969.

[130]Bianchi, *Interest Groups and Political Development in Turkey*, p. 260. Their frustration with both the TOB and its new leadership was reflected in the bitter statement made by the head of the of the Aegean Chamber of Industry, Şinasi Ertan. Warning that the industrialists would finally break away from the TOB once and for all, he blamed all evils, including the economic and political crises affecting Turkey, on the fact that the TOB was dominated by merchants (*tüccar*), *Cumhuriyet*, May 28, 1969.

[131]*Minutes*, 8/18/1971.

[132] Interview with an ISO member, Istanbul November 2, 1982.

[133]Another important founding member was Sakip Sabanci, whose family enterprises were widely considered the second largest in the country. In addition, in 1974, as the head of the Adana Chamber of

Industry, Sabanci became president of the Union of Chambers of Industry (*Sanayi Odalari Birliği*, SOB), an organization which replaced the defunct Organization of Cooperating Chambers of Industry.

[134]TÜSIAD, *The Turkish Economy, 1980* (Istanbul: TÜSIAD, 1980).

[135]*Minutes*, 8/18/1976 and 4/16/1980.

[136]Bianchi, *Interest Groups and Political Development in Turkey,* pp. 266-269.

7

The Road to Paralysis:
State-Business Relations

This chapter details the confusion and conflict which permeated state-business relations during the latter part of the 1960s and all of the 1970s. Private sector cleavages discussed in Chapter 6 were reflected in the proliferation of political parties. As political parties and private sector organizations became progressively embroiled in each other's affairs, their dialogue was increasingly characterized by acrimony and mutual suspicion. The loser in the process was the state which was deprived of its ability to produce coherent policies.

While the state could have used the private sector's divisions to bolster its limited autonomy, it chose to placate the different groups by using the resources at its disposal — specifically economic rents. This, however, had an opposite effect: it paralyzed the state, further accentuated the misallocation of resources described in Chapter 5, and set the stage for the 1980 military intervention. This was nowhere more apparent than in the private sector reaction to the 1970 stabilization measures.

At the center of these developments was the disintegration of the Justice Party (JP). In the 1960s and 1970s, as the party representing the various business interests, the Justice Party found itself under siege from competing private sector groups and new political parties, parties that vied for that segment of the political spectrum it hitherto dominated. The JP's problems played a critical role in hampering state officials from taking decisive action to remedy ISI's inherent and natural distortions. The following pages detail first those events — the revolt by Necmettin Erbakan at the heart of the TOB and the 1970 stabilization measures — which culminated in the disintegration of the JP, and then turn to how this party's leader Demirel worked to reunite the private sector in support of his party. The zeal with which Demirel approached his task contributed to the deepening stalemate by embroiling the private sector and its organizations into countless political struggles. Ultimately the deepening stalemate also paved the way for Turkey's 1980 economic and political transformation.

The JP under Siege

Ironically, because it was perceived as the party of business, the Justice Party had the greatest difficulty in managing the private sector, which continually asked it to meet impossible expectations. As heir to the banned Democrat Party of the 1950s, the JP's constituent base included the agricultural sector — specifically the commercialized regions of the West and South which had benefited most from the 1950s. In the 1960s most commercial groups and industrialists also backed the JP because, in their view, it represented the anti-thesis of the Republican People's Party (RPP). The RPP, still led by Ismet Inönü, the leader from the Etatist Era, continued to suffer from the memories of its authoritarian past and, paradoxically, also from the wartime Capital Levy (*Varlik Vergisi*). As one high ranking RPP official would admit, "the RPP continued to pay for imposing the Capital Levy because the business community's perception was one of 'a party capable of imposing such a tax is also capable of doing anything it wishes to the private sector.' This fear of the RPP prevailed despite the fact that a number of the functionaries responsible for this tax had, subsequently, left the RPP to join the opposition."[1]

As the discussion in Chapter 6 intimated, the Union of Chambers, TOB, was not only very strongly pro-Justice Party, but it allowed the JP and its leader Süleyman Demirel to interfere in its inner workings. In the mid-1960s, the influence wielded by the JP's leader gave the appearance that business interests were united under the tutelage of his party. In the 1965 national elections, both the TOB and the Istanbul Chamber of Commerce endorsed the JP despite the legal sanctions against such behavior.

The seemingly unanimous private-sector support of the JP masked the discontent brewing over the party's handling of parochial concerns. These would all surface in 1969 with the revolt at the TOB, the heart of Demirel's constituency.

A Rude Awakening: The Erbakan Revolt

Necmettin Erbakan's successful bid for the TOB's leadership was the first in a chain of events that would shake private sector confidence in the

Justice Party. As upset as industrialists and large city businessmen were over Erbakan's ascendancy, they were even more troubled by Demirel's methods to unseat him. In this respect 1969 proved a watershed year in JP-business — and consequently state-business — relations because, having been forced out of the TOB, Erbakan took his cause to the political arena. Throughout the 1970s he managed to disrupt the Demirel's attempts at rejuvenating the JP.

The TOB Revolt. Erbakan's rise came when dissatisfaction with the JP was spreading. Industrialists were cognizant of their relative weakness: accordingly their most serious problem was "that industry, unlike in other countries, does not carry sufficient clout to *impose* its own ideas on the government."[2] Hence, as Chapter 6 demonstrated, industry's desire to create its own representative organizations was, in the manufacturers' view, "necessary and vital, if they are to become an influential force in the political economy."[3]

Industrialists were not alone in expressing their frustration with the Justice Party's control over the TOB. It was the perceived neglect of Anatolian interests that enabled Erbakan to mount his 1969 challenge to Demirel's control over the TOB. Erbakan proved that discontent with Demirel and his party was much more widespread than anyone had previously anticipated. His revolt also set forth a series of events which, for the decade to come, would haunt state-business and intra-private sector relations. Even though the seeds of polarization in decision-making had long been planted, the rise of Erbakan and the JP's response to him served as catalysts for further acrimony.

Erbakan's success had as much to do with his excellent timing as it did with devious political maneuvering. He surprised both the TOB and Justice Party leaderships by disguising his true intentions. To deflect attention from himself, Erbakan announced his candidacy in the upcoming 1969 national elections for a parliamentary seat from the Konya region. Instead of campaigning for a parliamentary seat, he went to work canvassing potential delegates to the TOB convention and outmaneuvered the incumbent TOB leadership. On the eve of the TOB convention, realizing that something was amiss, Demirel and the TOB leadership tried to postpone the convention vote and buy time to woo back Erbakan's delegates. Unable to obtain a delay, the government sought and secured a court injunction against the holding of these elections.[4] The rebellious TOB General Council refused to obey the court order and Erbakan was duly elected as the organization's leader on May 24, 1969. The Demirel government responded by refusing to recognize the elections, thereby precipitating an unprecedented crisis in state-business relations.

The JP adopted an aggressive posture against the Erbakan revolt which, in the long-run, produced mixed results. Although Demirel managed to recapture the TOB from Erbakan, his tactics alienated a large segment of the business community. Demirel's response took three forms. First, he attacked the credibility of both Erbakan and the new TOB by denying the rebellious Union the standing a quasi-public institution is entitled. Second, he withheld the disbursement of import quotas and thus tried to cripple the organization financially. Third, he attempted to coopt Erbakan's Anatolian supporters back into a JP dominated TOB by promising to replace the organization's traditional leader, the Istanbul Chamber of Commerce (ITO), with an Anatolian chamber. The last objective was achieved soon after Erbakan's ouster when a Demirel ally and non-ITO member was selected as the new leader of the organization in new TOB elections held on January 5, 1970. For a while, ITO was excluded from any significant leadership role within the TOB.[5]

There were drawbacks to this approach. Industrialists were infuriated by the means employed, especially by the withholding of import quotas which made them the primary victims of the counter-attack. Since the quota freeze endangered the well-being of the industrial sector as a whole, industrialists perceived this as unfair punishment. If this undermined their confidence in the JP, it also forced them to play a mediating role because of what was at stake: import permits. A group led by chambers from the Aegean region negotiated with Erbakan to find a way out of the impasse. As a face-saving recourse and as a means of driving a wedge between the JP and industrialists, Erbakan, in exchange for his voluntary resignation from the TOB's leadership, demanded the following from Demirel: (1) the return of quota allocations to the TOB, (2) a government promise to never again revoke this TOB privilege, and (3) new TOB elections with joint Erbakan-JP slates and a promise to end political party interference in future TOB elections. The Aegean chambers readily accepted the first two conditions, but refused to transmit the third demand to the government.[6]

The mediation effort served to further politicize industrialists, which hitherto had remained on the sidelines. It also highlighted the limitations of the JP and Demirel. "We were forced to cooperate with the government and the party [JP] because of the delicate situation created by Erbakan. However, the day will come when the private sector will be strong enough that ISO will no longer be influenced by political parties."[7]

From the industrialists' perspective, Demirel's combative approach surfaced what had been an ill-disguised secret: the JP's interference in the

TOB and its associated chambers. ISO, in particular, was uneasy with the increased attention it and the rest of the private sector was attracting as a result of the Erbakan affair. Fearful that this awareness could, in turn, invite added scrutiny from other political parties and the press, and fuel the fires of polarization, the chamber asked for Demirel's assurance that he would limit and even end Justice Party interference in TOB elections. Demirel proved to be elusive on this matter,[8] betting that industrialists had, in the final analysis, no other recourse but to stay with him.

The Rise of a Political Star. Erbakan's temporary rise at the TOB forged the regional divisions within the private sector and, more importantly for him, propelled him into national politics. In 1969 he became an independent deputy from Konya, and later emerged as the leader of the National Order Party (*Milli Nizam Partisi*). Dedicated to an essentially populist platform that was laden with Islamic ideas, this party did not survive long and, in the aftermath of the 1971 military intervention, was banned by the Constitutional Court for allegedly undermining the country's secular foundations with the political use of religion.

Erbakan was undaunted. Some of his followers established the National Salvation Party (*Milli Selamet Partisi*), NSP, as an extension of the banned National Order Party. In 1973, as soon as the military had withdrawn from direct political involvement, Erbakan assumed the leadership of this new party which mirrored the political stance of its previous incarnation. Through his political activities and successes at the polls, Erbakan emerged as the main political representative of the small commercial elements of the Anatolian hinterland and, in some cases, of their counterparts in larger metropolitan areas.

1969 proved an important year from another perspective, as well. In the October 12 national elections the JP maintained its parliamentary majority, while losing considerable ground to the opposition.[9] Rightly or wrongly, the private sector saw this as a weakening of the party, thus fueling internal rebellions. The signs of polarization and extremism were visible everywhere. Another revolt did not take long to surface; it had been simmering for some time. A group of JP deputies with strong ties to Western Anatolia and the banned Democrat Party of the 1950s had been seeking the wherewithal to oust Demirel from the JP's leadership. By the end of 1970, their failure to do so led to the secession of a group of 41 of them, who formed the Democratic Party (DP).[10]

Amidst all these changes Demirel attempted the most ambitious restructuring effort of the Turkish economy. The 1970 stabilization measures were timely and well thought out. They also exacerbated his problems.

The 1970 Stabilization Measures

The stabilization measures introduced on August 10, 1970 came to represent the second turning point in JP-private sector relations. The Demirel government undertook what would prove to be the only wide ranging and *successful* stabilization program of the two decades. The measures accelerated the movement away from the JP, reinforced the breakaway political parties such as the Democratic Party, and seriously eroded the industrialists' confidence in the JP and its leadership. These measures carried a paradoxical lesson: the party responsible for their implementation was punished — despite the measures' unquestioned success. As a result, it would take ten years for such a program to be reintroduced. On January 24, 1980 the same set of personalities instituted comparable measures when the crisis of import substitution was upon Turkey with a vengeance. January 24, 1980 would represent the end of the ISI era in Turkey and the beginning of a new one. The events in 1970 proved to be decisive in shaping the state-business relations and ultimately the implementation of the 1980 measures.

The 1970 measures were unique in their long-term approach and internal consistency. The stabilization plan, which included a series of new taxes and a 66 percent devaluation of the lira, grew out of two developments: a foreign exchange shortfall and an anticipated large budget deficit triggered by a civil service reform. The first stage of the package, known as the Financing Law, was submitted to Parliament in May 1970. It included a new motor vehicle purchasing tax, a sales tax on luxury consumption, a "production" tax on assembly industry products, a property valuation tax, a lottery tax, and increases on inheritance duties and bank charges. These tax proposals were loudly criticized by all segments of the private sector, irrespective of their associational ties or geographical location. Only the agricultural sector had been spared any tax increase. In addition to raising revenue for the state, these tax increases were instituted to boost the manufacturing sector's competitiveness and to force the assembly industries to seek domestic sourcing for their imported components.

Industrialists and others interpreted the Financing Law, and the subsequent devaluation package, as a blow to the assembly industries' essence and, in particular, to the automotive sector. The TOB went so far as to reason that, since the JP had instituted measures advocated by the extreme left, the party must be siding with "these extremists" against the private sector.[11]

The new taxes did impact the assembly industries, but the dire predictions on the imminent demise of such industries proved premature. The blow dealt by the state was felt more acutely at the political level than at the economic: the private sector was shocked by the absence of prior notification and consultation.[12] The August devaluation was also strenuously opposed by the private sector, with the exception of agricultural interests. Again Demirel chose secrecy over prior consultation. "Prime Minister Demirel appears to have been convinced for some time that the lira should be devalued but had been unable to do so due to the opposition from within his own party. The industrialists in particular opposed the move, and they were among the key supporters of the Justice Party. The devaluation was announced shortly after Parliament adjourned, which suggests that the timing may have been influenced by that fact."[13]

Only the agricultural sector was spared the "adverse" impact of the reforms. The reason for safeguarding this sector was not the relatively small size of the plots, as the Finance Minister had officially claimed. Rather it was because Demirel could ill afford to further alienate this group when he was busy fending off a secession attempt by the old Democrat Party members. Unfortunately for Demirel, the concessions to agriculture did not suffice to prevail over the seceding deputies, and despite the program's resounding success, industrialists and others turned against him. As Table 5.10 demonstrated, with textiles leading the way, Turkish exports experienced a dramatic increase. The state's treasury was also filled with workers' remittances from Germany and elsewhere, propelling foreign exchange reserves to record levels. In 1970 Demirel's strategy clearly hinged upon an improving economy and, especially, improving foreign trade sector. In an interview some years later he said, "If only we could have held onto power until 1973, we would have become 'viable,' that is, balanced our trade and solved all of Turkey's problems."[14]

Just as the private sector had been shocked by the government's actions, Demirel and his party were equally surprised by the private sector's uncoordinated but hostile reaction.[15] He and his party were quickly cornered by the criticisms. The measures eroded private sector trust in the party as representative of its interests and reaffirmed the view some held of the government's disregard for Anatolia. With Erbakan and his allies hammering at the party from one direction, Demirel, in a meeting with industrialists in January 1971, gave into pressures from the latter and scrapped a series of hitherto unpublicized new tax measures.[16] By this time he was in such need of allies that regaining the industrialists — even temporarily — was crucial.

The success of the 1970 measures notwithstanding, Demirel and his party paid a heavy price in subsequent years. In the 1973 elections, the JP lost over a hundred seats to upstarts such as the Democratic Party and Erbakan's National Salvation Party (NSP). The JP not only lost its majority in Parliament, but came in second after Ecevit's Republican People's Party (RPP). Defeat at the hands of his political foes forced him to reconsider his basic strategy. In fact, the concession to industrialists was only the beginning of a process he undertook to reconstitute his party and political base.

Since the Turkish left, represented by the RPP and a few splinter parties, never managed to capture more than the 42 percent of the total votes cast, the main threat to the JP's majority status came from divisions on the right rather than a challenge from the left. Therefore, Demirel's strategy concentrated on the private sector which, while not responsible for all the divisions on the right, nonetheless had contributed the lion's share. His approach involved satisfying this sector's demands whenever possible. From 1973 onwards, he and his party had one goal in mind: to recapture the votes lost on right wing of the political spectrum. This goal was slowly achieved and with the victory at the October 1979 by-elections Demirel could claim that the JP had regained its 1965 strength.[17]

Balanced and successful as they were, the 1970 measures fell victim to the intra-party and state-business bargaining which marked most of the remainder of the decade. Had the 1970 program been maintained as designed, it would have moved Turkey away from substitution for the sake of substitution and toward a more balanced industrialization strategy, a shift which would have also encouraged export growth. Instead, the divisions caused the state to veer off its 1970 plan and condemn Turkey to 10 years of vacillation — which culminated in the 1980 economic transformation and military coup.

The 1970 measures failed for other reasons as well. Already weakened by concessions to the private sector, these stabilization measures were further compromised by the March 12, 1971 military ultimatum which forced the resignation of Demirel and his government. Demirel and Özal, the architect of the 1970 and 1980 stabilization programs, have both blamed the 1971 military intervention for interfering with the progress of the 1970 measures. In 1980, as Özal was briefing military commanders on the forthcoming stabilization measures, he reminded them of how their intervention in 1971 had derailed the earlier such attempt.[18] Despite such claims, the military's contribution was *not* decisive in 1970, a fact that even Özal acknowledged.

The 1970 stabilization package marked a turning point. From then on, fearing the impact of private sector retribution, governments and state bodies were to shy away from undertaking such measures. If the government was incapable of taking the lead, the disarray in the private sector meant that it would not take initiatives either. Thus, an impasse was born; an impasse fueled by a JP suffering from defections and losses at the polls.

The 1973 Elections and the Rise of the National Salvation Party

The Justice Party's loss of its parliamentary majority at the end of 1970 was also accompanied by a perceived decline in state authority. Increased working class agitation and student unrest reinforced this perception of a weakening state and party. The national elections in 1973, in which the JP lost its primary position, would demonstrate to Demirel how sizeable a price he and his party had to pay for their policies.

Before the elections were held, one other development was to occur. Within the military, unbeknownst to the public and politicians, arguments between radical and mainstream officers had undermined that institution's confidence in the government. On March 12, 1971 the military high command issued an ultimatum forcing Demirel's resignation.[19] Until the next general elections in October 1973, a series of above-party governments, comprised of members of Parliament and outsiders, held office with the support of officers. Confused in their mission, these governments did not leave much of an imprint on political-economy matters.[20] Instead, they concentrated on the eradication of terrorist groups and restoring state authority. During the interregnum, whereas the RPP transformed its character and leadership by moving toward a social-democratic synthesis with a new leader, Bülent Ecevit, the JP could do little to fight the brush fires on its right.

The military withdrew following the conclusion of the October 1973 elections. In these, the RPP emerged as the largest party, though shy of a majority. The results shocked most observers who had been predicting a JP plurality. The RPP received 33.3 percent of the vote and 185 seats; the JP, NSP and Democratic Party's figures were 29.8 percent and 149 seats, 11.8 percent and 48 seats, and 11.9 percent and 45 seats, respectively.[21] With 226 seats necessary for a majority in Parliament, the RPP was only 41 seats short which, in turn, transformed both the NSP and the new Democratic Party (DP) into instant kingmakers. Since DP members still held the RPP responsible for the 1960 coup — which had led to the overthrow of the original DP and the execution of some of its leaders — a RPP-DP coalition was not a realistic possibility. To the surprise of many, the secularist and social-democratic RPP managed to form a coalition government with the Islamicist and right-wing NSP. For Erbakan, denying the JP the power it sought represented an opportunity to pay Demirel back for his 1969 ouster from the TOB.

Erbakan's dream of a pay back was Demirel's nightmare, a nightmare that lasted for the rest of the decade. As discussed in the previous chapter, the NSP was successful in exploiting the perceived neglect of Anatolian business. Coupling an Islamic message with a strong emphasis on regional industrialization, the NSP was most successful in the East Central, Northeast and South Central regions of lesser development.[22]   By contrast, the Democratic Party argued that industrialization would *not* succeed without agricultural development and advocated support of that sector.[23] Not surprisingly, this message was best received in regions marked by low urban but high levels of rural development,[24] in other words, the relatively well-off agricultural areas of the Western Anatolia. Unlike the NSP, the Democratic Party turned out to be a one-election phenomenon. By the 1977 elections, the JP had successfully reabsorbed most of these defectors back into its fold. Despite the reversals it too would suffer in 1977, the NSP proved to be a more enduring movement.

The RPP-NSP coalition, which came to power in early 1974, did not last long enough to finish the year. Nonetheless, this relatively short period of joint rule proved eventful. The coalition agreement conferred on the NSP seven out of the twenty cabinet seats, including the two portfolios dealing with trade and industry. Erbakan became the Deputy Prime Minister in charge of coordinating economic affairs. This combination of influential cabinet posts enabled the NSP and Erbakan, in particular, to have a substantial hold on the Turkish political economy. Most importantly, the further elevation of Erbakan exacerbated the politicization of state-business relations, primarily because it now raised the stakes of the intra-private sector confrontations by introducing them into the inner workings of the state.

Initially there were divisions within the private sector on how to deal with the RPP-NSP coalition government. By then the TOB was firmly in control of Demirel's private-sector allies. TÜSIAD — which, as a new organization was anxious to demonstrate its clout — adopted a bellicose attitude. It organized a meeting of the private sector in April 1974, attended by the Aegean and Ankara Chambers of Industry and some commercial chambers. By contrast, ISO, the industrial chambers of Adana and Eskişehir, and ITO sought to establish a dialogue with the government and refused to attend this anti-government parley.[25]

If there were any doubts as to Erbakan's intentions, they did not last long. At the May 1974 annual TOB convention, Erbakan made a triumphant return to his old organization from which he had been unceremoniously forced out. This time he was addressing the delegates as Deputy Prime Minister in charge of coordinating economic affairs. He took the occasion to detail his own interpretation of the October 1973 national elections. Clearly elated by his party's success at the polls, he argued, "our people do not want unbalanced growth. . . [They] have expressed their displeasure with the lack of equity among regional areas and different groups. . . [The people] have said we want *real manufacturing* rather than assembly industries."[26] The emphasis on industrialization, specifically heavy industry, became one of Erbakan's trademarks. Although his speeches on the issue were the object of ridicule and scorn in the press and elsewhere, the continuous barrage on the subject captured significant attention.[27]

On the other hand, Demirel's hold on the TOB was very evident as the government's policies were severely criticized and its spokesmen, including Erbakan, were booed.[28] Soon after these meetings, the state-private sector confrontation reached a new high when, in what appeared to be a retaliatory move, the government decided to rescind the remaining TOB powers over foreign trade. The first to go was the import price control mechanism, which had been reinstituted to the TOB by the military-backed governments of the 1971-73 period.[29] Also revoked by the Minister of Trade, a NSP member, was the TOB's export price control authority. As the TOB loudly protested these moves, threatening "to defend private sector interests under any circumstances,"[30] the fact remained that the government's moves came at a time when, despite the resurgence of Demirel's allies, its influence had significantly diminished after years of infighting and the emergence of new organizations, such as TÜSIAD. Between the inter-party competition for the JP's share of the vote and the advent of coalition governments, state-business relations were further politicized. Neither side seemed to know how to deal with this new state of affairs. This became even more evident when the situation failed to improve with the dissolution of the RPP-NSP coalition.

Less than a year after its inception, this unstable coalition unraveled. Neither party ever trusted the other and, in the aftermath of the Cyprus invasions in the summer of 1974, Ecevit and the RPP sought to capitalize on their newly gained popularity by calling for new elections. With this in mind, Ecevit engineered the coalition's break-up. But his gamble did not pay off. Fearful of a RPP victory, all other parties banded to block the call for new elections. The collapse of the RPP-NSP coalition in the fall of 1974 was followed by the formation of a caretaker government composed of bureaucrats and a few politicians. This government was eventually replaced in March 1975 by the first of Demirel's National

Front (*Milli Cephe*) blocs, which brought together the two arch rivals — Demirel and Erbakan. Also included in this new coalition government were the small neo-fascist National Action Party of Alparslan Türkeş (3 seats) and the Republican Reliance Party of Turhan Feyzioğlu (13 seats), a right-of-center breakaway faction of the RPP. Thus, with the exception of the Democratic Party,[31] all the right wing parties were contained in the first National Front government.

The First National Front Government

The formation of the First National Front Coalition had two contradictory long-term consequences; while it temporarily consolidated Erbakan's role as a power broker in Turkish politics, it also enabled Demirel to take on his arch-rival within the confines of a coalition government and slowly usurp the latter's power base. The immediate result of this arrangement was a deepening of the impasse in decision-making circles as these two political leaders battled.

In the new cabinet, the NSP obtained eight of the thirty portfolios. As in the previous RPP-NSP coalition, Erbakan assumed the position of Deputy Prime Minister in charge of economic affairs and the Ministry of Industry and Technology was given to the NSP. The trade portfolio, however, went to a JP member.[32] Riddled with internal tensions because the coalition's parties, specifically the JP and NSP, were actively vying for each others constituents and votes, the government increasingly alienated the business community, which complained of the absence of a stable economic or political course.[33] ISO and other business organizations found themselves increasingly drawn into the political arena. The governments' fractions tried to use existing rivalries within the private sector to their advantage. One favorite tactic of Erbakan was to summon the heads of the industrial chambers at a moment's notice to Ankara without a predetermined agenda so as to minimize their prior cooperation, with the intent to undermine intra-sectoral unity.[34]

More importantly, Erbakan and the NSP used the Ministry of Industry to deny state incentive certificates to projects in the West, specifically in the Marmara region.[35] After two years of co-existence within the same government, the JP and NSP failed to agree on the location of a *single* project.[36] Disagreements between these two parties also delayed the promulgation of the 1977 Import Regime. This was a costly delay since without an import regime, firms could not apply for their import permits. As the government blamed such shortcomings on unrelated "problems" with the European Community, the NSP ventured to assume control of the distribution of import permits by transferring this responsibility from the JP-controlled Ministry of Trade to its own industry portfolio. This enabled the NSP to selectively issue permits and routinely deny them to its perceived enemies, especially assembly industries.[37]

During this first coalition period, an attempt was made to fashion an all-powerful business organization to encompass the entire private sector. Named the Free Enterprise Council (*Türk Hür Teşebbüs Konseyi*) this undertaking fell victim to intra-sectoral rivalries, jealousies and, most importantly, political interference. The idea had originated with the TISK leader, Halit Narin, as a means of enhancing the private sector's power vis à vis the labor unions.[38] Another — though less publicized — aim was to fortify private sector defenses against an increasingly erratic government. The Council itself was initially well received. Even ISO, the least politically adventurous of the chambers participated in its organizational meetings. The Council was comprised of five organizations: TISK, TÜSIAD, TOB, The Union of Agricultural Chambers and the Confederation of Tradesmen and Artisans. The leadership was to rotate among these constituent groups.

The Free Enterprise Council's failure grew out of the different constituent groups' own agendas. Some issues were petty: a struggle developed between the TOB's head Sezai Diblan and TISK president Halit Narin over who would be first to lead the Council. Others were more fundamental: while the TISK viewed the Council primarily as a bulwark against those forces "adamant on destroying the mixed economy," the agricultural sector, and especially the tradesmen's group, saw it as primarily an anti-RPP organization. The latter two clearly articulated this position when, in the council's first convention in January 1977, they asserted that the mistake of the 1973 elections — namely the RPP's success at the polls — should not be repeated. In fact, they even went further and argued that the private sector should unify under the JP's banner as it had been until 1969.[39] The TOB's position was more ambivalent. While its leadership was clearly for Demirel and sought to deliver him "an endorsement" in the upcoming elections,[40] others were reticent and even hostile to the idea of a pro-JP stand. For instance, the Eskişehir industry leader attacked the Council for being a disguised attempt by the JP at supplanting the TOB, which had eschewed all credibility.[41]

The overt political nature of the Council eventually drew fire from Ecevit, the RPP, Türk-İş — the more moderate of the two main trade union organizations — and even from some of the National Front members. This did not bode well for the industrial chambers that were already starting to feel the pinch of the oncoming economic crisis. SOB

leader Sabanci was forced to deny the political linkages between the JP
and the Council as well as the latter's anti-union character.[42] Ultimately,
the Council was disavowed by industrialists who feared its overt and
combative political attitudes. Even though this action spelled the end of
the Council, industrialists would not be able to remain above the political
fray as they found themselves, less than 6 months later, enmeshed in an
open political struggle of their own making with the government.

In 1977, with the economic situation deteriorating rapidly, the intra-
governmental conflicts hampering the allocations of import permits, and
the halt to foreign currency transfers, industrialists, in an unusual public
move, called for early national elections. SOB president Sabanci
admitted that this was the first time they had engaged themselves in an
open political declaration, but they felt that the worsening political and
economic conditions warranted such dire action.[43] What they feared of
course was loss of influence in the stalemated political atmosphere where
only the loudest voices were heard. At that time, their main concern
focused on the further politicization of the pending wheat price
supports. With Erbakan and Demirel struggling to broaden their bases,
industrialists were clearly worried about the generous and inflationary
support prices being granted what was, in their view, an undeserving
agricultural sector.

However, the industrialists' intervention in politics at this time can
also be seen as a clear-cut case of trying to ensure that their share of rents
and benefits were not parcelled out to the competition.

The 1977 Elections and the Deepening Stalemate

Just as the industrialists had wished, elections were held four months
ahead of schedule on June 5, 1977. Nonetheless, the situation continued
to deteriorate in their aftermath. The RPP increased both its share of the
vote and its parliamentary representation. This time, it fell just 13 seats
short of a parliamentary majority. To the RPP's 213 seats, the JP received
189, the NSP 24 and the NAP 16 seats. Hoping that defectors would rally
to it, the RPP tried to form a minority government. The new government
received immediate backing from both TÜSIAD and industrialists. This
represented a 180 degree turnaround on their part. The Eskişehir leader,
Mümtaz Zeytinoğlu, rationalized the switch by pointing out that the
alternative to the RPP and Ecevit consisted of Erbakan and his NSP, both
of whom had proven so disruptive to private sector interests in the
past.[44] Industrialists were eager to avoid another narrow coalition
government, and since Ecevit had come closest to the magical number of
226, he stood the best chance of denying Erbakan a share of power.[45]

A second reason for the industrialists' newfound sympathy for Ecevit and his party centered on overtures he had made to them during the electoral campaign. These overtures, spurned by the TOB because of its strong pro-JP leanings, nonetheless led industrialists to believe that since Ecevit enjoyed support of the DISK, the militant Revolutionary Trade Union Confederation, he alone could fashion a "social-contract" of the sort the British Labour Party had recently drafted. This is not to say that support for the minority RPP government was unanimous in industrial circles. Larger concerns were decidedly more positively disposed, while the smaller establishments, lacking political clout, remained apprehensive.

To most people's surprise, no miracle occurred and the minority government failed its first vote of confidence, forcing it to relinquish power to the second of Demirel's National Front coalitions.

The Second National Front Government and Ecevit's Return

While the JP had not regained its former strength, Demirel could find solace in the virtual disappearance of one of his primary rivals on the right — the Democratic Party — which had declined from 45 seats in the 1973 elections to just one. The NSP was also being worn down. Although it polled approximately the same number of votes (1,265 million in 1973 vs. 1,271 million in 1977), the NSP's share of the total vote declined from 11.8 to 8.6 percent and, in the process, lost half of its parliamentary representatives.[46] Therefore, Demirel's strategy of wearing down its competitors to his right seemed to be working.[47] Despite its diminished size in the new coalition, the NSP continued to retain the important industry portfolio and Erbakan remained as Deputy Prime Minister.

The NSP suffered reversals in all parts of the country — except in the Southeast and in Konya, Erbakan's home province. In Istanbul, it registered a 20 percent decline. These reversals in the party's fortunes did not render it any more accommodating of Western business interests than before. Even the JP, whose share of the vote in Istanbul remained stable, complained to ISO members about the lack of support it had been getting in the region. When the trade minister was asked to speed up the promulgation of the 1977 Import Regime, he attributed the delay in legislation to the antipathy to business circles within the JP which, "as the defender of private enterprise," had not received enough votes in Istanbul.[48] The JP was clearly incensed at the welcome Ecevit had received from Istanbul's leading industrialists. This was another indication of the costs and consequences of the politicization of private sector roles.

The Second National Front Government proved no better at handling its internal tensions than its predecessor. Economic decision making remained hostage to JP-NSP squabbles: the 10 percent September 1977 devaluation, promised to the IMF, was implemented by the Treasury without cabinet approval because the NSP was refusing to sign any such authorization.[49] Even long-standing JP supporters found the situation intolerable. Ibrahim Bodur, ISO's General Council president, directly challenged the government's legitimacy when he publicly stated that "they [ISO] would not even entertain the idea of a dialogue with a government devoid of all credibility."[50] Industrialists blamed all the country's ills on this Second National Front government. Hence, a collective sigh of relief greeted the news of this coalition's eventual demise and its replacement by a new RPP government in early 1978. This time the RPP, which managed to attract enough independents and JP defectors with promises of ministerial positions, had more than the 226 parliamentary seats needed. However, the inclusion in the cabinet of eleven outsiders meant, as one of its ministers argued, "a coalition with eleven political parties."[51]

The new government quickly proved that it was not the panacea sought by industrialists. They alone had supported its formation and rumors abounded about their money being lavishly spent on recruiting JP defectors. Industrialists found that the new government could not deliver on its promises of a clear and well thought out policy. When the RPP government finally devalued the currency in March 1978 (see Chapter 6), it refused to increase the prices for fertilizers and petroleum for fear of alienating the average consumer. In fact, the government was caught between the IMF's demands for serious stabilization measures — as a precondition for the release of desperately needed foreign currency — and opposition to both IMF mandates and tampering with the value of the lira.

Some of the problems encountered by Ecevit were inherited. In fact, it is during his tenure that over five and a half billion dollars in short-term loans, incurred by the National Front coalitions, were temporarily rescheduled, relieving the economy from its yearly large debt bill. It is also during this government's tenure that the U.S. embargo on arms sales to Turkey, imposed after the Cyprus invasions, was ended, again relieving some of the pressure on the balance of payments.

Nonetheless, the pervasiveness of commodity shortages, and the accelerating street and political violence soured relations between the government and industrialists. Previously held suspicions were fast resuscitated. Industrialists were quick to question the RPP's commitment to free enterprise. For its part, the government dismissed private sector complaints as hyperbole, especially since — by TÜSIAD's own admission — 1978 had been a banner year for corporate profits. Ecevit was also convinced that industrialists had used back channels to ask the IMF *not* to extend any credit to his government.[52]

The confrontation between the two exploded into the public domain in May 1979 when TÜSIAD, in the aftermath of the inconclusive March 1979 stabilization measures, commenced a widespread newspaper campaign against the government. This campaign was significant in two respects. First, there was no precedent for a private sector organization mounting such a challenge against an incumbent Turkish government. Second, the organization acted unilaterally without seeking the consent of other private sector groups. In view of their quasi-legal standing, the chambers would have been in serious difficulty had they openly cooperated in advance with TÜSIAD. Nevertheless, lack of prior knowledge still created a dilemma for the chambers. While uneasy over this act of defiance, most felt obliged to align themselves with TÜSIAD's in order to create a semblance of private sector unity.

The industrial chambers' position was further complicated by the timing of the campaign's launch, which immediately followed a joint meeting of all the executive councils of the chambers comprising the SOB, the Union of Chambers of Industry. Given their crisscrossing membership ties with TÜSIAD, the ad campaign was interpreted by the public and government alike as a joint ISO/SOB/TÜSIAD venture. Irrespective of its own disenchantment with government policies, ISO was embarrassed by the timing of the offensive and by its ignorance of it during its two-month preparation, in which some of its own members had taken part.[53] Nevertheless, ISO tried to put the best light on the event by arguing that the ad campaign did not represent a break with the government, but rather an indication that more cooperation and discussions were needed to bridge the gap between the two. Stung by this unprecedented criticism, Ecevit and the RPP promised to call in the public prosecutor and seek legal sanctions.

With this bold challenge TÜSIAD managed to upstage both the TOB and the chambers, and established itself as the private sector's most important spokesgroup. It was duly rewarded when, in 1981, the military rulers upgraded its status and conferred it with legal standing and legitimacy. Ecevit's government did not survive long as it lost the 1979 by-elections to the JP which proved once again that its policy of slowly regaining its lost votes was paying off. This time the private sector welcomed the new minority-based Demirel government, even though it relied on the "outside" support of the two right wing parties, the NSP and NAP. It is this government which finally instituted the radical measures that were to represent the beginning of Turkey's break with its past industrial policy, and especially with ISI.

The Politics of Indecision

Turmoil within the private sector and its reflection in the political arena created an atmosphere of confusion and uncertainty. The various governments, whether led by Demirel or Ecevit, could not provide the needed leadership because they themselves were unable to speak with one voice. On the other hand, the private sector's lack of consensus destroyed any chance of coordinated action or policy proposal. In such an atmosphere of uncertainty, short-term considerations prevailed.

No organization was immune to the debilitating disharmony, including TÜSIAD. In a meeting with the Minister for Industry in February 1979, "while some TÜSIAD members complained about the problems of industry, the inability to generate profits, the decline in production, the fact that some would probably be out of business next year. . . other members said they were perfectly satisfied and that they had never had such a prosperous and happy year. Naturally, at the end of the meeting the minister told us that he did not know who among us to believe."[54] This meeting was ostensibly called by TÜSIAD in an attempt to convince the Ecevit government of the need for reform and concerted action.

While state authorities correctly perceived the discord, they were unable to offer concrete suggestions. In fact, as one ex-RPP cabinet member argued, "with the probable exception of the 1979 TÜSIAD-led campaign against the RPP government, the private sector has not had a common, proficient, genuine and long-term perspective on any policy issue."[55] TÜSIAD's campaign may have been effective in galvanizing the private sector, but its success was limited since its was restricted in scope to a single negative objective: bringing down a government. Therefore, this campaign could not be translated into a broader and more constructive set of proposals. In reality, when it had tried to push for changes in broad policy objectives, other segments of the private sector blocked these prospective modifications (Chapter 6). Later, in 1980, Özal strongly urged that, in order to avoid some of the pitfalls of 1970, all private sector groups — whether they be industrialists, commercial or agricultural interests — be completely ignored, and that economic decision making be centralized under his authority.[56]

The practice which best exemplified the absurdity of the deadlock occurred during the period when foreign exchange reserves were almost non-existent. Called "cash against goods," or "cash against documents" imports (*mal mukabili ithalat*), a grossly illegal and widely abused system of importing products was developed as a means of salvaging the import-dependent manufacturing sector. The operating principle of the system was quite simple: importers/industrialists devised ways to circumvent the Central Bank and gain access to foreign currency abroad in order to finance their imports. The private sector was cognizant of both the illegalities and corruption involved in this practice.[57] Only TÜSIAD was critical of the long-term implications and estimated that, in two short years, non-guaranteed trade arrears resulting from this practice had reached $1.7 billion owed to 98,000 claim holders abroad.[58] On the other hand, in a meeting with Ecevit in March 1979, SOB president Sabanci demanded that the government continue to turn a blind eye to this grossly illegal practice.[59] The government obliged.

In another revealing case, the Ecevit government yielded to the demands of industrialists. To encourage and facilitate Turkish exports, Ecevit's government decided to establish an Export Council in which the private sector representatives were to play a significant role. Industrialists objected to the "private sector representatives" designation as being too broad and demanded that membership requirement be amended to Chamber of Industry representatives *only*, thus eliminating agriculture — the most significant export sector — and other competitors from within the TOB.[60] The government once again acceded.

Why did the Turkish state repeatedly give in? It could not have been because the Turkish private sector was singularly powerful. This sector perceived itself as weak and at the mercy of the state: "in the West [industrialized societies], the private sector has a right to express its opinions. Here this right is given [by the state] only as charity, we are made to feel unwanted in our own household."[61]

Yet the examples cited above, which demonstrated the extent to which even the RPP went out of its way to accommodate private sector interests, imply that the state was not as powerful as the private sector perceived it to be. Ironically, despite its widely held image among businessmen of harboring anti-private sector biases, the RPP felt frustrated by what its own leadership (including Ecevit) perceived as a pattern of concessions to the private sector, one that was far more extensive than any other party.

Divided as it was, the private sector could have easily fallen prey to state manipulation. But this did not happen. Because of the proliferation of political parties and private sector cleavages, a complex political dynamic was produced. In such an atmosphere of increased politicization, every struggle and every issue had a political ramification.

The state was not manipulated by private sector interests either. Instead, it was overwhelmed with demands. In large measure, this was the normal by-product of a dynamic identified by Charles Lindblom and accentuated by the extensive state involvement in the market that is associated with ISI. As Lindblom argues, "knowing that [business] must have some privileges and knowing that government officials fully understand that simple fact, businessmen ask for a great deal. They also routinely protest any proposal to reduce any of their own privileges. They are not highly motivated to understand their own needs. It might weaken them in governmental negotiations to do so. Hence they often predict dire consequences when a new regulation is imposed on them, yet thereafter quickly find ways to perform under it."[62]

Instead of appreciating this dynamic, successive Turkish governments simply buckled under the pressure. In the parlance of the Turkish political economy, the state gave in to all demands, however contradictory they were. What kept the system going was the state's ability to mediate the different demands through the system of rent distribution. Economic rents, which cushioned all from the vagaries of international competition and prevented the formulation and adoption of new ideas, helped to maintain the status quo. It is therefore not surprising that the state regained some of its autonomy when, as a result of the intensification of the economic crisis, sources of economic rents dried up.

The 1970 stabilization measures had already demonstrated that there were solutions to Turkey's problems. All that had to be done was to reapply them. But it took the collapse of the economy in 1979 to convince both state and society of the need to implement radical change.

Notes

[1] Interview with a leading RPP member, Ankara November 2, 1982. See Chapter 3, footnote 35 for further details on the Capital Levy.

[2] *Minutes*, 11/20/1968, emphasis added.

[3] *Minutes*, 10/17/1973.

[4] The government offered the rather flimsy excuse that since the International Union of Chambers of Commerce was to convene its meetings in Istanbul later that year, an experienced TOB leadership was necessary to shepherd the international visitors.

[5] Bianchi, *Interest Groups and Political Development in Turkey*, pp. 257-258.

[6] With demands 1 and 2, he was clearly trying to score points with industrialists, *Minutes*, 7/16/1969.

[7]*Minutes*, 1/21/1970.

[8]*Minutes*, 6/21/1972.

[9]The JP's share of the vote declined from 52.9 percent in 1965 to 46.5.

[10]Of the 41, 26 were kicked out of the party following their February 13, 1970 negative votes on the budget resolution that forced Demirel's resignation. The remaining fifteen left at the end of the year to join the new party.

[11]TOB, *Devalüasyon - Yeni Vergiler ve Otomotiv Sanayi* (Ankara: TOB, 1971), pp. 15-17; Mükerrem Hiç et. al., *Montaj Sanayi: Gelişmesi Sorunlari ve Ekonomimizde Yeri* (Istanbul: Ekonomik ve Sosyal Etüdler Konferans Heyeti, 1973), pp. 71-85.

[12]According to the Aegean Chamber of Industry president, the government had promised to consult with them during the preparation of the package, *Cumhuriyet*, May 30, 1970.

[13]Anne Krueger, *Foreign Trade Regimes and Economic Development: Turkey* (New York: National Bureau of Economic Research, 1974), p. 312. The devaluation had been anticipated for immediately after the 1969 elections, but defectors from the JP, who openly criticized the impending move, may have had a hand in the delay.

[14]Cüneyt Arcayürek, *Demirel Dönemi, 12 Mart Darbesi: 1965-1971* (Ankara: Bilgi Yayinevi, 1985), p. 324.

[15]Some of the reaction was detailed in the previous chapter, under the headings Import Substituting Industrialization, and Foreign Trade and Exchange rate policy.

[16]*Minutes*, 2/17/1971.

[17]Arcayürek, *Demirel Dönemi, 12 Mart Darbesi: 1965-1971*, p. 321. 1965 represented the high point of the party's fortunes.

[18]Emin Çölaşan, *24 Ocak: Bir Dönemin Perde Arkasi* (Istanbul: Milliyet Yayinlari, 1983), pp. 113-115, 301.

[19]The 1971 coup was really a countercoup designed to forestall a more radical move by more junior officers. To co-opt the junior officers, the high command issued a pronunciamento which also reflected many of the radicals' wishes, including land reform. This led unions and other left-wing organizations to support the coup. However, they were soon to be disappointed because with the chain of command safeguarded, the service chiefs quickly retired their rebellious underlings and the direction of the new regime took a decidedly authoritarian bent.

[20]One exception was the revocation of TOB's right to issue import licenses. See Chapter 6 for further details.

[21]Feroz Ahmad, *The Turkish Experiment in Democracy* (Boulder:

Westview, 1977), p. 319.

[22]South Central was not as underdeveloped as the other two, but it contained Konya.

[23]Muzaffer Sencer, *Türkiye'de Siyasal Partilerin Sosyal Temelleri* (Istanbul: May Yayinlari, 1974), p. 380.

[24]Ergun Özbudun and Frank Tachau, "Social Change and Electoral Behavior in Turkey: Toward a 'Critical Realignment,'" *International Journal of Middle East Studies*, Vol. 6 (1975), p. 476.

[25]ISO informed TÜSIAD that it was too early to criticize a government which had agreed to undertake a dialogue, *Minutes*, 4/17/1974 and *Cumhuriyet*, April 5, 1974. ISO's main concern focused on discouraging a government already viewed as hostile to its interests. On the other hand, ISO had to be careful not to snub TÜSIAD, which was in violation of their previously determined strategy, *Minutes*, 6/19/1974. Eskişehir and Adana, on the other hand, were more appreciative of the fact that this government, on paper at least, promised to pour considerable sums of money into the industrialization of Anatolia, *Cumhuriyet*, April 5, 1974.

[26]TOB, *XXIX. TOB Genel Kurulu* (Ankara: TOB, 1974), p. 63, emphasis added.

[27]Interview with a member of that coalition government, Ankara, November 11, 1982.

[28]*Cumhuriyet*, May 31, 1974.

[29]*Cumhuriyet*, June 3, 1974.

[30]*Cumhuriyet*, June 3, 1974.

[31]Having all defected from the JP, the members of the Democratic Party could not have been expected to support Demirel.

[32]Ahmad, *The Turkish Experiment in Democracy*, pp. 360-361.

[33]*Minutes*, 12/22/1976.

[34]*Minutes*, 6/18/1975.

[35]*Minutes*, 5/12/1976.

[36]*Cumhuriyet*, February 11, 1977.

[37]*Cumhuriyet*, January 13, 1977 and *Cumhuriyet*, February 11, 1977.

[38]*Minutes*, 1/19/1977.

[39]TOB, *Türk Hür Teşebbüs Konseyi: I. Genel Kurul* (Ankara: TOB, 1977), p. 82.

[40]Bianchi, *Interest Groups and Political Development in Turkey*, p. 272.

[41]Eskişehir Sanayi Odasi, *Eskişehir Sanayi Odasinin 10. Yili ve Mümtaz Zeytinoğlu* (Istanbul: Eskişehir Sanayi Odasi Yayinlari, 1981), p. 405.

[42]*Cumhuriyet*, February 16, 1977.

[43]*Cumhuriyet*, February 16, 1977.

[44]Eskişehir Sanayi Odasi, *Eskişehir Sanayi Odasinin 10. Yili ve Mümtaz Zeytinoğlu*, pp. 439-446.

[45]The disruptiveness of Erbakan and his group was also openly acknowledged by Turgut Özal when he was preparing his 1980 stabilization plan: an ironic admission given that his brother was part of the NSP and he himself had made an unsuccessful run for a parliamentary seat under the NSP banner. Çölaşan, *24 Ocak: Bir Dönemin Perde Arkasi*, p. 301. The industrialists' first preference was for a broad-based RPP-JP coalition. This was an unlikely outcome since it would have damaged Demirel's attempts to recapture the political right's dispersed voters.

[46]*Cumhuriyet*, June 14, 1977.

[47]In fact, he was even hoping that 7 or 8 more parliamentarians could be persuaded to join the JP's ranks from the NSP, further depleting his adversary's bargaining power. See Cüneyt Arcayürek, *Demokrasinin Sonbahari: 1977-1978* (Ankara: Bilgi Yayinevi, 1985), p. 212.

[48]*Minutes*, 10/19/1977 and *Cumhuriyet*, October 20, 1977.

[49]Ironically, while they came from different perspectives the NSP and industrialists agreed on one issue: opposition to devaluation. Erbakan's motives were purely nationalistic, he was not about to "give in" to foreign demands.

[50]*Cumhuriyet*, October 20, 1977

[51]Interview with a member of that cabinet, Ankara, November 9, 1982, PM.

[52]One of the bitter complaints of industrialists consisted of the *kur farki* issue discussed in Chapter 6. For the government's views, see Cüneyt Arcayürek, *Müdahalenin Ayak Sesleri* (Ankara: Bilgi Yayinevi, 1985), pp. 245, 320.

[53]*Minutes*, 5/16/1979.

[54]*Minutes*, 2/21/1979.

[55]Interview, Ankara, November 12, 1982.

[56]Çölaşan, *24 Ocak: Bir Dönemin Perde Arkasi*, pp. 294, 310, 317.

[57]*Minutes*, 1/17/1979. Accordingly, an individual needing imports would finance the purchase of goods by buying black market dollars from Turkish workers abroad or by using his/her own illegal foreign bank accounts. This was necessary since no foreign supplier aware of Turkey's payment problems was willing to ship goods on credit. Having paid the foreign supplier, the Turkish importer/industrialist would then

deposit the cost of the goods in Turkish liras at the Turkish Central Bank. However, the Central Bank, which had no foreign exchange to spare, was unable to transfer funds for an indeterminable amount of time. The importer/industrialist then had to pretend to Turkish state authorities that the supplier was willing to accept the Central Bank promise of payment at some future point in time and expedite the purchases. In reality the foreign supplier had already been paid. The absurdity lay in the fact that many of the 98,000 foreign claimants on Turkish Central Bank arrears were, in fact, Turkish citizens waiting to be paid for their own financing schemes.

[58]TÜSIAD, *The Turkish Economy, 1980* (Istanbul: TÜSIAD, 1980), p. 50.

[59]*Cumhuriyet*, March 14, 1979.

[60]*Minutes*, 4/19/1978.

[61]*Cumhuriyet*, January 19, 1979.

[62]Charles Lindblom, *Politics and Markets* (New York: Basic Books: 1977), p. 179.

8

Regaining Autonomy: the Making of a Bureaucratic Authoritarian Regime

On January 24, 1980, the Demirel government announced what would turn out to be the most significant set of economic measures since 1960. Intent on revitalizing the economy with the new program, the government abandoned the inward-oriented, import substitution guided political economy in favor of an export-driven one. The new program, supported initially by most segments of the private sector, represented a radical departure from past policies and practices, and has received much of the credit for turning Turkey around in a few short years. Its success, however, came at a price. Besieged on all sides by the centrifugal forces of society, the Demirel government succumbed to a military coup less than nine months after the promulgation of the January 24 measures. The autonomy the democratic state had derived from the private sector support proved temporary, if not illusory. It was the new military regime which regained the state's autonomy.

The first section of this chapter discusses the implementation of the January 24 measures and shows how the September coup ensured success. The second section discusses the engineering of the BA state in Turkey. Finally, the chapter concludes by comparing the Turkish experience with those of some Latin American countries, such as Argentina, and shows how this case is not without its parallels.

The 1980 Transformation

The January 24, 1980 Programme

The waning months of 1979 ushered an increasing sense of despair and frustration as the economy failed to recover from previous resuscitation attempts. Following the off-year fall elections, in which Ecevit and his party were completely routed, Demirel assembled a minority government which relied on the outside support of two less than reliable partners: the National Salvation Party (NSP) and the National Action Party (NAP). This peculiar arrangement was the consequence of two factors. First, having collaborated in coalition governments on two previous occasions, Demirel and the Justice Party (JP) were unwilling to repeat their experiences with these two extremist parties. Second, in view of the desperate economic conditions awaiting any new government, the NSP and NAP were not anxious to share in the blame for what to them seemed certain defeat and failure. Both sides, however, agreed on the need to remove Ecevit and the Republicans from power. Thus, a compromise was reached. Paradoxically, it is the minority coalition's homogeneity which provided Demirel with the much needed internal consistency of views, a fact that had eluded him during the National Front coalitions of the 1970s.

The new Demirel government quickly came to the conclusion that, short of a bold set of new initiatives and measures, the Turkish economy would be incapable of shaking off its sluggishness and declining fortunes. Hence, the government decided to gamble and implement a major long-term restructuring program, advocated by Prime Minister Demirel and his chief economic czar, the SPO chief, Turgut Özal. The program was designed to dismantle the import-substituting edifice and transform the inward-oriented political economy into an export-oriented one.

From the outset, the success of the January 24, 1980 measures depended on three crucial ingredients: (1) a rescheduling of Turkey's debt, (2) the cooperation of the various domestic groups, and (3) time for the results to sprout. The first was necessary to stimulate the foreign trade sector and resume the inflow of new money into Turkey. These objectives could only be achieved with the major international lending institutions' stamp of approval. Other creditors — commercial banks and other governmental institutions — were unlikely to extend new loans and credits to Turkey without the IMF and the World Bank's lead. Past attempts at restructuring had fallen short of Turkey's needs and expectations,[1] the Turkish government needed to convince the international lending agencies of the seriousness with which it approached this task.

The second and third ingredients were more difficult to obtain because the transformation desired entailed enormous, if not prohibitive, political dangers for Demirel and his party. After all, a much less ambitious program in 1970 had undermined the party's dominant position. Therefore, the sacrifices now required from the public risked jeopardizing the JP's hard-won political comeback. On the other hand, what made the risks acceptable can be traced to four distinct differences from the situation in 1970. First, the prevailing sense of desperation that accompanied the economic paralysis had been absent in 1970. Second, to bolster Turkey's position in the wake of the Iranian Revolution, the advanced industrialized states promised external assistance in the form of credits and, most notably, foreign exchange. This too was unlike 1970 when the government could not rely on any external sources of assistance. Third, in another departure from previous precedents, Özal went out of his way to obtain the military high command's prior consent. Finally, the government benefited from a sense of self-confidence stemming from the resounding successes it had achieved at the polls in the October partial elections.

Özal presented the package to his colleagues and the nation as measures of the last resort. First, in his November 1979 memorandum to the Prime Minister, Özal argued that the radical measures were unavoidable since another year of indecision could only lead to a collapse of the Turkish state. Given the prevailing crisis atmosphere, he feared that, at the hands of an unforgiving electorate, an indecisive Justice Party would suffer the same fate as its predecessor, Ecevit's RPP. Therefore, by instituting a bold new plan, the Justice Party could hope to be rewarded in early elections for confronting the hard choices ahead.[2] In the January 24, 1980 cabinet meeting, when outlining the program, he argued that the consequences of not adopting the proposed measures would be dire: the inflation rate would quickly surpass the 120 percent mark, the unemployment rate would reach unbearable levels, and the deteriorating economic conditions would aggravate the already intolerable levels of anarchy and terrorism.

Özal also set forth the following priorities for the plan: (1) combat inflation, (2) increase foreign currency receipts, (3) increase capacity utilization of existing plants and equipment, (4) increase exports, (5) eliminate black market operations and scarcities, (6) speed up investments decisions, which would increase employment, and (7) improve the distribution of income to end what he called the "disappearance of the middle class."[3] These pointed to one fundamental objective: the jettisoning of Turkey's inward-oriented economic structure.

The measures were divided between those which could be introduced through government edicts and regulations and those which required parliamentary approval. Whereas exchange rate determination fell within the purview of the government, tax reform required parliamentary approval. Accordingly, the first measure to be announced on January 24, 1980 was a devaluation of the lira by almost 49 percent: from 47.10 TL to the dollar to 70 TL. The size of the devaluation was unexpected: it even surpassed IMF demands. The devaluation was the first step in what was hoped would develop into a system of flexible exchange rates, an objective finally achieved on May 1, 1981. Both the Demirel government and the subsequent military administration continued to impose periodic mini-devaluations, which kept the currency apace of the changes in its real value. This constant adjustment of the currency was the first and foremost requirement of the stand-by agreement signed by the government with the IMF. Other measures to revamp the foreign trade sector included export incentives in the form of credits or foreign exchange to exporters, and the liberalization of import regulations and of the laws governing the entry of foreign capital. On the domestic front, price control mechanisms were abolished together with some of the selected subsidies. The prices of public sector products were repeatedly increased by significant amounts to close the gap in State Economic Enterprises' budgets. The government also announced its intention to reform the tax system, although, as in the past, it proved unable to do so when confronted with opposition inside and outside Parliament. It would be up to the post-September 1980 military authorities to implement the tax reform package. Another significant measure, which was envisaged in the January package and realized on July 1, 1980, was the freeing of domestic interest rates. This move enabled banks and other savings institutions to charge the "prevailing market rates" on deposits and loans.

The package, which was designed to streamline the economy and specifically the manufacturing sector, also produced an immediate adverse reaction by deepening the existing recession. Domestic demand was reduced by adhering to IMF prescriptions of a tight monetary policy. The credit squeeze added to inventories and seriously endangered mid-sized manufacturing concerns which did not enjoy ready access to funds from privately owned banks. Interest rates continued to climb, despite the larger banks' attempts to negotiate a "Gentlemen's Agreement" to avert the practice of paying unofficial premiums to large depositors. By mid 1981, 12-24 month time deposits, which in January 1980 were earning an average of 12 percent, had officially climbed to over 40 percent and much higher unofficially.[4]

Having relied in the past on the expansionary effects of cheap credit, the consumer durable industries were particularly affected by the credit squeeze which effectively eliminated middle- and low-income groups from the market. In 1982, at a time when the rate of inflation exceeded 35 percent, these industries were forced to offer a variety of incentives, including interest-free long-term payment plans to attract prospective consumers. Depressed domestic demand and rising inventories increased the pressure to export on the various sectors, most notably on manufacturing. When exporting, the cost structure of domestic industries proved to be a serious hurdle. A case in point was the OYAK-Renault automobile company which, compelled to export because of the collapse of the domestic market, had to sustain a loss of more than $2,000 per car exported.[5]

As Özal explained to industrialists, the severe costs were part and parcel of the price Turkey had to pay for the eventual success of the stabilization-transformation package: "the problems facing the country cannot be resolved with short-term temporary measures. Only a program such as theirs, with an anticipated implementation duration of *five years*, can do the job of opening up the economy to foreign competition and encourage exports."[6]

The Private Sector and the January 24 Measures

The private sector's initial reaction to the January 24, 1980 measures was favorable. Even ISO, which hitherto had resisted any and all devaluations, initially welcomed the new programme. As on previous occasions, the chamber's most immediate concern was the replenishment of foreign exchange reserves and, in this case, if the IMF and other international lending institutions needed to see a serious package to be persuaded to extend credit, then ISO was ready to go along.

There were other factors operating on ISO. For one, the 1979 consensus within the private sector to push for new measures had led to its isolation. Hence, this organization and its membership had been subjected to enormous pressures to follow the lead of others. Second, ISO's position had become untenable as a result of the economy's poor performance following the 1979 Ecevit measures, which the chamber had backed but others criticized. Private Western donors were unlikely to extend credit under these circumstances. Therefore, it is not surprising that ISO did an about face and endorsed the January 24 measures as the best possible solution under the circumstances.[7] This change in ISO's public stance was so dramatic that some ISO members were concerned that the general public and labor unions would misinterpret it as an endorsement of the government.[8]

On the other hand, the kind of transformation Özal envisaged did not bode well for the future of many establishments which had benefited extensively from past ISI-inspired policies. While some were willing to wait out the effect of the measures, others — especially those accustomed to receiving large shares of economic rents — were unlikely to survive an extended period of competition and market contraction. In the aftermath of the 1980 measures, the private sector splintered along three categories: (1) those concerns immediately threatened by the new measures, (2) those which could temporarily weather the difficult period ahead, and (3) those which were poised to take advantage of the new opportunities and grow rapidly. This division became more evident after the freeing of interest rates. The first category included mostly medium sized companies which had relied exclusively on the domestic market and were unable to afford interest rate hikes. Among these were some large enterprises and even subsidiaries of the major Turkish conglomerates. The most noteworthy was Asil Çelik, the steel producing subsidiary of Koç Holding which, hovered on the verge of bankruptcy.

The second category consisted of the mostly larger holding corporations which, by virtue of their size, could adopt a wait and see attitude. They had access to their own banks' funds and could temporarily withstand losses stemming from "exporting" their inventories. The main import substituting corporations were in this category. Finally, the third group of companies, comprised of entities which were enthusiastically backed by Özal, were, by virtue of the nature of their products, either uniquely well-suited to export, as in the case of textile industries, or involved in Middle East construction projects where a company's religious affiliation mattered a great deal to potential customers.[9] While Çukurova Holding represented the first type of company, Enka Holding, a construction company, became an example of a diversified export concern closely allied with Özal and his policies. This type of differentiation was exactly what Özal had in mind: a shakeout of industries with those best able to survive the competition remaining alive and others disappearing.

The private sector's enthusiasm for the new measures would not last long. Discontent among the first of the categories discussed would spread to the second category, large import substituting concerns, and lead to Özal's dismissal in the summer 1982.

Ushering in a New Era: The September 12, 1980 Coup

Time, and especially the five years Özal had anticipated the stabilization programs would need, was a luxury the Demirel government could not afford. On September 12, 1980 — ten months after taking office — his government was overthrown. The new military rulers dissolved Parliament, exiled or arrested almost all of the political party leaders, and quickly got on with the task of restructuring the Turkish political system.

The coup came at the peak of Prime Minister Demirel's problems within parliament and the forces aligned outside it. In city streets or in the small hamlets, the anarchy and political violence, which had recommenced in the mid-seventies, knew no bounds. The violence between left- and right-wing groups progressively worsened as they attacked each other with an unparalleled ferocity and savagery. Despite the imposition of martial law, which gave security forces wide discretionary powers to deal with the violence, the number of fatalities averaged twenty a day, with many more wounded. Simultaneously, a record number of workers were on strike, especially in Istanbul and in the textile and metal goods producing sectors (Table 5.15). Some strikes were the direct result of the DISK's, the Revolutionary Workers' Confederation, struggle against the January 24, 1980 measures. Others had been provoked by employers who, suffering from the effects of declining demand, were, by TÜSIAD's own admission, perfectly content to continue depleting their inventories through attrition and without having to go through the difficult and costly lay-off procedures.[10]

In addition to the violence in the streets and the dismal economic conditions, Parliament had been deadlocked since April 1980 over the selection of a new President of the Republic to replace Fahri Korutürk, whose term had expired. Since the incumbent could not constitutionally succeed himself, an acting president, whose presence further symbolized the drift towards anarchy, had been installed. The parliamentary deadlock took a spin for the worse when a temporary alliance, designed to harass and bring down the government without triggering new national elections, was forged between Ecevit's RPP and Erbakan's NSP.[11] The two allies forced votes of no confidence on individual ministers (rather than the government as a whole) and, with Demirel's government's minority status, the outcome of these votes was a foregone conclusion. The first to succumb was the Minister for Foreign Affairs.[12] With another such vote scheduled, this time targeting the Finance Minister, the military moved in.

The coup did not come as a complete surprise. Rumors of an impending move by soldiers had been in the offing throughout the year.[13] The military high command had also made its displeasure public on numerous occasions, the most important of which was contained in a New Year ultimatum to all political leaders warning them of possible action. This warning in fact delayed the promulgation of the January 24, 1980 measures as Demirel and Özal scrambled to determine the imminence and likelihood of a new coup. The ultimatum also propelled Özal to discuss the outlines of the stabilization measures with the higher echelons of the Armed Forces.[14]

The September 12, 1980 intervention had two sets of political economic consequences. In the first place, it boosted, and even rescued, the January 24, 1980 measures. Second, it paved the way for the restructuring of the state's political foundations, without which the long-term economic transformation would not have materialized. So to understand the long-term implications of the intervention and the new regime, we turn to how the intervention was instrumental in buying time for Özal's stabilization plan.

How Necessary was the Coup? By the time the military intervened on September 12, 1980, the January 24 measures had significantly impacted the economy. Nevertheless, despite the abundant of evidence of a transformation, the measures were still in their infancy and their long-term economic success was not by any means guaranteed. Could the liberalization policies instituted in January of 1980 have survived without the coup? The answer is unquestionably no.

In assuming office, the officers did not betray any evidence of undue concern or anxiety about the prevailing economic conditions. This is not to say that they were unaware of these or unknowledgeable about the January 24 package. From a national security point of view, they could not remain indifferent to deteriorating economic conditions which led to reduced imports of military hardware and supplies, forcing them to curtail the training of troops and use of ammunition. This seeming indifference to the economy at the beginning of the military interregnum was due to two factors. First, unlike the cases of most Latin American counterparts, stabilization measures had already been imposed in advance of the coup by a civilian leadership. Second, since Özal had briefed the military high command on at least on three occasions about the nature and progress of the stabilization plan, the ruling generals were very aware of developments on that front. So long as existing policies appeared to be producing results, the coup makers were perfectly content to maintain them. Therefore, one of the first proclamations (No. 5) issued by the new ruling National Security Council, NSC,[15] stated that the January, 24 1980 stabilization measures were to be continued. To further demonstrate its commitment to the new programme, the NSC picked Turgut Özal as Deputy Prime Minister and Minister of State in charge of economic matters, even before settling on who would lead the next cabinet.

If January 24, 1980 had not taken place, would the armed forces in Turkey have emulated their Latin American counterparts and instituted orthodox liberalization policies on their own? Demirel has argued that the officers would not have dared to intervene had the stabilization package not been in place. If the military intervention occurred in 1980, rather than in 1979, it is because the generals were averse to taking office under unfavorable conditions.[16] Kenan Evren, the general who overthrew Demirel, echoed these thoughts. Evren maintained that a program such as this one required a government intent on remaining in power for an extended period of time — five to ten years. Because his was envisaged to be a short transitional regime, the military could not have contemplated the imposition of such wide-ranging measures.[17]

From a political perspective, the coup provided the January 24 program with forward momentum. Despite the initial positive results and the international lending agency support for the measures, the Demirel government was facing an impasse at the political level. The parliamentary deadlock reached in April over the election of a new president had slowed the progress of the January 24 package. The government had not been able to push through a tax reform bill it needed to ensure the measures' success. In view of past governments' large budget deficits, tax reform legislation was needed first to raise additional revenues, and second to relieve pressure on the salaried classes which had borne the brunt of the inflation tax. In fact, in the immediate aftermath of the 1980 military takeover, Özal's first recommendation to the new leaders was to implement the tax reform.[18] The most controversial aspect of the tax reform proposal involved the agricultural sector which hitherto had successfully managed to avoid paying taxes. As Özal himself would later admit, without such a reform the government would never have been able to balance its budget.[19]

However, the political problems that hindered the Demirel government from making the measures work were far more comprehensive than its inability to persuade parliament to adopt its tax reform proposals. As Özal had foreseen, in light of the precarious state of its political life, the uncertainty surrounding the government severely tested its capabilities and durability. The hope was that Parliament would "soon" dissolve itself and that new elections would ensue.

Long after the government's overthrow, Özal would still cling to the belief that early national elections had been possible in 1980.[20] Nevertheless, in the summer of 1980, under the long shadow of internecine party conflict, it was clear to everyone that even if early elections represented the only viable solution, they were not on Parliament's agenda. The reason was relatively simple. Given the JP's recent resurgence in the 1979 by-elections, new elections could have heralded its total victory. Such a victory would have resulted in the goal Demirel had been furiously striving for during the 1970s: the re-emergence of the JP as the dominant political party after having re-absorbed the contending political forces on its right-wing. Therefore, starting with Erbakan and his NSP, no party would be willing to risk such an outcome.

Paradoxically, Demirel's minority government was becoming the victim of its own success. The NSP had been supporting the government from the "outside." The government's early successes in the economic realm meant that the NSP could no longer afford to support it since continuing to do so might have ensured a JP victory in the next scheduled election.

In the prevailing crisis atmosphere of the final months, the Demirel government's energies were consumed by the ongoing parliamentary deadlock, the violence in the streets and the need to constantly maneuver among hostile groups. It was distracted from the necessity to concentrate on the stabilization program. Only a miracle could have saved the government and, by extension, the stabilization plan from collapse. Not surprisingly, Ecevit and Erbakan, who were intent on bringing down the government, had been extremely critical of the January 24 measures. Ecevit, with some foresight, even claimed that since the measures were a take-off on Latin American examples, they could not be sustained under a democratic system.

The military takeover relieved the Justice Party of its political problems and of maintaining the economic course under what were deteriorating economic conditions. These economic problems were, for the most part, beyond the control of Turkish authorities. The rapid rise in oil prices following the revolution in Iran constituted the most serious of these problems, further hampering the government's ability to control its domestic inflation and its balance of payments deficits. Similarly, rising international interest rates made the cost of borrowing prohibitive and debt servicing a very expensive endeavor.

Even though the Demirel-Özal measures contained an element of forcefulness and long-term thinking reminiscent of the 1970 package, the demands of democratic systems still weighed heavily on the government. For instance, in order to remain within money emission limits set by the IMF, Özal tried in vain to persuade Demirel to reduce the support prices for state purchases of wheat by lowering the purchase price to internationally acceptable levels. By contrast, after the coup the NSC not only implemented this request, but it even went along with Özal's radical suggestion to import wheat in an attempt to bring down prices.[21]

This is not to say that Özal succeeded in obtaining every one of his demands. He was, for instance, denied the positions he had demanded in the government. From the very beginning he had appealed for a much greater concentration of power than the military rulers were willing to concede. He insisted on the position he ultimately was assigned to, Deputy Prime Minister in charge of coordinating economic policies, and on attaching the Ministries of Finance and Treasury to himself The ruling officers refused on the grounds that this would be unconstitutional.[22] In addition, Özal's relations with the new Prime Minister, Bülend Ulusu, were riddled with tension. Ulusu, who until August 30, 1980 had been commander in chief of the Navy and thus an active participant in the coup preparations,[23] resented the fact that Özal had, in effect, been selected before him. There were also serious disagreements between Özal, a dedicated free-marketer prepared to tolerate a certain degree of chaos in the marketplace in order to let market forces take shape, and Ulusu, a military officer, who felt more at home with the orderly operation of such forces. One such serious clash occurred in November 1980 over the extension of price controls beyond their date of termination. Özal objected and threatened to resign when Ulusu decided to extend their duration.[24]

Despite their publicly known ambivalence over the January 24, 1980 measures, the military rulers nevertheless continued to implement them in view of the support the package had received abroad. In a press conference shortly after a few days after the coup, General Evren stated that, in the absence of new and major hurdles, the incoming military regime was intent on sticking with the January 24 program. Yet, he also appointed Adnan Başer Kafaoğlu, a critic of Özal and his policies, as his own economics advisor.

The military regime's commitment to protecting Özal was short-lived. As criticisms mounted, because of the financial scandal and panic in the summer 1982, triggered by the flight of the largest of the "bankers," Özal was forced to resign from the government. His propensity to advocate minimal intervention with market forces made him a convenient scapegoat upon whom this scandal and the ensuing panic could be blamed, even though he was not directly responsible for them. In fact, in a weak regulatory environment resulting from the generally underdeveloped nature of financial markets, these "bankers" had mushroomed beyond anyone's imagination. His dismissal, however, was widely interpreted as a victory for the import substituting concerns and, specifically, for the two largest ones, the Koç and Sabancı groups which had exerted a great deal of pressure on the military.[25]   One of the major issues, which brought the simmering confrontation between Özal and the largest holding corporations into the open, was his resolute refusal to bail out the ailing Asil Çelik, the steel making subsidiary of Koç Holding. It was Özal's successor, Kafaoğlu, who ultimately engineered the state takeover of this steel complex.

Özal had identified steadfastness against demands from all groups, and especially from the private sector, as the cardinal ingredient for his measures' success. This had been the primary lesson derived from the 1970 stabilization package. By the time of his "resignation," the measures had gained sufficient momentum for his successor, Kafaoğlu, to stay the course — despite promises of significant changes.

In general, the coup gave the measures a new lease on life. Meaningful opposition from any segment of the private sector, the working class, the parliament and the various political parties was eliminated overnight. As a leading member of the industrial class also pointed out, "the absence of government-opposition conflict is a great stroke of luck because now *rapid* and *dynamic* decision-making is possible."[26]   More significant than the dynamism of the decision making itself was its internal consistency. By using the military as a shield, Özal managed to direct the various state agencies to design policies with the desired level of cohesion and continuity.

The Making of a Bureaucratic Authoritarian Regime?

Turkey's political economic crisis in the late 1970s and the subsequent 1980 military intervention bear a striking resemblance to the coups and severe economic crises experienced by many Latin American countries in the 1960s and 1970s. Starting with Brazil in 1964, followed by Argentina in 1966, Chile and Uruguay in 1973, and finally Argentina again in 1976, numerous semi-industrialized Latin American societies succumbed to problems attributed to the decline or "exhaustion" of import substitution: violence and breakdown of social order threatening the very existence of the regimes themselves. In all the cases listed above, the military intervened to preserve the unity of the state, control the violence and institute long-ranging economic and political reforms. From an economic perspective, the military regimes did away with ISI-inspired developmental strategies and accompanying populist policies.

The new regimes, labeled by Guillermo O'Donnell as Bureaucratic Authoritarian, represented an authoritarian backlash to the expansive and inclusionary politics which had characterized Latin America ever since the days of such populist leaders as Peron and Vargas. Although O'Donnell's BA model has come under severe criticism, it nonetheless presents an adequate organizing concept with which to look at the post-1980 developments in Turkey.[27]

The Economics of the New Order

From an economic standpoint, 1980 was the beginning of the transformation of Turkey's political economy from its ISI-inspired attitudes and structures to a more dynamic and open system. The January 24, 1980 measures served as the catalyst for the changeover, and during the course of 1984 the government introduced a number of new measures to consolidate the gains achieved.

The most striking shift has occurred in the structure of the foreign trade sector. In 1979, foreign trade accounted for 11.5 percent of GNP, whereas this figure climbed to 37.2 percent by 1988. Export performance has even been more dramatic, registering a rise from 3.4 to 16.7 percent of GNP. During the 1979-1987 period, whereas the Gross Domestic Product increased by less than 50 percent and imports by 300 percent, exports jumped by 450 percent. These developments were accompanied by a qualitative change in the export picture; since 1982, manufacturing sales no longer constitute the bulk of exports as exports gained a measure of diversity.[28]

This transformation has exacted a price; it has come at the expense of further indebtedness and consistently declining real wage rates. The Turkish foreign debt increased by 2.5 times since 1980. Even more alarming for Turkey has been the changing nature of the foreign debt as short-term debt, which had been reduced from 25 percent of the total in 1979, to 15 percent in 1980, and then to 10 percent in 1982, started to rise in 1984 reaching almost 23 percent by 1987.[29] In the long-run, and especially in view of the problems faced by the large debtor nations of Latin America, the over-dependence on short-term financing can potentially lead to crises of confidence, crises characteristic of the

1970s. Moreover, the decline in real wages since 1979 — by almost 30 and 50 percent for private and public sector employees — has not been accompanied by significant improvements in the unemployment picture (Table 8.1).

Table 8.1: Unemployment Rate (including disguised unemployment, %)

1979	1980	1981	1982	1983	1984	1985	1986	1987
14.0	14.8	15.2	15.6	16.1	16.1	16.3	15.8	15.2

Source: OECD, *Economic Surveys, Turkey* (various years) and TÜSIAD, *The Turkish Economy* (various years).

With respect to the deepening proposition advanced by O'Donnell, it can be argued that deepening — the vertical integration of the industrial structure through an increase in state and/or international capital investments in heavy industries — not only failed to materialize, but did not figure among the priorities of the January 24, 1980 measures. In line with the Latin American experience, Turkish efforts at restructuring the economy also consisted of traditional orthodox remedies, mainly designed to buttress the sagging export sector.[30]

Table 8.2: Distribution of Incentive Certificates to the Manufacturing Sector (%, at current prices)

	1977	1978	1979	1980	1981	1982	1983	1984
Manufacturing	68.8	87.2	90.1	78.1	49.1	41.0	47.4	50.4
of which								
consumer goods	6.7	9.1	9.0	22.2	26.0	30.8	32.6	53.8
intermediate goods	55.2	52.6	57.0	41.5	17.5	29.1	42.0	27.4
investment goods	37.8	38.2	35.0	36.1	56.6	38.8	21.1	18.8

Source: TÜSIAD, *The Turkish Economy* (various years) and DPT, *Annual Programs* (various years).

Two measures that indicate the governments' disinterest in deepening are the gross domestic capital formation ratios and the distribution of incentive certificates to and within the manufacturing sector. On the first score, the gross fixed capital formation as a percentage of GNP declined from 24.1 percent in 1977 to 20.4, 18.9 and

18.3 in 1979, 1982 and 1984, respectively.[31] As Table 8.2 indicates, the pattern in the government's distribution of incentive certificates reflects a move away from industries in the intermediate and investment sectors that would satisfy the deepening requirements. This change in investment priorities is a natural reflection of the consumer goods sector's export potential and especially of textiles, which received the lion's share of certificates.

Restructuring the Political System

The officers who came to power on September 12, 1980 had an ambitious plan for restructuring Turkish political institutions. The objectives of the intervention were quickly spelled out by the new military ruler, General Kenan Evren. The military leaders were particularly opposed to the previous liberal-minded 1961 Constitution and the weak political structures it had engendered. They proposed a new constitution and a new electoral system that would eliminate the shortcomings of the previous regime. In other words, this was to be the coup d'état that would end all coups. While no time limit was set by the ruling junta, the officers made it plain that theirs would not assume the characteristics of a Latin American coup with a long stay in power. In comparison to other military regimes of this type, the Turkish transition back to civilian rule was relatively quick; within three years civilians were back in power.[32]

The incoming military rulers intended to create a new order — one that would be more stable and less prone to polarization and politicization. While their 1960 predecessors had been primarily interested in freeing society from the previous authoritarian controls, the 1980 military rulers had a different vision. Their new order was to be more restrictive of individual liberties because, as far as Evren was concerned, the liberal 1961 Constitution was the underlying cause of the violence and chaos that engendered the 1980 coup.[33] In the final analysis, in the new political system the state was given a much better chance of enhancing its autonomy.

This was achieved through two distinct sets of changes: (1) those that reduce potential political deadlocks and bottlenecks within state institutions, and (2) those designed to reduce the potential of societal groups for mobilization and conflict. Among the modifications included in the first category were the replacement of a bicameral legislature with a unicameral one and the strengthening of the office of the President. Although the political system does not emulate the French presidential one, the Turkish president's new powers are considerably enhanced so as to serve as a real check on the behavior of the parliament.[34] The decision to abolish the bicameral legislature in favor of a unicameral one, which eliminated one more possible avenue for conflict among parties, also provided the public with the sense (and possibly with the reality) of a more efficient system of government.

However, it is the second category — changes designed to reduce polarization and politicization of societal groups — where the state's powers were visibly enhanced. Not surprisingly, the groups most affected have been the ones that experienced the greatest degree of mobilization in the 1970s: workers, students and, to a lesser extent, professional associations. The 1961 Constitution had ushered in a new age in capital-labor relations by granting workers the right to strike and to collective bargaining, and by refusing to restrict these permissions. The 1982 Constitution, by contrast, severely restricted them.

New restrictions were also introduced on the activities of labor unions. The new constitution requires unions to abstain from all political activity, prohibits them from supporting *or* receiving any support from political parties, and from collaborating with any of the quasi-public associations, such as those representing the different professions. As an added measure of control, unions are required to deposit their funds in state-owned banking institutions. These restrictions effectively curbed the unions' bargaining power and helped institutionalize a lesser economic role in society for them, ensuring, in O'Donnell's terms, the economic exclusion of the "popular sectors."

Similar corporatist restrictions were extended to other parts of civil society. Professional organizations and associations were also prohibited from supporting or receiving support from political parties. In addition, they were put under the tutelage of individual ministries and were required to maintain their headquarters in the national capital, Ankara. If deemed necessary, regional governors were empowered to remove remove the leaderships of trade union and professional organizations from office, including those of business associations. Universities lost their cherished autonomy when, despite the objections of its hand-picked Constituent Assembly, the military rulers decided to elevate in stature and importance the Higher Educational Council, YÖK, a new body it had created to centralize all decision making in Turkish universities, by making it a constitutional body.

Clearly, all these changes were intended to depoliticize society, reduce the influence of highly mobilized groups and increase the state's ability to monitor and control their activities, especially those on the extreme political spectrum's left and right wings. Thus, future civilian regimes will be better equipped than those in the 1970s to deal with the praetorianization of society. The constitutional modifications have effectively retrenched the political power of the organized working class leading, as O'Donnell would argue, to its political exclusion. The impact of economic and political changes designed to curtail working class ambitions was not lost on members of the bourgeoisie. Reflecting the perception that a major reversal in the distribution of power in society had occurred, Halit Narin, chairman of the Turkish Employers Confederation, TISK, commented that "the workers have had their day and now it is our turn."[35]

The two categories of constitutional changes discussed above were buttressed by new laws on political parties and electoral procedures. Determined to halt the proliferation of small parties and the resulting political stalemates, the military set out to deliberately create a two-party system modeled, according to Prime Minister Ulusu, on the British system; "one party would emulate the defunct Justice Party of Demirel [although Demirel was banned from having any role] and the other would resemble the British Labour Party. In other words, it would be statist in orientation."[36] To ensure the emergence of a two-party system, electoral provisions were crafted to favor larger parties. A party, for instance, was required to win at least 10 percent of the national vote total in order to get even one representative elected to the National Assembly. Additional restrictions were introduced at the district level further discouraging the smaller parties.[37]

During the transition to civilian rule, the military vetoed the formation of political parties and the participation of individuals as a final attempt at political engineering.[38] The officers made liberal use of their veto power to eliminate any potential opposition, not only because they intended to shape the country's future political landscape, but because they had already picked the winner of the first elections. Their favorite party was the newly constituted center-right National Democracy Party (NDP). If the NDP was destined to become the majority party in the new parliament, the loyal opposition was to consist of another of the military's creations, the Populist Party (PP), led by Necdet Calp, a lifelong bureaucrat and undersecretary at the Prime Minister's office who previously had served the Republican People's Party. To the distress of the officers, their best laid plans did not materialize, and the 1983 elections were not won by either the NDP or the PP, but rather by an unexpected newcomer, Turgut Özal and his Motherland Party.[39]

Özal was well served by his forced 1982 resignation. He took advantage of the hiatus to form a brand new political party and, given his popularity abroad with Turkey's major supporters in western governments and agencies, the military could not subject him or his party to the same veto process. Thus, on the eve of the elections, he and his Motherland Party were the only non-military sponsored entities contesting the vote and, as such, benefited from a public backlash which sought to punish the official military parties, especially the NDP, for their arrogance. Özal's solid win, under the new electoral system, assured him uncontested supremacy of the economic decision-making prerogatives for the duration of the parliamentary session.

Conclusions

The officers responsible for the September 1980 coup had clearly intended for their efforts to be long-lasting. If the post-1980 regime had all the trademarks of a BA state, it was the intentional result of a complex process of social engineering. At one level or another, almost all the constitutional, institutional and practical changes implemented — with the exception of deepening — fulfilled O'Donnell's requisites for a BA state.

The Turkish rendition of the BA state ultimately transformed the balance of power in the private sector by creating an atmosphere in which the state could pursue orthodox economic policies without interference from the vested interests in that sector. Armed with this newly gained autonomy, the state was able to eliminate the basic import substituting premise of the political economy, and the economic rents upon which the industrial sector had been built. Under such conditions the state could nurture new groups, such as exporters of goods and services, which previously would not have seen the light of day.

The coup and the post-1983 era have allowed for the emergence of new constellations of power within the private sector which have a genuine stake in maintaining the export drive and the new political-economic direction. This is not to say that there are no vestiges of the the import substituting days. On the contrary, as soon as the balance of payments picture improved in the post-coup period, those industrialists who had attributed the pre-1980 economic crisis to a temporary lack of foreign exchange demanded that the stabilization measures be scaled back. This time, the state was empowered to refuse to accommodate their demands. The economic transformation's endurance can also be seen in the positions taken by the new post-1983 opposition parties which have joined the political discourse in the aftermath of the transition back to democracy. Despite their dislike for Özal and their misgivings about some of the results of the post-1980 economic measures, they agree that, for the most part, a return to the 1970s economic positions is not a realistic option.

The Turkish case is not without its parallels. In Argentina, during the post-Peronist years of 1955-1966, the inter-sectoral cleavages and struggles within the private sector was even more pronounced than those in Turkey. There, the main business organizations clashed vehemently with each other.[40] As was the case in Turkey, the inter-sectoral business clashes revolved around issues of representation and economic policy. Often the conflict assumed zero-sum terms. In the final analysis, the clashes between the main philosophies and protagonists in the Argentine business sector assumed the characteristics of street-level polarization. In the 1960s, unable to get a "fair hearing" for their views, the losers in the competition — the adherents of orthodox economic policies — forged links with society's anti-democratic forces. They sought to have their economic philosophies accepted by force and opted to de-legitimize the existing regime and encouraged the 1966 military takeover.[41]

In the final analysis, as the discussion on the post-1980 era in Turkey has shown, the stalemate of the 1960s and 1970s had to be resolved by a military intervention. This end result was avoidable. What Turkey needed was not the forced jettisoning of import substitution. Rather, it needed an autonomous state apparatus which was confident and strong enough to effectively remedy the debilitating side-effects of ISI and its private sector cleavages. Instead, faced with the disintegration of the import substitution efforts, the state sowed the seeds of its own impotence. It tried to simultaneously please all its constituents, new and old, at the expense of a determined and well thought-out economic direction.

Notes

[1] For a discussion of these negotiations and the role of the various institutions see Peter Wolff, *Stabilization Policy and Structural Adjustment in Turkey, 1980-1985* (Berlin: German Development Institute, 1987), pp. 69-79.

[2] Emin Çölaşan, *24 Ocak: Bir Dönemin Perde Arkasi* (Istanbul, Milliyet Yayinlari, 1983), pp. 289-299.

[3] Çölaşan, *24 Ocak: Bir Dönemin Perde Arkasi*, p. 314.

[4] In addition, a new phenomenon emerged in the relatively undeveloped Turkish credit market: that of "bankers." Unaffiliated with any bank, yet calling themselves "bankers," less-than-scrupulous

individuals promised considerably higher rates of return on deposits than established banks and successfully managed to attract large amounts of funds from the public. Unregulated, the "bankers" later induced one of the most severe domestic crises the military-appointed government would have to confront.

[5]*İşveren*, (a TISK publication), December 1980, p. 20. This represented approximately a 20 percent loss per unit.

[6]*Minutes*, 8/20/1980, emphasis added. The international financial institutions also allotted for a five year period for achieving the essential objectives of the stabilization program.

[7]*Minutes*, 5/21/1980.

[8]*Minutes*, 2/20/1980.

[9]Also included in this last category were "export companies" which, modelled after the Japanese or Korean examples, were designed to take advantage of export economies of scale.

[10]TÜSIAD, *The Turkish Economy, 1981* (Istanbul: TÜSIAD , 1981), p. 103.

[11]Ecevit argued that national elections should not be called without first choosing a new president of the Republic. In fact, both he and Erbakan feared the possible results of new elections given the much improved performance of Demirel and his party in the October by-elections. Hence, their aim was to force the government to resign so that they could form a new governing coalition.

[12]It is worth noting that the Foreign Minister's downfall occurred as a result of a no confidence resolution proposed by the NSP over Israel's announcement that the whole of Jerusalem would now constitute its capital. The NSP, which had always wanted an immediate end to Turkey's relations with Israel, used this event as a pretext to bring down the Foreign Minister.

[13]As early as the fall 1978, the Chief of Staff, Kenan Evren, had assembled a small group of officers to study the bases for a coup, Mehmet Ali Birand, *12 Eylül: Saat 04.00* (Istanbul: Milliyet Yayinlari, 1984), p. 64.

[14]Çölaşan, *24 Ocak: Bir Dönemin Perde Arkasi*, pp. 101-111.

[15]The NSC was composed of five generals, the Chief of Staff, heads of the Army, Navy, Air Force and Gendarmerie.

[16]*Milliyet*, January 24, 1990. Demirel does not discuss the probability of the situation worsening.

[17]*Milliyet*, January 24, 1990.

[18]Emin Çölaşan, *12 Eylül Ekonomisinin Perde Arkasi* (Istanbul:

Milliyet Yayinlari, 1984), p.

[19]Quoted in Osman Ulagay, *24 Ocak Deneyimi Üzerine* (Istanbul: Hil Yayin, 1983), p. 18. Özal made these comments on the second anniversary of the January 24 measures. These thoughts were also echoed by Dündar Soyer, head of the Izmir Chamber of Commerce and later a member of the Constituent Assembly nominated by the National Security Council, Ulagay, *24 Ocak Deneyimi Üzerine*, p. 19.

[20]Interview with Özal, *Yanki* (weekly) 1981, No. 561.

[21]Since international prices were lower than local producers were willing to offer the state, the government saved money, admittedly at the expense of foreign exchange outlays. Nonetheless, by buying abroad the government remained within the limits set by the IMF in the 3-year stand-by agreement. Çölaşan, *12 Eylül Ekonomisinin Perde Arkasi*, pp. 255-58.

[22]It was ironic for the military high command to use this constitutionality argument when they themselves had overthrown a constitutionally elected government. Özal, however, tried to convince them of the necessity of his assuming all the positions he had been demanding by arguing that, while his position in the Demirel cabinet had been "lower" than such ministers of finance and trade, in reality he had been more powerful than them because he had the Prime Minister's complete support who was a *political force*, Çölaşan, *12 Eylül Ekonomisinin Perde Arkasi*, pp. 59-60. He succeeded in convincing the military to appoint one of his allies, Kaya Erdem, Minister of Finance and forced the resignation of an opponent in another critical position: President of the Central Bank.

[23]Had the coup taken place as initially scheduled in July 1980, then Ulusu would have been one of the generals in the NSC ruling the country. However, having reached the mandatory retirement age, he retired on August 30, 1980 and his successor assumed his position in the NSC.

[24]Özal often complained that he and his advisors were outvoted in cabinet meetings on economic issues by people who did not understand the issues involved. Therefore, he would often find excuses not to attend the cabinet meetings, Çölaşan, *12 Eylül Ekonomisinin Perde Arkasi*, pp. 200-201.

[25]Interview with an ex-Minister of Finance, Istanbul November 5, 1982. For more information on the bankers please see footnote 4 above.

[26]Minutes, 2/17/1982, emphasis added.

[27]Refer to the discussion of the BA state in chapters 1 and 2 of this book. The essential components of O'Donnell's definition of the BA

state are: 1) that its principal social basis is the upper bourgeoisie, 2) at the institutional level, the BA state is controlled by two elements; those in charge of coercion and those whose principal task is to "normalize" the economy, 3) focus on the political exclusion of the previously activated popular classes, 4) the political exclusion leads to the suppression of political citizenship and democracy, 5) economic exclusion of these same classes, 6) the depoliticization of the social issues, 7) the closing off of channels of representation, where only those in control of formal institutions have access to decision making, Guillermo O'Donnell, *Bureaucratic Authoritarianism: Argentina, 1966-1973, in Comparative Perspective* (California: University of California Press, 1988), pp. 31-33. This refurbished definition omits his more controversial deepening hypothesis included in the earlier versions of the definition.

[28]The dramatic improvement in post-1980 export performance was significantly helped by the onset of the Iran-Iraq War in September 1980. Turkish exports to Iran and Iraq rose from $44.7 million and $69.5 million in 1978, to $1,079 million and $961 million in 1985, respectively. At a time of a global recession, the two warring nations' inability to gain regular access to the international marketplace provided Turkey with a unique opportunity as the only country bordering both of them. For more analysis of the economic and political implications of the Gulf War on Turkey, see Henri J. Barkey, "The Silent Victor: Turkey's Role in the Gulf War," in Efraim Karsh (ed.), *The Iran Iraq War: Impact and Implications* (London: Macmillan, 1989), pp. 133-154.

[29]The increasing reliance on short term financing raises the possibility that long-term debt is being converted into short-term obligations. Dani Rodrik, "External Debt and Economic Performance in Turkey," in Tevfik Nas and Mehmet Odekon (eds.), *Liberalization and the Turkish Economy* (Connecticut: Greenwood Press, 1988), p. 173.

[30]This is not to say that there were no supporters of the deepening process. Among the private sector, the Eskişehir Chamber of Industry was the most vocal proponent of deepening through the collaboration of the state with the domestic private sector.

[31]TÜSIAD, *The Turkish Economy, 1985* (Istanbul: TÜSIAD, 1985), p. 15.

[32]For more details on Turkey's return to civilian rule and the intricacies of its transition, see Henri J. Barkey, "Why Military Regimes Fail: The Perils of Transition," *Armed Forces and Society*, Vol. 16, No. 2 (Winter 1990), pp. 169-192.

[33]Cüneyt Arcayürek, *Demokrasi Dur: 12 Eylül 1980* (Istanbul: Bilgi

Yayinevi, 1986), p. 511.

[34]Christian Rumpf, "The Military, the Presidency, and the Constitution: Comparisons between the Weimar Republic, France 1958, and Turkey 1982," in Metin Heper and Ahmet Evin (eds), *State, Democracy and the Military: Turkey in the 1980s* (West Berlin: Walter de Gruyter, 1988), p. 231.

[35]*Yanki*, No. 634, p. 38.

[36]Yavuz Donat, *Buyruklu Demokrasi: 1980-1983* (Istanbul: Bilgi Yayinevi, 1987), p. 328. Ulusu, had a curious interpretation of British Labour Party's politics and orientation. What he may have had in mind was a party in the tradition of Ismet Inönü's RPP, Ecevit's predecessor.

[37]It is thanks to these types of changes that Turgut Özal's Motherland Party managed to remain the ruling party when, in the November 1987 elections, it received 36 percent of the total votes cast, yet captured more than 60 percent of the seats in the assembly.

[38]For a discussion of the vetoes used by the military, see Birol Ali Yeşilada, "Problems of Political Development in the Third Turkish Republic," *Polity*, Vol XXI, No. 2 (Winter 1988), pp. 357-361.

[39]For details on the problems faced by the military during the transition, see Barkey, "Why Military Regimes Fail: The Perils of Transition."

[40]The two protagonists in Argentina were the Argentine Industrial Union, which comprised of the larger and generally more externally oriented corporations, and the General Economic Confederation, composed of the smaller and more nationalistic establishments. The conflict between these two were often joined by other interested organizations, such as the Chambers of Commerce. Jorge Niosi, *Les Entrepreneurs dans la Politique Argentine* (Montréal, Canada: Presses de L'Université du Québec, 1976), pp. 146-149.

[41]Marcelo Cavarozzi, "Political Cycles in Argentina since 1955," in Guillermo O'Donnell, Phillipe Schmitter and Lawrence Whitehead (eds.), *Transitions from Authoritarian Rule: Latin America* (Baltimore: Johns Hopkins University Press, 1986), p. 28.

Selected Bibliography

Official Sources

DPT. *Yillik Programlar* (Annual Reports).
ISO. *Minutes* (Minutes of the Istanbul Chamber of Industry's Executive Council Meetings)
OECD. *Turkey: Annual Surveys.*
TOB. *Iktisadi Rapor* (Economic Report, Annual).
TÜSIAD. *The Turkish Economy* (Annual Reports)

Turkish Newspapers, Weeklies and Journals

Cumhuriyet (Daily)
Görüş (Viewpoint, TÜSIAD Monthly)
Işveren (Employers, TISK Monthly)
Istanbul Sanayi Odasi Dergisi (Istanbul Chamber of Industry Journal, Monthly)
Mesaj (Bi-monthly)
Milliyet (Daily)
Nokta (Weekly)
Rapor (Daily)
Resmi Gazete (Official Gazette)
Yanki (Weekly)

Books and Articles

Abou-el-Haj, Rifat A. "The Ottoman Vezir and Pasha Households 1683-1703: A Preliminary Report," *American Journal of Oriental Studies*, 94: 438-447, 1974.

Ahmad, Feroz. *The Turkish Experiment in Democracy*, Boulder: Westview, 1977.

Alexander, Alec P. "Industrial Entrepreneurship in Turkey: Origins and Growth," *Economic Development and Cultural Change*, 8: 349-365, 1960.

Arcayürek, Cüneyt. *Demirel Dönemi, 12 Mart Darbesi: 1965-1971* (The Demirel Era: 1965-1971), Ankara: Bilgi Yayinevi, 1985.

————. *Demokrasi Dur: 12 Eylül 1980* (Democracy Stop: September 12, 1980), Ankara: Bilgi Yayinevi, 1986.

————. *Demokrasinin Sonbahari: 1977-1978* (The Autumn of Democracy), Ankara: Bilgi Yayinevi, 1985.

————. *Müdahalenin Ayak Sesleri* (The Footsteps of the Intervention), Ankara: Bilgi Yayinevi, 1985.

Ariman, Abdurrahman. *Türkiye'de Sermaye Yoğunlaşmasi ve Sermaye Gruplarinin Oluşumu* (The Concentration of Capital and the Formation of Capital Groups in Turkey), Istanbul: Istanbul Technical University, Unpublished Doctoral Dissertation Thesis, 1981.

Ayres, Robert. "The 'Social Pact' as Anti-Inflationary Policy: The Argentine Experience since 1973," *World Politics*, 28 (4): 473-501, 1976.

Babüroğlu, Oğuz N. *A Theory of Stalemated Social Systems and Vortical Organizational Environment: The Turkish Experience and Beyond*, Philadelphia: University of Pennsylvania, Unpublished Doctoral Dissertation Thesis, 1987.

Baer, Werner. "Import Substitution and Industrialization in Latin America: Experiences and Interpretations," *Latin American Research Review*, 7 (1): 95-122, 1972.

Balassa, Bela. *Growth Policies and the Exchange Rate in Turkey*. Washington, D.C.: World Bank, 1981.

Barkey, Henri J. "The Silent Victor: Turkey's Role in the Iran-Iraq War," Efraim Karsh (editor), *The Iran-Iraq War: Impact and Implications*, London: Macmillan, 133-153, 1989.

————. "Why Military Regimes Fail: The Perils of Transition," *Armed Forces and Society*, 16, (2): 169-192, 1990.

Bianchi, Robert. *Interest Groups and Political Development in Turkey*, Princeton: Princeton University Press, 1984.

Birand, Mehmet Ali. *12 Eylül: Saat 04.00* (September 12: 04.00 AM), Istanbul: Milliyet Yayinlari, 1984.

Boratav, Korkut. *Türkiye'de Devletçilik* (Ankara: Savaş Yayinlari, 1982.

Bulmuş, Ismail. "Türkiye'de Tarimsal Taban Fiyat Politikasi ve Etkileri," (Agricultural Support Price Policies in Turkey), *ODTÜ Gelişme Dergisi*, Special Issue, 541-574, 1981.

Bulutay, Tuncer. "Türkiye'nin 1950-1980 Dönemindeki Iktisadi Büyümesi Üzerine Düşünceler" (Reflections on the Economic Growth of Turkey 1950-1980), *ODTÜ Gelişme Dergisi*, Special Issue, 493-540, 1981.

Bulutoğlu, Kenan. *Bunalim ve Çikiş* (Crisis and Resolution), Istanbul: Tekin Yayinevi, 1980.

Cardoso, Fernando Enrique. "Associated-Dependent Development: Theoretical and Practical Implications," in Alfred Stepan, *Authoritarian Brazil*, New Haven: Yale University Press, 1976.

Cardoso, Fernando Enrique, and Faletto, Enzo. *Dependency and Development in Latin America*, Berkeley: University of California Press, 1979.

Cavarozzi, Marcelo. "Political Cycles in Argentina since 1955," in Guillermo O'Donnell, Phillipe Schmitter and Lawrence Whitehead (editors), *Transitions from Authoritarian Rule: Latin America*, Baltimore: Johns Hopkins University Press, 1986.

Cem, Ismail. *Siyaset Yazilari* (Political Writings), Istanbul: Cem Yayinevi, 1980.

————. *12 Mart* (March 12), Istanbul: Cem Yayinevi, 1978.

Cohen, Youssef. *The Manipulation of Consent: The State and Working-Class Consciousness in Brazil*, Pittsburgh: Pittsburgh University Press, 1989.

————. "Democracy from Above: The Political Origins of Military Dictatorship in Brazil," *World Politics*, 40 (1): 30-54, 1987.

Çölaşan, Emin. *12 Eylül Ekonomisinin Perde Arkasi* (Behind The Scenes of the September 12 Political Economy), Istanbul: Milliyet Yayinlari, 1984.

————. *24 Ocak: Bir Dönemin Perde Arkasi* (Behind The Scenes of an Era), Istanbul: Milliyet Yayinlari, 1983.

Demirel, Süleyman. *1971 Buhrani ve Aydinliğa Doğru* (The 1971 Crisis and the Road to a Solution), Ankara: Doğuş Yayinevi, 1973.

Derviş, Kemal, and Robinson, Sherman. "Structure of Income Inequality in Turkey," in Ergun Özbudun and Aydin Ulusan (editors), *The Political Economy of Income Distribution in Turkey*, New York: Holmes and Meier, 83-122, 1980

Devlet Istatistik Enstitüsü. *Imalat Sanayii: Istihdam, Üretim, Eğilim, 1978 (III) - 1979 (III)* (Manufacturing Industry: Employment, Production, Expectation 1978 (III) - 1979 (III)) Ankara: DPT, 1980.

Diaz-Alejandro, Carlos. "Southern Cone Stabilization Plans," in W. R. Cline and S. Weintraub (eds.), *Economic Stabilization in Developing Countries* (Washington, D.C.: Brookings, 119-148, 1981.

Dodd, C. H. *The Crisis of Turkish Democracy*, Great Britain: Euthen Press, 1983.

Donat, Yavuz. *Buyruklu Demokrasi: 1980-1983* (Democracy on Command), Istanbul: Bilgi Yayinevi, 1987.

DPT. *Beşinci Beş Yillik Kalkinma Plani: 1975-1989* (The Fifth Five Year Development Plan: 1979-1983), Ankara: DPT, 1985.

————. *Kamu Yatirimlarinin Kalkinmada Öncelikli Yöreler ve Diğer Iller Itibariyla Dağilimi* (Distribution of Public Investments According to Regions and Developmental Priorities), Ankara: DPT, 1982.

————. *Dördüncü Beş Yillik Kalkinma Plani: 1979-1983* (The Fourth Five Year Development Plan: 1979-1983), Ankara: DPT, 1979.

————. *Yeni Strateji ve Kalkinma Plani: Üçüncü BeşYil 1973-1977* (New Strategy and the Third Development Plan: 1973-1977), Ankara: DPT, 1973.

————. *Second Five Year Development Plan: 1968-1972*, Ankara, DPT, 1969.

————. *Kalkinma Plani: Birinci Beş Yil* (Developmental Plan: First Five Years), Ankara: DPT, 1963.

Ebiri, Kutlay. "Turkish Apertura, Part I," *ODTÜ, Gelişme Dergisi* 7 (3-4): 209-254, 1980.

Ecevit, Bülent. *Bu Düzen Değişmelidir* (This System Must Change), Istanbul: Tekin Yayinevi, 1978.

Economic Commission for Latin America. "The Growth and Decline of Import Substitution in Brazil," *Economic Commission for Latin America*, March 1964.

Ekonomik ve Sosyal Etüdler Konferans Heyeti. *1972 Sonbaharinda Türkiye'nin Iktisadi Durumu* (Turkey's Economic Situation in the Autumn of 1972), Istanbul: Ekonomik ve Sosyal Etüdler Konferans Heyeti, 1973.

Eralp, Atila. "Türkiye'de Izlenen Ithal Ikameci Kalkinma Stratejisi ve Yabanci Sermaye" (Import Substitution Strategy and Foreign Capital in Turkey), *ODTÜ Gelişme Dergisi*, Special Issue, 613-634, 1981.

Eskişehir Sanayi Odasi, *Eskişehir Sanayi Odasinin 10. Yili ve Mümtaz Zeytinoğlu* (The Eskişehir Chamber of Industry's Tenth Year and Mümtaz Zeytinoğlu), Istanbul: Eskişehir Sanayi Odasi Yayinlari, 1981.

Evans, Peter. *Dependent Development*, Princeton: Princeton University Press, 1979.

Evin, Ahmet. *Modern Turkey: Continuity and Change*, Opladen, West Germany: Leske und Bundrich, 1984.

Frey, Frederick. "Patterns of Elite Politics in Turkey," in George Lenczowski (editor), *Political Elites in the Middle East*, Washington, D.C.: American Research Enterprise, 1975.

Frieden, Jeff. "Sectoral Conflict and U.S. Foreign Economic Policy," in G. J. Ikenberry, D. Lake and M. Mastanduno (editors), *The State and*

American Foreign Economic Policy, New York: Cornell University Press, 1989.

Furtado, Celso. *Economic Development of Latin America*, London: Cambridge University Press, 1970.

Gerekçeli Anayasa (The Constitution Explained), Istanbul: Değişim Yayinlari, 1984.

Gerschenkron, Alexander. *Economic Backwardness in Historical Perspective*, Cambridge, Mass.: Belknap Press, 1962.

Gevgilili, Ali. *Türkiye'de 1971 Rejimi* (The 1971 Regime in Turkey), Istanbul: Milliyet Yayinlari, 1973.

—————. *Yükseliş ve Düşüş* (Ascendacy and Fall), Istanbul: Altin Kitaplar Matbaasi, 1981.

Giritli, Ismet. *Fifty Years of Turkish Development: 1919-1969*, Istanbul: Fakülteler Matbaasi, 1969.

Goldstein, Judith. "Ideas, Institutions, and American Trade Policy," in G. J.Ikenberry, D. Lake and M. Mastanduno (editors), *The State and American Foreign Economic Policy*, New York: Cornell University Press, 1989.

—————. "The Political Economy of Trade: The Institutions of Protection," *American Political Science Review*, 80 (1): 161-184, 1986.

Gourevitch, Peter. *Politics in Hard Times: Comparative Responses to International Economic Crises*, New York: Cornell University Press, 1989.

Grunwald, Joseph. "Some Reflections on Latin American Industrialization Policy," *Journal of Political Econmy*, 78 (4), 1970.

Hale, William. *The Political and Economic Development of Turkey*, New York: St. Martin's Press, 1981.

Hamilton, Nora. *The Limits of State Autonomy*, Princeton: Princeton University Press, 1982.

Harris, George. *Turkey: Coping with Crisis*, Boulder: Westview, 1985.

Heper, Metin. "Recent Instability in Turkish Politics: End of a Monocentrist Policy," *International Journal of Turkish Studies*, 1(1), 1981-1982.

Heper, Metin, and Evin, Ahmet (editors). *State, Democracy and the Military: Turkey in the 1980s*, West Berlin: Walter de Gruyter, 1988.

Hershlag, Zvi Y. *Turkey: The Challenge of Growth*, Leiden: Brill, 1968.

Hiç, Mükerrem et al. *Montaj Sanayi: Gelişmesi, Sorunlari ve Ekonomimizdeki Yeri* (Assembly Industry: Its Development, Problems and Place in the Economy), Istanbul: Ekonomik ve Sosyal Etüdler Konferans Heyeti, 1973.

Hirschman, Albert. *National Power and the Structure of Foreign Trade*, Berkeley: University of California Press, 1980.

—————. "The Turn to Authoritarianism and the Search for Economic Determinants," in David Collier (editor), *The New Authoritarianism in Latin America*, Princeton: Princeton University Press, 1979.

—————. "The Political Economy of Import Substituting Industrialization," in Albert Hirschman, *A Bias for Hope*, New Haven: Yale University Press, 1971.

Horowitz, Irving Louis, and Trimberger, Ellen Kay. "State Power and Military Nationalism in Latin America," *Comparative Politics* January 1976.

Ikenberry, G. J., Lake, D. and Mastanduno, M. (editors), *The State and American Foreign Economic Policy*, New York: Cornell University Press, 1989.

Iktisadi Araştirmalar Vakfi. *Ortak Pazar Karşisinda Türk Sanayiinin Durumu* (The State of Turkish Industry in View of the Common Market), Istanbul: Iktisadi Araştirmalar Vakfi, 1970.

Inalcik, Halil. "Military and Fiscal Transformation in the Ottoman Empire, 1600-1700," *Archivum Ottomanicum*, 6: 283-337, 1980.

—————. *The Ottoman Empire, The Classical Age 1300-1600*, New York: Weidenfeld and Nicolson, 1973.

—————. "The Ottoman Economic Mind and Aspects of the Ottoman Economy," in M.A. Cook (editor), *Studies in the Economic History of the Middle East*, London: Oxford University Press, 1970.

—————. "Capital Formation in the Ottoman Empire," *Journal of Economic History*, 29 (1): 97-140, 1969.

—————. "Land Problems in Turkish History," *Muslim World*, 45: 1955.

ISO. *Türk Otomotiv Sanayi'nin Gelişimi ve Yan Sanayi ile Ilişkiler* (The Development of the Automotive Industry and its Relations with Subsidiary Industries), Istanbul: ISO, 1981.

—————. *Türkiye'nin Dişa Açilma Stratejisi Içinde Ihracat Sorunu ve Sinai Ürünlerin Ihracatini Arttirma Imkânlari* (The Problem of Exports and the Possibilities of Increasing Exports of Manufactured Goods), Istanbul: ISO, 1981.

—————. *Yatirimlari Finanse Eden Kuruluşlar* (Institutions which Finance Investments), Istanbul: ISO, 1981.

—————. *Ekonomik Yaşantiya Iliskin Alinmasi Gerekli Önlemler Hakkinda Görüş ve Öneriler* (Reflections and Suggestions Regarding Needed Economic Measures), Istanbul: ISO, 1979.

—————. *Türkiye ve Istanbul Sanayiinde Son Gelişmeler* (The Latest Developments in Turkey and Istanbul's Industry), Istanbul: ISO, 1970.

ITO. *Cumhuriyetimizin 50 Yillik Ekonomik Kalkinmasinda: Özel Teşebüsün Rolü* (The Role of Private Enterprise in the Republic's 50 Years of Economic Development), Istanbul: ITO, 1974.

―――――. *AET Karşisinda Türk Sanayi*, (Turkish Industry in the Face of the EEC), Istanbul: ITO, 1967.

Johnson, Leland L. "Problems of Import Substitution: The Chilean Automotive Industry," *Economic Development and Cultural Change*, 15 (2): 202-216, 1967.

Kaldor, Nicholas. "Türk Vergi Sistemi Üzerine Rapor" (Report on the Turkish Tax System), *Toplum ve Bilim*, 15-16, 1981-1982.

Kamhi, Jak. "Dayanikli Tüketim Mallari Sanayi," in *2. Türkiye Iktisat Kongresi* Ankara: DPT, Vol. 6, 1981.

Kaufman, Robert. "Industrial Change and Authoritarian Rule in Latin America: A Concrete Review of the Bureaucratic-Authoritarian Model," in David Collier (editor), *The New Authoritarianism in Latin America*, Princeton: Princeton University Press, 165-254, 1979.

Keesing, Donald. "Outward-Looking Policies and Economic Development," *The Economic Journal*, 77: 303-320, 1967.

Kerwin, Robert. "Private Enterprise in Turkish Industrial Development," *Middle East Journal*, 5 (1): 21-38, 1951.

Keyder, Çağlar. *The Definition of a Peripheral Economy: Turkey 1923-1929*, Cambridge: Cambridge University Press, 1981.

―――――. "The Political Economy of Turkish Democracy," *New Left Review*, No. 115, (May June), 1979.

Kili, Suna. *Türk Anayasalari* (Turkish Constitutions), Istanbul: Tekin Yayinevi, 1982.

Korum, Uğur. "The Structure of Interdependence of the Public and Private Sectors in the Turkish Manufacturing Industry," in Mükerrem Hiç (editor), *Turkey's and Other Countries' Experience with the Mixed Economy*, Istanbul: Istanbul University Faculty of Economics, 459-516, 1979.

―――――. *Türk Imalat Sanayi ve Ithal Ikamesi: Bir Değerlendirme* (The Turkish Manufacturing Sector and Import Substitution: An Analysis), Ankara: Siyasal Bilgiler Fakültesi Yayini, 1977.

Krueger, Anne. "Inflation and Trade Regime Objectives," in W. R. Cline and S. Weintraub (editors), *Economic Stabilization in Developing Countries*, Washington, D.C., Brookings, 1981.

―――――. *Foreign Trade Regimes and Economic Development: Turkey*, New York: National Bureau of Economic Research, 1974.

―――――. "The Political Economy of Rent Seeking Society," *The American Economic Review*, 64 (3): 291-303, 1974.

Krueger, Anne, and Tuncer, Baran. "Estimating Total Factor Productivity Growth in a Developing Country," *World Bank Staff Working Paper*, No. 422, Washington, D.C.: World Bank, 1980.

Kurth, James. "Industrial Change and Political Change: A European Perspective," in David Collier (editor), *The New Authoritarianism in Latin America*, Princeton: Princeton University Press, 1979.

Kurth, James. "The Political Consequences of the Product Cycle: Industrial History and Political Outcomes," *International Organization*, 33 (1): 1-35, 1979.

Landau, Jacob, Özbudun, Ergun, and Tachau, Frank (editors). *Electoral Politics in the Middle-East*, London: Croom Helm, 1982.

Lewis, Bernard. *The Emergence of Modern Turkey*, New York: Oxford University Press, 1979.

Lindblom, Charles. *Politics and Markets*, New York: Basic Books, 1977.

Lubell, H., Mathieson, D., Smith, R., and Viraph, B., *The Turkish Import Regime*, Ankara: AID, 1968.

Malloy, James M. "Authoritarianism and Corporatism in Latin America: The Modal Pattern," in James M. Malloy (editor), *Authoritarianism and Corporatism in Latin America*, Pittsburgh, Pittsburgh University Press, 1977.

Mamlakis, Nikos. "Theory of Sectoral Clashes," *Latin American Research Review*, 4 (3): 9-46, 1969.

Miliband, Ralph. "Poulantzas and the Capitalist State," *New Left Review*, 82 November-December 1973.

—————. *The State in Capitalist Society*, New York: Basic Books, 1969.

Niosi, Jorge. *Les Entrepreneurs dans la Politique Argentine* Montréal, Canada: Presses de L'Université du Québec, 1976.

Nordlinger, Eric A. *On the Autonomy of the Democratic State*, Cambridge, Mass: Harvard University Press, 1981.

Nurkse, Ragnar. "Some International Aspects of the Problem of Economic Development," in A. N. Argawala and S. P. Singh (editors), *The Economics of Underdevelopment*, New York: Oxford University Press, 1971.

O'Donnell, Guillermo. *Bureaucratic Authoritarianism: Argentina, 1966-1973, in Comparative Perspective*, California: University of California Press, 1988.

—————. "Reflections on the Pattern of Change in the Bureaucratic Authoritarian State," *Latin American Research Review*, 13 (1): 3-38, 1978.

—————. "State and Alliances in Argentina, 1956-1976," *Journal of Development Studies*, 15: 3-33, 1978.

————. *Modernization and Bureaucratic Authoritarianism*, Berkeley: University of California Press, 1979.

————. "Tensions in the Bureaucratic-Authoritarian State and the Question of Democracy," in David Collier (editor), *The New Authoritarianism in Latin America*, New Jersey: Princeton University Press, 1979.

————. "Corporatism and the Question of the State," in James M. Malloy (editor), *Authoritarianism and Corporatism in Latin America*, Pittsburgh: Pittsburgh University Press, 1977.

Okyar, Osman. "The Role of the State in the Economic Life of the 19th Century Ottoman Empire," *Asian and African Studies*, 14: 143-164, 1980.

————. "Development Background of the Turkish Economy: 1923-1973," *International Journal of Middle East Studies*, 10: 325-344, 1979.

————. "The Concept of Etatism," *Economic Journal*, 75: 98-111, 1965.

Oyan, Oğuz. *Dışa Açılma ve Mali Politikalar, Türkiye 1980-1989* (Monetary Policies and Economic Opening in Turkey 1980-1989), Ankara: V Yayinlari, 1989.

Ökte, Faik. *The Tragedy of the Turkish Capital Tax* (translated by Geoffrey Cox), London: Croom Helm, 1987.

Öncü, Ayşe. "Chambers of Industry in Turkey: An Inquiry into State-Industry Relations as a Distributive Domain," in Ergun Özbudun and Aydin Ulusan (editors), *The Political Economy of Income Distribution in Turkey*, New York: Holmes and Meier, 455-480, 1980.

Özbudun, Ergun. *Social Change and Political Participation in Turkey*, Princeton: Princeton University Press, 1976.

Özbudun, Ergun, and Tachau, Frank. "Social Change and Electoral Behavior in Turkey: Toward a 'Critical Realignment,'" *International Journal of Middle East Studies*, 6: 460-480, 1975.

Pamuk, Şevket. "Ithal Ikamesi, Döviz Darboğazlari ve Türkiye 1947-1979," (Import Substitution, Foreign Currency Bottlenecks and Turkey 1947-1979) in Korkut Boratav, Çağlar Keyder and Şevket Pamuk, *Krizin Gelişimi ve Türkiye'nin Alternatif Sorunu* (The Development of the Crisis and the Problem of Alternatives in Turkey), Istanbul: Kaynak Yayinlari, 36-68, 1984.

Pevsner, Lucille W. *Turkey's Political Crisis*, New York: Praeger, 1984.

Poulantzas, Nicos. *Political Power and Social Classes*, London: New Left Books, 1973.

Remmer, Karen, and Merkx, Gilbert. "Bureaucratic-Authoritarianism Revisited," *Latin American Research Review*, 17 (2): 3-40, 1982.

Robock, Stefan H. "Industrialization Through Import Substitution or Export Industries: A False Dichotomy," in J. W. Markham and G. F.

Papanek (editors), *Industrial Organization and Economic Development*, Boston: Houghton Mifflin, 1970.

Rodrik, Dani. "External Debt and Economic Performance in Turkey," in Tevfik Nas and Mehmet Odekon (editors), *Liberalization and the Turkish Economy*, Connecticut: Greenwood Press, 1988.

Rueschemeyer, Dietrich, and Evans, Peter. "The State and Economic Transformation: Toward an Analysis of the Conditions Underlying Effective Intervention," in Peter Evans, Dietrich Rueschemeyer and Theda Skocpol (editors), *Bringing the State Back in*, New York: Cambridge University Press, 1985.

Rumpf, Christian. "The Military, the Presidency, and the Constitution: Comparisons between the Weimar Republic, France 1958, and Turkey 1982," in Metin Heper and Ahmet Evin (editors), *State, Democracy and the Military: Turkey in the 1980s*, West Berlin: Walter de Gruyter, 1988.

Sanayi Odalari Birliği. *IV üncü Beş Yillik Plan Için Sanayileşme Stratejisi'ne Ilişkin Görüş ve Öneriler* (Views and Proposals Concerning the Industrialization Strategy in the Fourth Five Year Development Plan), Ankara: Sanayi Odalari Birliği, 1976

Saybaşili, Kemal. "Türkiye'de Özel Teşebbüs ve Ekonomi Politikasi," (The Turkish Private Sector and Economic Policies) *ODTÜ Gelişme Dergisi* 13: 83-98, 1976.

—————. "Chambers of Commerce and Industry, Political Parties and Governments: The British and Turkish Cases," *ODTÜ Gelişme Dergisi* 11, 1975.

Sencer, Muzaffer. *Osmanli Toplum Yapisi* (Ottoman Social Structure), Istanbul: May Yayinlari, 1982.

—————. *Türkiye'de Siyasal Partilerin Sosyal Temelleri* (The Social Bases of Turkish Political Parties), Istanbul: May Yayinlari, 1974.

Serra, Jose. "Three Mistaken Theses Regarding the Connection between Industrialization and Authoritarian Regimes," in David Collier (editor), *The New Authoritarianism in Latin America*, Princeton: Princeton University Press, 1979.

Sevimay, Hayri. *Bankalar Sistemi ve Kredi Düzeninin Eleştirisi* (A Critique of the Banking and Credit System), Eskişehir: Eskişehir Sanayi Odasi Yayinlari, 1971.

Seyidoğlu, Halil. *Türkiye'de Sanayileşme ve Diş Ticaret Politikasi* (Industrialization and Foreign Trade Policy in Turkey), Ankara: Turhan Kitabevi, 1982.

Sheahan, John. *Patterns of Development in Latin America*, Princeton: Princeton University Press, 1987.

──────. "Market-Oriented Economic Policies and Political Repression in Latin America," *Economic Development and Cultural Change*, 28 (2): 264-89, 1980.

Simpson, Dwight. "Development as a Process: The Menderes Phase in Turkey," *Middle East Journal*, 19: 141-152, 1965.

Singer, Morris. *The Economic Advance of Turkey*, Ankara: Turkish Economic Society, 1977.

Skidmore, Thomas. *Politics in Brazil: 1930-1964*, New York: Oxford University Press, 1986.

──────. "The Politics of Economic Stabilization in Post-War Latin America," in James Malloy (editor), *Authoritarianism and Corporatism in Latin America*, Pittsburgh: Pittsburgh University Press, 149-190, 1977.

Skocpol, Theda. *State and Social Revolutions*, New York: Cambridge University Press, 1979.

Stein, Barbara, and Stein, Stanley. *The Colonial Heritage of Latin America*, New York: Oxford University Press, 1970.

Stepan, Alfred (editor). *Authoritarian Brazil*, New Haven: Yale University Press, 1976.

Sunar, Ilkay. *State and Society in Turkey's Development*, Ankara: Siyasal Bilgiler Fakültesi Yayinlari, 1974.

Şaylan, Gencay. "Planlama ve Bürokrasi," (Bureaucracy and Planning), *ODTÜ Gelişme Dergisi*, Special Issue, 183-206, 1981.

Tachau, Frank. "The Anatomy of Political and Social Change: Turkish Parties, Parliaments and Elections," *Comparative Politics*, 5: 551-573, 1973.

Tekeli, Ilhan, and Ilkin, Selim. *Savaş Sonrasi Ortaminda 1947 Türkiye Iktisadi Kalkinma Plani* (The 1947 Turkish Economic Development Plan in the Post-War Period), Ankara: ODTÜ Yayinlari, 1974.

TOB. *Bankalar Kanunundaki Değişikliklere Ilişkin Görüşler ve Öneriler* (Reflections on the Proposed Changes in the Banking Law), Ankara: TOB, 1979.

──────. *Türk Hür Teşebbüs Konseyi: I. Genel Kurul* (Free Enterprise Council: 1st Annual Convention), Ankara: TOB, 1979.

──────. *Ödemeler Dengesi Sorunlari* (Balance of Payments Problems), Ankara: TOB, 1978.

Ödemeler Dengesi Sorunlari (Balance of Payments Problems), Ankara: TOB, 1978.

──────. *XXIX. TOB Genel Kurulu* (29th Annual Convention), Ankara: TOB, 1974.

──────. *XXVIII TOB Genel Kurulu* (28th Annual Convention), Ankara: TOB, 1973.

————. *Devalüasyon — Yeni Vergiler ve Otomotiv Sanayi* (The Devaluation — New Taxes and the Automotive Industry), Ankara: TOB, 1971.

————. *Özel Sektörün Yabanci Sermaye Hakkinda Görüşü* (Private Sector Views on Foreign Capital), Ankara: TOB, 1966.

————. *Beş Yillik Kalkinma Planinin Uygulanmasi ve Hazirlanacak 1965 Yili Programi Hakkinda Özel Sektörün Görüş ve Teklifleri* (The Private Sector's Views and Suggestions Regarding the Five Year Development Plan and the 1965 Plan), Ankara: TOB, 1964.

Trimberger, Ellen K. *Revolution from Above: Military Bureaucrats and Development in Japan, Turkey, Egypt and Peru*, New Brunswick: Transaction Books, 1978.

Tuncer, Baran. "Türkiye'nin Sanayileşmesi ve Sanayi Politikalari," in Ekonomik ve Sosyal Etüdler Konferans Heyeti, *Diş Ticaret ve Ekonomik Gelişme* (Foreign Trade and Economic Development), Istanbul: Ekonomik ve Sosyal Etüdler Konferans Heyeti, 1979.

Turgut, Hulusi. *12 Eylül Partileri* (Political Parties of September 12), Istanbul: ABC Yayinlari, 1986.

Tüzün, Gürel. "Bunalim, Ekonomi Politikalari, Planlama ve Devlet: Bir Yaklaşim Önerisi," (Crisis, Economic Policies and the State: An Approach), *ODTÜ, Gelişme Dergisi*, Special Issue, 3-18, 1981.

Ulagay, Osman. *24 Ocak Deneyimi Üzerine* (On the January 24 Experiment), Istanbul: Hil Yayin, 1983.

Uras, Güngör. *Türkiye'de Yabanci Sermaye Yatirimlari* (Foreign Direct Investments in Turkey), Istanbul: Formül Matbaasi, 1979.

Üstünel, Besim. "Problems of Development Financing: The Turkish Case," *Journal of Development Studies*, 3, 130-154, 1967.

Veinstein, Gilles "Trésor Public et Fortunes Privées dans l'Empire Ottoman (milieu XVIe - début XIX siècles)," *Actes des Journés d'études Bendor* Vol. 3-4, 1979.

Waisman, Carlos H. *Reversal of Development in Argentina*, Princeton: Princeton University Press, 1987.

Wallerstein, Michael. "On the Collapse of Democracy in Brazil," *Latin American Research Review*, 15 (1): 3-49, 1980.

Walsted, Bertil. *State Manufacturing Enterprises in a Mixed Economy*, Baltimore: Johns Hopkins University Press, 1980.

Warren, Bill. *Inflation and Wages in Underdeveloped Countries*, London: Frank Cass, 1977.

Weber, Max. *Economy and Society*, Gunther Roth and Claus Wittich (editors) Berkeley: University of California Press, 1978.

Weicker, Walter. *The Modernization of Turkey*, New York: Holmes and Meier Publishers, 1981.

————. *The Turkish Revolution 1960-1961*, Washington, D.C.: Brookings, 1963.

Wilde, A. "Conversations among Gentlemen: Oligarchical Democracy in Colombia," in Juan Linz and Alfred Stepan (editors), *The Breakdown of Democratic Regimes: Latin America*, Baltimore: Johns Hopkins University Press, 1978.

Wolff, Peter. *Stabilization Policy and Structural Adjustment in Turkey, 1980-1985*, Berlin: German Development Institute, 1987.

World Bank. *Turkey: Industrialization and Trade Strategy*, Washington, D.C.: World Bank, 1982.

————. *Turkey: Prospects and Problems for an Expanding Economy*, Washington, D.C.: World Bank, 1975.

Yaşa, Memduh. *Cumhuriyet Dönemi Türkiye Ekonomisi* (Turkey's Economy during the Republican Era), Istanbul: Akbank Yayinlari, 1980.

Yeşilada, Birol Ali. "Problems of Political Development in the Third Turkish Republic," *Polity*, 21 (2), 1988.

Yüzgün, Arslan. *Cumhuriyet Dönemi Türk Banka Sistemi 1923-1981* (Turkish Banking System during the Republican Era 1923-1981), Istanbul: Der Yayinevi, 1982.

Zarkovic, M. *Issues in Indian Agricultural Development*, Boulder: Westview, 1987.

Zeytinoğlu, Mümtaz. *Ulusal Sanayi* (National Industry), Istanbul: Çağdaş Yayinlari, 1981.

Index

Aegean Chamber of Industry, 137

Agricultural sector, 63, 80(&
    table), 110, 128, 129-130
  under Democrat Party, 53, 54
  employment in, 80, 81(table)
  under Etatism, 48, 50
  exchange rates and, 12, 119
  growth of, 67(table)
  investment in, 68(table),
    101(table)
  Justice Party and, 150
  price supports, 27-28, 129
  taxation of, 145(n85), 181

Akbank, 125(table)

Argentina, 1, 5, 9, 10, 11, 14, 15,
    24, 25, 30, 32, 33, 36(n15), 62,
    184, 191

Argentine Industrial Union,
    195(n40)

Ariman, Abdurrahman, 89

Army Mutual Assistance
    Corporation (OYAK), 89-90,
    115

Artisans, 110

Asil Çelik, 178, 184

Assembly industries (*montaj
    sanayi*), 67, 73, 76(n26), 86,
    114-115, 120, 154-155, 159

Assembly Industry Guidelines,
    73, 114-115

Atatürk, Kemal, 43, 45, 46, 47-48,
    50, 51, 52, 61

Automobile industry, 13, 69, 115,
    126, 141(n18)

Automotive Indisutrialists
    Association, 115

Ayans, 41

Balance of payments, 5, 7, 54, 69,
    97-98

Balassa, Bela, 96

Bank credits, 123-125

"Bankers," 191-192(n4)

Banking, 80(table), 81(table),
    112, 123-125, 144(n63)

Batur, Sirri Enver, 131

Bayar, Celal, 47, 48, 51

Berker, Feyyaz, 129

Bianchi, Robert, 138

Bilateral Trade List, 71, 78(n38)

Bismarck, 3

Black market, 100

Bodur, Ibrahim, 164

Brazil, 1, 5, 9-10, 11, 13, 14, 15,
    17, 30, 36(n15), 46-47, 184

Bureaucracy, 61

Bureaucratic Authoritarian (BA)
    states, 1, 2
  autonomy of, 29-30
  characteristics of, 193-194(n27)
  ISI and, 13, 14-16
  making of, 184-190
  technocracy in, 15

Calp, Necdet, 189

Capital
  accumulation, 46, 123, 186
  concentration, 89-90,
    90(table), 96-97, 97(table)
  market, 123

Capital Levy, *See Varlik
    Vergisi*